Can the Third World Survive?

CAN THE THIRD WORLD SURVIVE?

JACQUES LOUP

THE JOHNS HOPKINS UNIVERSITY PRESS
Baltimore and London

Originally published in France as *Le Tiers-Monde peut-il survivre?*
© 1980 by Economica

English translation copyright © 1983 by The Johns Hopkins University Press
All rights reserved
Printed in the United States of America

Johns Hopkins Paperbacks edition, 1983
Second printing, 1984

The Johns Hopkins University Press, Baltimore, Maryland 21218
The Johns Hopkins Press Ltd., London

Library of Congress Cataloging in Publication Data

Loup, Jacques.
  Can the Third World survive?

  Translation of: Le Tiers-monde peut-il survivre?
  Includes bibliographical references and index.
  1. Underdeveloped areas. I. Title.
HC59.7.L6713   1983   330.9172′4   82–9945
ISBN 0–8018–2765–5   AACR2
ISBN 0–8018–2766–3 (pbk.)

to Anne

CONTENTS

TABLES AND FIGURES

TABLES

FIGURES

INTRODUCTION

At the beginning of the 1980s, the development of the Third World once again emerges as a fashionable subject. In the first years of the decade, a flurry of international gatherings drew the world's attention to these countries' predicament. In 1980 the Independent Commission on International Development Issues, over which the former German Chancellor Willy Brandt presided, submitted its report, and later in the same year, a Special Session of the United Nations launched the third Development Decade. The following year witnessed two development-related international conferences — on new and renewable energies and on the specific problems of the thirty-one "least developed countries" — and one world "premiere" when twenty-two ministers and heads of state met to discuss the main issues of poverty and development. As a result of this summit, 1983 might see the start of "Global Negotiations," a planetary bargaining session covering all aspects of North-South economic relations.

It might, however, be safer not to have any illusions about the duration and outcome of this new spurt of interest. Perhaps the present excitement is only the latest manifestation of a cyclical phenomenon that, every ten years or so, compels the international community to express a sudden concern about the Third World's situation — before it rapidly returns to more important matters. Thus, the Pearson report, published at the end of the sixties, was soon forgotten, and the Development Strategy adopted for the previous decade was neglected after a few years; as for the world conferences and summits of the North-South dialogue, they have thus far yielded so few concrete results that we may be justified in doubting that the attention they still receive will last for long.

Yet circumstances have changed considerably since 1970. In the economic sphere the last ten years have witnessed unexpected upheavals, and many traditional ways of thought have been called into question. The shocks of the years 1972 to 1975 have led economists to take another look at the future of growth; at the same time the content and quality of this growth have been challenged in the Third World. A feeling of failure and anxiety now seems to prevail among many economists and political leaders: it is frequently said that three decades of growth have yielded only disappointing results for the developing countries, and it is generally believed that the coming years will be even more difficult.

To a certain extent this situation may appear paradoxical. For the developing countries the last thirty years have seen unprecedented economic growth. Since the end of World War II, these countries' average income per capita has more than doubled, their food production has been multiplied by two and a half, and, from Brazil to South Korea, their new industries are now challenging the firms of the developed world. Furthermore, the progress achieved has not been limited to the economic sector: in the areas of health, education, and housing, exceptional results have also been obtained.

Neither can this discouragement be explained by a slowdown of growth. In fact, this growth was just as exceptionally rapid during the Second Development Decade — the decade of the seventies — as it had been during the previous one. Yet, while the first decade was generally deemed a success, the second has frequently been considered a failure.

The present feelings of frustration and impatience are presumably due not so much to the pace of growth as to the problems this growth has been unable to solve. In this respect, the last decade brought growing evidence of numerous failures. At the beginning of the eighties, still more than 400 million people suffer from malnutrition, and the number of "absolute" poor, those who survive with an income below seventy-five dollars per capita, is probably twice as high. There are about 600 million illiterate adults in the Third World today, and, during this very year, some 15 million children under five years of age are likely to die of hunger. Moreover, the economic growth of the developing countries has been very unequally shared, and, for a billion people living in the poorest of these countries, the last thirty years have brought an increase in real income of only two to three dollars (1980 value!) per year. Ten years ago, undoubtedly, we were not totally unaware of these problems, but it was still possible for us to believe that the ongoing economic growth would enable us to solve them. The fact that such confidence has become extremely rare today is no doubt a telling sign of the changes that have taken place during the last decade.

While certain failures of growth have now become evident, the very possibility of its continuation appears doubtful today. The shocks of the last decade have shaken the optimism of the late sixties, and the prospects for the year 2000 have considerably darkened. The period of rapid economic expansion that the world experienced after World War II is probably now over; in addition, there is cause to fear that the problems we have been unable or unwilling to solve during the previous decades — those, for instance, of energy, unemployment, and hunger — will take on an added urgency in the coming years.

These doubts and worries have made the last years a time of questioning and searching. The patterns of growth pursued by the developing countries in the fifties and sixties have been called into question, and many beliefs have been abandoned. Chancellor Brandt sums up the spirit of this contestation when he writes: "The hope that faster economic growth in developing countries by itself would benefit the broad masses of poor people has not been fulfilled," and many would agree with him that "development strategies which used to aim at increasing production as a whole will have to be modified and supplemented in order to achieve a fairer distribution of incomes taking into account the essential needs of the poorest strata and the urgency of providing employment for them." [1]

While the need for change in development strategies is clearly felt today, the possible alternatives have so far been less precisely formulated. Ideas and proposals have not been lacking, but they have rarely gone beyond the level of objectives or even slogans. Basic needs, self-sufficiency, collective self-reliance — so many battle cries that, as yet, have had more political or emotional appeal than operational and concrete import.

This book does not claim to propose such an alternative, much less to present a blueprint for action. My endeavor is much more modest and would at most aim at shedding some light on the ongoing debate. In the first part of the book I shall thus try to describe briefly the results of three decades of growth in the Third World. A reflection on alternative development strategies can begin only with an objective evaluation of the experience of past strategies; we cannot dismiss the orientations followed in recent decades without a clearer understanding not only of their failures but also of their successes. In this respect, it would probably not be difficult to "prove," by concentrating on certain aspects of this experience, that the last thirty years have constituted an unprecedented success; by pointing out certain problems it would be equally easy to show that they have in fact witnessed some very significant failures. Total objectivity in this area is probably an illusion; yet it is only from an evaluation of past experiences, carried out as impartially as we can, that we shall eventually be able to formulate alternative strategies.

These results are relatively easy to estimate with regard to the changes in certain economic data (gross domestic product, income per capita, value added of the different sectors, etc.). They are harder to appreciate, however, if we want to measure how the last three decades have affected living conditions. In this area, the scarcity and unreliability of statistics permit the most subjective interpretations. To avoid this bias as much as possible, I have resorted time and again to the estimates and evaluations of international organizations — at the risk perhaps of tiring the reader.

In the second part of the book I shall attempt to present some of the major problems that will confront the developing countries in the coming decades. Perhaps the only excuse for dealing here with questions as diverse as population, food, and poverty is that I am an expert in none of these areas. But certainly it is necessary to evaluate the most important among these problems in order to define development strategies that will enable us to face them. An analysis of these issues is also valuable because it reveals certain common elements: in the three areas mentioned above, for instance, the same necessity appears of a reorientation of development actions toward the poorest strata and toward the rural sector.

As I have said, I do not intend to offer any "alternative strategy" here. The heterogeneity of the Third World is now more obvious than ever, and it would be an illusion to look for *one* strategy that would answer the diverse problems of Bangladesh, the Ivory Coast, and Mexico. In the last three decades, the gap between developed and developing countries has grown still wider, but the gaps within the Third World itself have also increased. In fact, the feeling of failure that is now widespread after these thirty years of exceptional growth in the developing countries is largely due to the stagnation of the poorest among these nations. These countries — the "poverty belt" of sub-Saharan Africa and the Indian subcontinent — today account for half the Third World population. As the end of the century draws near, the future of these billion people will become the real challenge of development.

The few elements of a strategy that I propose in the third part of the book concern mainly these low-income countries. Different though they may be, these nations — the poorest among the poor — do share certain common characteristics, the main one probably being the overwhelming importance of the agricultural sector in production and employment. But while the orientations I propose are more specifically intended for the particular circumstances of these countries, certain of them would also be relevant to the situation of many of the more advanced countries.

In this last part I insist essentially on measures or policies aiming to increase the productivity and incomes of the poorest, in contrast to measures of a "social" nature (to use a distinction that is contested today). This is, of course, not because I consider the latter measures useless or harmful. On the contrary, I think that the most positive aspect of the "basic needs" approach is its call for a reorientation of government efforts toward the poorest, in the areas of education, health, or the supply of certain goods such as drinking water and electricity. But this needful reorientation must not make us forget the necessity of growth; the examples of Sri Lanka and Tanzania are here to show that the will for justice cannot without danger neglect the obligation of productivity.

This very problem is now, I think, at the center of the ongoing debate on the development of the Third World. The experience of the fifties and sixties taught us that growth and development were not synonymous terms; we know today that growth of the gross domestic product will not necessarily improve the living conditions of the poorest. Few people would now deny that growth must be redefined to take into account the needs of the most destitute categories. But the sharing of poverty is not a solution, and eventually the improvement in the well-being of the poorest will require an increase in production. In the coming years the reconciliation of the imperative of justice with the necessity of growth may indeed constitute the greatest challenge of world poverty.

1
THREE DECADES OF DEVELOPMENT

1

ECONOMIC GROWTH SINCE WORLD WAR II

In the field of economics, as in many other related fields, the period since World War II has been exceptional. When a European or a Japanese recalls the crippled state of his country immediately after the war, he is bound to acknowledge that many changes have taken place since then. Although we are aware that growth in the developed countries has been characterized by extreme rapidity, we seldom perceive the full extent of the transformation that has occurred during the same period in the Third World countries. We know about their political vicissitudes, beginning with their accession to independence, but we seldom realize that for the Third World countries too, if not for them above all, the last thirty years have been distinguished by highly important changes in the demographic, economic, and social fields.

THE POPULATION EXPLOSION

During the last three decades the population of the developing countries (excluding China) has approximately doubled, rising from one billion in 1950 to over two billion in 1980. This rate of growth (about 2.4 percent annually) is unprecedented not only in the history of these countries but also in the history of the developed world. It is thus estimated that before World War I the population of the countries that are now the developing ones increased at a rate distinctly lower than 1 percent and remained below 2 percent until 1940.[1] As for the now-developed countries, at the beginning of industrialization their population increased at a much slower rate, about 1 percent.[2]

This population explosion caught the experts by surprise. Even in 1951 a United Nations survey for the period 1950 to 1980 still forecast annual

3

increases of 0.7 to 1.3 percent for Africa and Asia. It was only during the sixties, with the publication of the censuses made at the beginning of that decade, that the experts and the public learned of an "explosion" which had already been going on for over ten years.

This accelerated growth of population was mainly due to the rapid and unexpected decrease in mortality in all these countries. In the Third World mortality decreased about five times faster than it did in the developed countries when they were at a similar stage of development. In eight years, from 1945 to 1953, the fall in the death rate in Sri Lanka was roughly equivalent to the decline in this rate in Sweden in a whole century, from 1771 to 1871. In the majority of these countries this reduction in mortality was the outcome of postwar campaigns to conquer the main infectious diseases: malaria, smallpox, and cholera. Thanks to these campaigns and to subsequent improvements in the health sector, the Third World has now reached mortality rates of about 10 to 20 per 1,000 — rates which the developed countries did not attain until about 1900, and in some instances, even 1925.

During the same period the crude birthrates in the Third World also decreased, from an average of about 43 per 1,000 in 1955 to 34 per 1,000 in 1978. This decrease, which was initially less rapid than the fall in the death rate, later accelerated: from 1960–1965 to 1975–1980 the average crude birthrate of the Third World went from 40 per 1,000 to 34 per 1,000, while the death rate went from 17 per 1,000 to 12 per 1,000. (See Table 1.1.)

One of the most striking consequences of the population increase in the Third World has been the even bigger explosion in the rate of urbanization. Thirty years ago the urban population of these countries was about 250 million; today it has reached some 800 million. An unprecedented rural exodus has caused this urban growth to be much more rapid than the growth of the total population itself: consequently, the urban population has significantly increased in proportion to the total population. In 1950 one person out of five in the Third World was a townsman; today the ratio is one to three. This extraordinary pace of urbanization is most clearly manifested by the proliferation of huge built-up areas. Thirty years ago only six cities in the entire world — and they included only one Third World city (Buenos Aires) — had over five million inhabitants; in 1975 this was the case for 21 cities, and 10 of them were in the developing countries.

In recent decades urban growth has proceeded more than twice as rapidly in the developing as in the developed countries during the same period. Moreover, the rate has been faster than it was in the latter countries during a comparable stage of their development. From 1950 to 1980 the annual increase in the urban population of the Third World exceeded 4 percent, a rate which the developed countries attained only occasionally, and much later in their development. In this field too we see that the

TABLE 1.1 Main Demographic Indicators, 1950–1980

Area	Population (millions)		Crude birthrate (per 1,000)		Crude death rate (per 1,000)		Rate of natural increase (per 1,000)	
	1950	1980	1960–65	1975–80	1960–65	1975–80	1960–65	1975–80
World	2,513	4,415	34.0	28.9	14.4	11.3	19.6	17.6
More developed regions	832	1,131	20.3	15.6	9.0	9.4	11.3	6.2
Less developed regions	1,681	3,284	40.0	33.6	16.8	12.0	23.2	20.4
Africa	219	469	47.6	46.0	22.4	17.1	25.2	28.9
Latin America	164	368	39.9	35.4	11.5	8.4	28.4	27.0
North America	166	246	22.8	15.3	9.2	9.0	13.6	6.3
East Asia	673	1,136	32.2	21.7	12.8	8.6	19.4	13.1
South Asia	706	1,422	44.1	38.9	19.8	14.1	24.3	24.8
Europe	392	484	18.7	14.5	10.2	10.6	8.3	3.9
Oceania	13	23	26.7	21.6	10.5	9.0	17.3	12.6
U.S.S.R.	180	267	22.3	18.3	7.2	8.9	14.4	9.4

SOURCE: United Nations, *The World Population Situation in 1979* (New York, 1980).

postwar experience of the developing countries cannot be compared to the experience of the developed countries during their early years of industrialization.

GROWTH OF THE GROSS DOMESTIC PRODUCT

While the growth of population in the Third World countries since the Second World War has been rapid, their economic growth has been just as exceptional — and just as unexpected.

The scarcity of statistics for the period before 1950 precludes any accurate assessment of the economic growth of these countries before the middle of the century. Nevertheless, Paul Bairoch estimates that, from 1900 to 1952-1954, the average annual rate of growth was about 2.1 percent for the gross domestic product (GDP) of these countries (excluding China) and approximately 0.8 percent for their GDP per capita. There is a distinct change of pace after the Second World War. From 1950 to 1980, GDP increased at an annual rate of approximately 5.3 percent and GDP per capita, at about 3.0 percent.

The exceptional nature of this growth becomes even more evident when we compare it to the limited achievements of the now-developed countries of Europe and of the United States at the beginning of their industrialization, that is to say, during the nineteenth century. During this period the average annual growth rates of their GDPs ranged from 2.0 percent to 2.5 percent, and those of their GDP per capita, from 1.2 percent to 1.7 percent.[3] These are less than half the rates realized by the developing countries since World War II. Even Japan, whose growth has been exceptionally rapid, has had a long-term growth rate inferior to that maintained by the developing world throughout three decades. Moreover, from 1950 to 1980 the GDP per capita of the developing countries (excluding China) grew almost as fast as it did in the developed countries (3.0 percent against 3.2 percent).

It is thus not surprising that this rapid growth was not foreseen at the beginning of the fifties by the few economists concerned with the future economic evolution of the "underdeveloped regions." Even the forecasts made in the sixties — following a decade of growth at the remarkably high rate of 4.4 percent — proved deceptively low, at least for the majority of the developing countries.

For economists currently attempting to foresee the future growth of the developing countries, it may be a useful exercise to compare certain forecasts made in the sixties with the actual economic results. For instance, in 1961 Rosenstein-Rodan forecast that, aside from the European countries, only one country would realize an average annual growth rate of GDP per capita of 3 percent during the 1961-1976 period.[4] In fact, however, 18 of the 66 countries which he covered reached or exceeded this figure. The same writer proved equally unfortunate in picking the winners of this growth race. Thus, India was to experience the most rapid growth: this country already was at the take-off stage. In fact, however, the annual growth rate of per capita GDP in India was only about 1.3 percent during this period. Among the laggards, on the other hand, Rosenstein-Rodan chose South Korea, Singapore, and Thailand, predicting growth rates of per capita GDP below 1.5 percent. In fact these countries realized rates four to five times higher than this figure. As a rule the forecasts made during the sixties proved insufficiently optimistic.

In 1961 the General Assembly of the United Nations designated the period 1961–1970 the first United Nations Development Decade. Each member country was requested to set its own goal, "aiming at a 5% minimum annual growth rate of national income at the end of the Decade." [5] At the time, this target was considered exceedingly ambitious, if not unrealistic. Yet the actual rate proved to be as high as 5.4 percent. Moreover, the growth rate increased during the decade, rising from 5.1 percent during the first half to 5.8 percent during the second. Encouraged by these results, the General Assembly inaugurated the second Development Decade, nine years later, with the proposal that "the average annual growth rate of the gross product of the developing countries during the . . . Decade . . . should be at least 6%." [6] This time, however, the goal was not attained. Although a rate of 5.9 percent was reached during the first half of the seventies, the overall growth of these countries slowed down after the recession of 1974–1975. The estimates made by the U.N. Secretariat cite 5.5 percent as the average annual growth rate for the whole decade.

THE GAP BETWEEN DEVELOPED AND DEVELOPING COUNTRIES

The situation that we have studied appears so far to be quite satisfactory. In spite of unprecedented population increases, all the developing countries have attained high rates of economic growth. Indeed, these rates are higher than those of the developed countries at a comparable stage of development. If we examine these results more closely, however, we can see that the situation is in fact less encouraging.

Since the average GDP per capita of the developing countries has increased during recent decades less rapidly than that of the developed countries with market economies, the gap between these two groups has consequently widened slightly (see Table 1.2). This gap was 1 to 12.6 in 1950 and reached 1 to 13.2 in 1975. [7] However insignificant it may appear, this increase was the continuation of a trend which can be traced back to

TABLE 1.2   Population and Annual Growth Rate of Gross Domestic Product (GDP), 1961–1975

Country group	Population (1970)	
	No. (millions)	% of world total
Developing countries	1,638	60.1
Developed market economies	739	27.1
Developed planned economies	348	12.8

SOURCE: "Development Trends since 1960 and Their Implications for a New International Development Strategy," *United Nations Journal of Development Planning* (New York), no. 13 (1979).

the beginning of the industrialization of the developed countries and had become more evident during the first half of the present century: between 1900 and 1950 this gap doubled.

The gap between countries can be measured in terms of a *relative* gap (ratio of the average GDPs per capita) or of an *absolute* gap (difference of these average GDPs per capita measured in constant prices — that is to say, by eliminating the changes due to inflation). A little elementary algebra enables us to see that a country's (or group of countries') relative gap vis-à-vis another, more advanced country will decrease if the rate of growth of its GDP per capita is higher than its predecessor's. This, however, would not guarantee a short-term decrease in the absolute gap. Of course, if the less developed countries maintain a high growth rate of their GDP per capita over a sufficiently long period, they will eventually decrease this absolute gap and catch up with the slower-growing advanced countries. But this process may require considerable time, and in the meanwhile the absolute gap will probably increase before it decreases.[8]

Understandably, then, a slight increase in the relative gap between developing and developed countries has gone hand in hand with a significant rise in the absolute gap. Measured in dollars (constant 1974 prices), this gap more than doubled between 1950 and 1975, rising from $2,200 to $4,800. Moreover, apart from Libya, no developing country was able to reduce its absolute gap with the developed countries during this period: even for South Korea and Taiwan this gap doubled between these two dates.

These rather disappointing results clearly indicate that the reduction of the gap is not a suitable development objective. Indeed, a reduction of the absolute gap appears unfeasible for the next few decades. Even if the developed countries managed to maintain, over the long term, an annual growth rate of their GDP per capita equaling the rate realized from 1950 to 1980 (3.2 percent) and if the developing countries achieved an average rate twice as high, the absolute gap between the two groups would continue to

Growth rate of GDP (%)			Growth rate of GDP per capita (%)		
1961–65	1966–70	1971–75	1961–65	1966–70	1971–75
5.1	5.8	5.9	2.5	3.1	3.2
5.2	4.5	2.8	3.9	3.4	1.8
6.1	7.4	6.3	4.8	6.4	5.5

increase for some sixty years. In this regard, the reduction of the relative gap might prove a more feasible target. One may, however, question the significance of such a target as far as the well-being of the population is concerned: after all, this well-being should presumably be the ultimate aim of development. At any rate, the history of the last three decades indicates that even this target would not be easily attainable.

If the reduction of the gap (absolute or relative) is thus rejected as an objective of development strategies, are there any other quantitative targets which could be retained as a goal for the international community? A priori, the idea of setting a goal for the average GDP per capita (growth rate or desirable minimum) seems more satisfactory. But, as we shall see in Chapter 2, such an "average" also gives rise to problems.

THE GAPS AMONG DEVELOPING COUNTRIES

While the overall growth rate of developing countries has been remarkably high during the last three decades, this average performance conceals important variations among countries or groups of countries. Table 1.3 shows the growth rates of different categories of countries, grouped according to their per capita income. As can be seen in this table, the growth rates of these countries seem directly related to their income per capita: from 1950 to 1980 the countries in the middle-income category grew faster than those in the low-income group. Such a relationship is quite understandable, however: at the end of a sufficiently long period, the richest countries will be the ones that have grown most rapidly, irrespective of their initial ranking.

Nevertheless, it would not be completely accurate to conclude that the countries that were richest in 1950 have achieved the highest growth rate. For instance, with regard to regions, in 1950 per capita GDP in Latin America was higher than in the Middle East, but it subsequently increased at half the rate maintained by the latter region. And in the middle of the century, GDP per capita in East Asia stood below what it was in Africa,

TABLE 1.3 Gross National Product (GNP) per Person, 1950–1980

Country group	GNP per capita (1980 dollars)			Av. annual growth rate (%)	
	1950	1960	1980	1950–60	1960–80
Low-income countries	170	180	250	0.6	1.7
Middle-income countries	640	820	1,580	2.5	3.3
Industrialized countries	4,130	5,580	10,660	3.1	3.3

SOURCE: World Bank, *World Development Report* (Washington, D.C., 1981).

NOTE: Data exclude all nonmarket countries.

but it has since increased more than twice as rapidly. In spite of this, the classification of the developing countries according to their GDP per capita hardly varied between 1950 and 1980.[9] With a few exceptions, the first in the race in 1980 were already at the forefront in 1950. Yet, while this classification has undergone little change, the distances have substantially increased: the absolute gap between the first and the last country (in constant dollars) has more than trebled since 1950.[10]

Since 1950, then, the growth of the developing world has been marked by a pattern of "divergent development."[11] This is not entirely novel: gaps existed among developing countries in the nineteenth century, and from 1900 to 1950, they were already growing larger. Yet the acceleration of this process in recent decades more clearly reveals several groups of Third World countries whose problems and economic performance differ fundamentally from each other. To take two extremes – even though we thereby oversimplify – we can contrast a small group of fast-growing countries, mainly located in Latin America and East Asia, with the majority of sub-Saharan African and South Asian countries, characterized by low income and slow growth. The contrast between the newly industrializing countries, already formidable competitors in international trade, and the poorest countries, forever imprisoned in the vicious circle of poverty, now becomes strikingly evident.

Leaving aside for the time being the case of the few capital-surplus oil-producing countries, we could order the other developing countries between the two extreme types above, without distinguishing any gap, any quantum leap, which would separate one group of countries from another. In fact, if we ranked these countries according to their per capita GDP, we would obtain a regular gradation from Bangladesh to Spain without any apparent discontinuity. While it is difficult to perceive where the border lies between the developed and the developing countries (Singapore, for instance, has the same GDP per capita as Ireland), it is also hard to recognize any thresholds which would help us to distinguish explicitly the poorest countries or the middle-income countries. Although they do not form a

TABLE 1.4   Growth Rates of GDP in Developing Countries after Adjustment for Relative Price Changes

(percentages)

Country group	Growth rate of GDP			Growth rate of GDP per capita		
	1961–65	1966–70	1971–75	1961–65	1966–70	1971–75
All developing countries	4.9	5.8	9.4	2.3	3.1	6.5
Oil-exporting developing countries	4.6	7.0	24.6	1.9	4.1	21.2
Other developing countries	4.9	5.6	5.0	2.3	2.9	2.3

SOURCE: See Table 1.2.

NOTE: GDP in constant 1970 prices adjusted to reflect changes in the terms of trade.

homogeneous whole, neither can the developing countries be divided into several clearly distinct and identifiable categories.

The above analysis does not include an important aspect of the inequality existing among the different countries. The aggregates from the national accounts that are used to measure economic growth (GDP, GDP per capita) are appropriately calculated in constant prices, in order to separate "real" growth from a mere rise in prices. This method is justified when the terms of trade do not change too abruptly, that is to say, when the ratios of the prices of the various products recorded in the national accounts remain at least comparatively stable through the years. It is much less satisfactory, however, when the terms of trade undergo rapid modifications. An obvious example is the quadrupling of oil prices in 1973–1974: if in calculating the GDP of the member countries of the Organization of Petroleum Exporting Countries (OPEC) at *constant 1970 prices,* we were to take $1.80 as the price for a barrel of oil (the price that prevailed in 1970), the macroeconomic indicators so computed for these countries would not adequately convey the fundamental change that has taken place. We must therefore alter our calculations to take into consideration the changes which have occurred in the terms of trade, while continuing to "neutralize" the inflation effect linked to the *general* rise in prices. Table 1.4 shows the effect of the oil price increase on the growth of the oil-producing countries' *real* per capita GDP.

During the sixties the real GDP per capita of the oil-exporting countries increased at an annual rate of 3 percent; from 1971 to 1975 the corresponding rate was approximately 21 percent. For the other developing countries, however, the annual rate decreased slightly during the 1971–1975 period in comparison to the previous decade. For the poorest among these countries this decrease was substantial; the annual growth rate of their real GDP per capita fell from 1.7 percent during the sixties to 0.2 percent from 1971 to 1975.[12] The rise in oil prices has unquestionably

TABLE 1.5 Growth of Agricultural Production in
Developing Countries, 1966–1975

Country group	Annual growth rate (%)		Ratio of agricultural production to GDP in 1975 (%)
	1966–70	1971–75	
Countries with 1970 GDP per capita below $200	2.4	1.4	38.6
Countries with 1970 GDP per capita of $200–$400	2.8	3.4	22.5
Countries with 1970 GDP per capita above $400	2.9	4.9	10.8
All developing countries	2.6	2.6	20.9

SOURCE: See Table 1.2.

introduced a new dimension in the growth of the petroleum-exporting countries. Although it is unlikely that their future GDP growth rates will compare to those achieved at the beginning of the seventies,[13] their oil resources clearly place these countries in a special category today.

The differences that were already evident in the sixties within the developing world (the new industrial countries against the poorest ones) were thus supplemented in the seventies by the contrast between the oil-producing and the oil-importing countries. Today, more than ever before, we must recognize that there is not one but several Third Worlds, each of which has its own problems and potential.

EVOLUTION OF THE VARIOUS ECONOMIC SECTORS

We can reinforce our analysis of growth in recent decades by tracing the evolution of the main economic sectors: agriculture, industry, and trade. We must distinguish herein the different categories of countries, because, as we have seen, the economic results have varied considerably from one group to another.

Agriculture

During the first Development Decade (1961–1970) the agricultural production of the Third World (excluding China) increased at an annual rate of 2.9 percent. For the second Decade, the United Nations set a target of 4 percent growth in agricultural production, even though no such target had been set for the first Decade. The rate achieved, however, was only around 2.8 percent. Since population increased at an annual rate of 2.4 percent during these two decades, agricultural production per capita remained virtually stagnant for twenty years.

These results look even more discouraging when we analyze this evolution by category of country. As Table 1.5 shows, the poorest countries are

TABLE 1.6   Annual Growth Rates of World Manufacturing
Value Added, 1960–1975
(percentages)

Years	Developing countries	Developed market economies	Developed planned economies
1960–1965	6.7	6.7	9.1
1965–1970	6.0	5.3	9.4
1970–1975	8.7	3.2	9.0

SOURCE: United Nations Industrial Development Organization (UNIDO), *World Industry since 1960: Progress and Prospects* (New York, 1979).

in fact the ones which have progressed the least rapidly. In this category (which, as we have seen, includes primarily the countries of sub-Saharan Africa and of South Asia) agricultural production during the sixties increased about as rapidly as population, thus causing the stagnation of per capita production. Moreover, production per capita *decreased* during the first half of the following decade. In Chapter 7 we shall examine the implications for nutrition of these disappointing results.

Within the category of middle- and high-income countries, agricultural progress from 1960 to 1975 was not uniform. Generally, the countries whose agricultural production increased the most rapidly were the ones in which the contribution of agriculture to GDP was comparatively less important. On the other hand, the countries where the agricultural sector and, in particular, the sector of traditional food production still played an important role were the ones which achieved the lowest growth rates. In many cases, this has resulted in a relative impoverishment of the countryside and, consequently, an acceleration of the exodus toward the towns.

In the agricultural sector we thus witness an already familiar evolution: encouraging progress among the most advanced countries and persistent stagnation among the poorest ones. For the latter countries the continuing sluggishness of the agricultural sector is especially alarming, since it has resulted in an absolute deterioration in their general situation.

Industry

In the fifties and sixties the development strategies of Third World countries placed considerable emphasis on industry, which was considered the "noble" sector of the economy. More recently, the fear evinced by the developed countries with regard to the industrial competition of the Third World could lead us to believe that, in this sphere at least, the efforts of the developing countries have been successful. What exactly has been the result of several decades of industrial endeavor?

In the Third World during the last two decades, value added increased faster in the industrial sector than in the agricultural sector. In fact, as Table 1.6 indicates, since 1965 the manufacturing value added (MVA) of

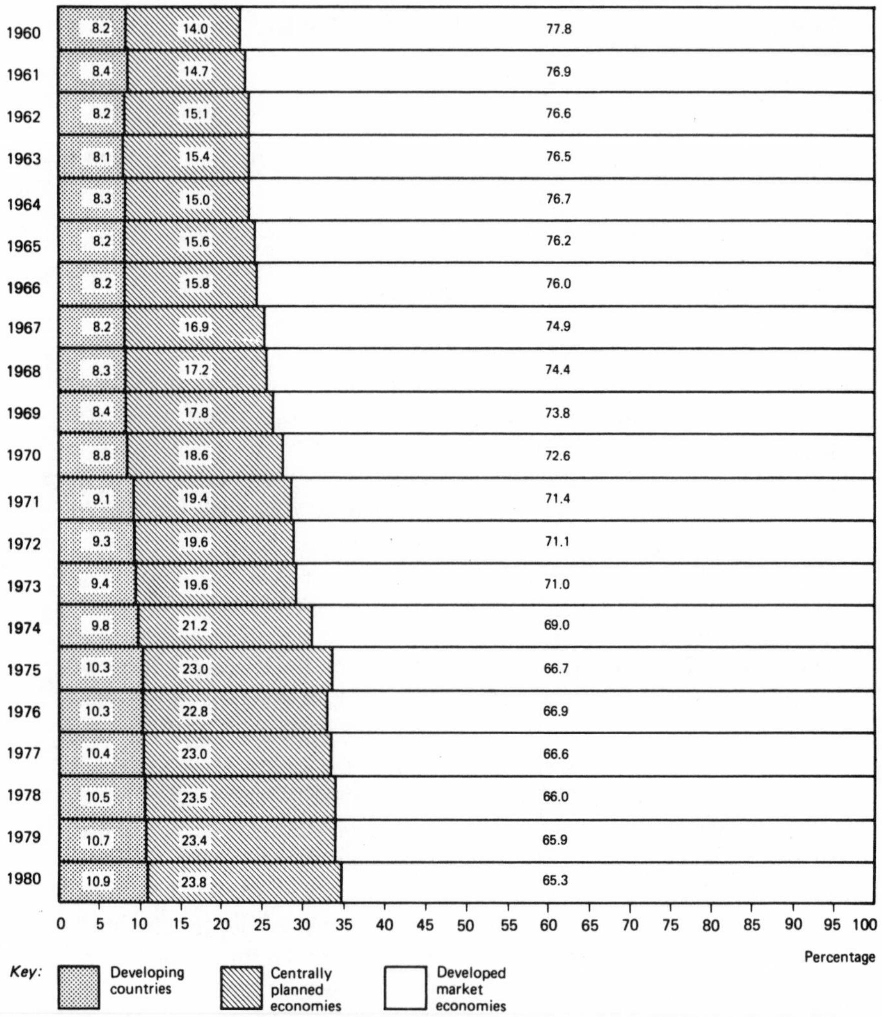

	Developing countries	Centrally planned economies	Developed market economies
1960	8.2	14.0	77.8
1961	8.4	14.7	76.9
1962	8.2	15.1	76.6
1963	8.1	15.4	76.5
1964	8.3	15.0	76.7
1965	8.2	15.6	76.2
1966	8.2	15.8	76.0
1967	8.2	16.9	74.9
1968	8.3	17.2	74.4
1969	8.4	17.8	73.8
1970	8.8	18.6	72.6
1971	9.1	19.4	71.4
1972	9.3	19.6	71.1
1973	9.4	19.6	71.0
1974	9.8	21.2	69.0
1975	10.3	23.0	66.7
1976	10.3	22.8	66.9
1977	10.4	23.0	66.6
1978	10.5	23.5	66.0
1979	10.7	23.4	65.9
1980	10.9	23.8	65.3

0 5 10 15 20 25 30 35 40 45 50 55 60 65 70 75 80 85 90 95 100

Percentage

Key: Developing countries   Centrally planned economies   Developed market economies

Source: UNIDO data base; information supplied by the United Nations Office of Development Research and Policy Analysis and the United Nations Statistical Office; United Nations, *Monthly Bulletin of Statistics,* November 1980; and estimates by the UNIDO secretariat.

Note: Data for 1980 are preliminary estimates.

FIGURE 1.1.   Share in world manufacturing value added, by economic grouping, 1960–1980. From United Nations Industrial Development Organization (UNIDO), *World Industry in 1980* (New York, 1981), p. 29.

14

TABLE 1.7 Contribution of Selected Developing Countries to the Increase in Manufacturing Value Added of the Third World, 1966–1975

Country	Contribution (%)
Brazil	23.9
Mexico	10.7
Argentina	9.4
Republic of Korea	8.2
India	5.9
Turkey	5.0
Iran	2.9
Indonesia	2.5
Hong Kong	2.4
Thailand	2.3
All countries above	73.2

SOURCE: See Table 1.6.

NOTE: Calculated in 1970 prices.

the developing countries has increased more rapidly than the MVA of the developed market economies. As a result of this performance the share of the developing countries in world MVA has risen during the last twenty years. The increase is relative, however: these countries supplied 8.2 percent of world MVA in 1960 and still only 10.9 percent in 1980 (Fig. 1.1). We are still far from the goal, set by the second General Conference of the United Nations Industrial Development Organization (UNIDO) at Lima in 1975, of raising this percentage to 25 percent by the year 2000.

Although the industrialization of the Third World is a reality, we should not exaggerate its pace, which, for instance, remains slower than the industrial growth of the socialist countries. We must also note that this industrialization has so far taken place among a comparatively small, though increasing number of developing countries. From 1966 to 1975 four countries representing 11 percent of the population of the developing world contributed over half the increase of the MVA of the developing countries, and eight countries, with 17 percent of the total population, produced about two-thirds of it. (See Table 1.7.)

Finally, if we analyze the growth rates of manufacturing value added, we can see that in this case too, the advances of the poorest countries have been the most limited (see Table 1.8). In the African countries the growth of manufactured production has been particularly slow; today these countries are far behind the other developing countries. In 1975 manufactured production represented approximately 5 percent of the GDP of the African developing countries as opposed to 16 percent for the Asian ones and 25 percent for those of Latin America and the West Indies.[14]

TABLE 1.8   Growth of Industrial Production in Developing Countries, 1966–1975
(percentages)

Country group	Annual growth rate		Proportion of manufacturing value added in GDP, 1975
	1966–70	1971–75	
Countries with 1970 GDP per capita below $200	5.0	4.7	12.7
Countries with 1970 GDP per capita of $200–$400	10.1	10.5	16.7
Countries with 1970 GDP per capita above $400	7.8	8.1	23.1
All developing countries	7.4	7.7	19.0

SOURCE: See Table 1.2.

In all categories of developing countries, irrespective of income level, growth of industrial production has been characterized by the expansion of heavy industries: chemicals, iron and steel, machinery and equipment. This expansion has been more rapid than the growth of the food industry or the textile, clothing, and shoe industries. It is worth emphasizing this point, because a European or an American aware of the recent increase in the imports of clothing and shoes coming from the Third World may be inclined to believe that it is the *light* industries which have developed most rapidly in these countries.

During the last two decades, in fact, the industrialization programs of many Third World countries have undergone a significant change of direction. After World War II industrialization in most of these countries concentrated on the creation of import-substituting industries. Since the early sixties, however, the possibilities of substitution have begun to dwindle; consequently, a fundamental reorientation has taken place in certain countries, especially in East Asia and Latin America. These countries have endeavored to develop their exports of manufactured goods, mostly to developed countries. In numerous countries the export industries have thereby contributed substantially to the industrialization process during recent years.

Trade

The trade performance of the developing countries has aroused considerable interest lately. The developed countries, painfully aware since 1973 of their dependence on imports from OPEC, have also encountered a new aggressiveness among the developing countries with regard to industrial exports. Confronted with this double "Third World challenge," all the rich countries have endeavored to expand their exports in order to reduce

TABLE 1.9   Annual Growth Rates of International Trade of
Developing Countries, 1961–1975

(percentages)

Country group	Exports			Imports		
	1961–65	1966–70	1971–75	1961–65	1966–70	1971–75
Countries with 1970 GDP per capita below $200	4.7	4.8	4.0	3.9	4.5	7.3
Countries with 1970 GDP per capita of $200–$400	4.7	6.0	6.3	2.3	8.2	10.6
Countries with 1970 GDP per capita above $400	7.9	7.8	4.4	4.5	9.8	15.1
All developing countries	6.3	6.7	4.8	3.8	7.9	12.2
Oil-exporting developing countries	9.8	8.6	3.5	3.5	8.8	26.3
Non–oil-exporting developing countries	5.1	5.9	5.3	3.8	7.7	6.7

SOURCE: See Table 1.2.

the deficits in their trade balances. This explains the increased attention paid to the exports as much as to the imports of the developing countries.

How have the commercial relations of the Third World evolved in recent decades? As we have seen, the period since the Second World War has been characterized by rapid economic growth in all developed countries ("capitalist" or socialist) and developing countries. This growth has been accompanied and sustained by continuous liberalization of international trade, including, in particular, a general reduction of the tariffs protecting the developed countries of the Organization for Economic Cooperation and Development (OECD). These two factors, rapid economic growth and liberalization of trade, have led to an exceptional expansion of international trade. From 1960 to 1975 world exports increased at an annual volume of 7.1 percent. Exports of developed countries grew at an unprecedented rate (7.5 percent annually during the above period), but the developing countries' exports also increased rapidly (5.9 percent annually).

The exports of the developing countries, like the exports of the industrialized countries, suffered from the effects of the recession of 1974–1975. While the volume of these exports had risen at an annual rate of more than 6 percent during the sixties, the rate fell to 4.7 percent during the seventies, far below the minimum goal set by the International Development Strategy. Table 1.9 shows that the poorest countries have increasingly fallen behind in the commercial sphere, as they have in the other sectors considered above; this deterioration touches exports as well as imports.

A noticeable characteristic of the exports of the developing countries during recent years has been their growing diversification. Between 1960

TABLE 1.10   Evolution of Exports of Developing Countries, 1960–1975, in Constant 1975 Prices

(percentages)

Type of export	Exports		Increase in exports, 1960–75	Av. annual growth rate	
	1960	1975		Developing countries	World
Fuel and energy	39	40	42	6.2	6.3
Agricultural products	43	27	16	2.6	4.2
Nonfuel minerals	7	7	6	4.8	3.9
Manufactures	11	26	36	12.3	8.9
All merchandise exports	100	100	100	5.9	7.1

SOURCE: World Bank, "The Changing Composition of Developing Countries' Exports," Staff Working Paper, January 1979.

and 1980 the share of primary products (including fuels) in exports shrank, while the share of manufactured products rose from 11 percent to 37 percent; according to the World Bank it could exceed 50 percent before the end of the present decade. These characteristics of the export trade are shown in Table 1.10. Although the Third World only recently began to export manufactured goods, these exports have grown at a remarkable rate. They rose, in current dollars, from $4.6 billion in 1965 to about $101 billion in 1980, an increase of more than twentyfold. In 1965 there were only three developing countries whose exports of manufactured products, measured in constant 1975 dollars, exceeded $1 billion; in 1978 there were fourteen.

Yet we should not overestimate the present importance for the Third World of this twofold trend of industrialization and expansion of manufactured exports. We have already seen that the developing countries still produce only a small share (10.9 percent) of the world MVA and that the recent growth of this share is due mainly to the contribution of a handful of countries. The situation is similar with regard to manufactured exports. In 1980 the developing countries contributed only 9 percent of world exports of these goods; at the same time the share of the developed countries with market economies was 83 percent.[15] Moreover, the bulk of Third World manufactured exports is still provided by a few countries undergoing rapid industrialization, even though, as we have seen, the number of these exporting countries is growing. In 1978 ten countries, representing 45 percent of the Third World's population, supplied over 75 percent of its manufactured exports, and of those ten, three countries, with less than 3 percent of the total population, furnished over 40 percent. At the other extreme, the poorest developing countries (with GDPs per capita below $360), which account for 56 percent of the Third World's population, were responsible for less than 8 percent of these exports.

If we now turn to the imports of the developing countries, we observe rapid growth here as well (Table 1.9). It has been particularly high since 1973–1974 because of the rise in the foreign exchange earnings of the OPEC countries. As a result, the maximum rate of 7 percent set for the seventies by the International Development Strategy has been surpassed.

The developed countries with market economies supply two-thirds of the developing countries' imports. These sales from the "North" to the "South" constitute approximately 22 to 24 percent of the total exports of these developed countries. This proportion is higher for manufactured products (26 percent); in fact, during the last three decades the developing countries have become one of the most important outlets for the industrialized countries' manufactured exports. This trend has become even more pronounced lately because of the recent rise in the purchasing power of the oil-producing countries: from 1970 to 1976 the developing countries doubled the volume of their manufactured imports, which rose from $39 billion to $78 billion (in constant 1970 prices).

What conclusions can we draw at the end of this rapid survey of three decades of economic development — at least of such development as can be apprehended through the principal macroeconomic indicators? The first impression is that the results have been, to say the least, unequal. Side by side with achievements that have surpassed the most optimistic forecasts are alarming weaknesses or shortcomings.

The Third World has experienced nearly a third of a century of exceptional growth. On the average, between 1950 and 1980 the gross domestic product per capita more than doubled. This rapid increase in the average income is all the more remarkable considering that the total population of these countries also rose simultaneously at an unprecedented rate. The manufacturing sector has increased particularly fast — faster, in fact, than GDP itself; and at the present time manufactures contribute as much to GDP in the Third World as agriculture.[16]

Yet these overall results conceal the near stagnation of the poorest countries. Some forty countries, accounting for over a billion people, have experienced only very limited growth of their GDP per capita (approximately 1.3 percent annually); in thirty years their inhabitants' average annual income has risen from $170 to $250 (in 1980 dollars). Two regions of the world, sub-Saharan Africa and the Indian subcontinent, form this hard core of poverty, which, in contrast to the rest of the Third World, has been marked by slow development in all the sectors of economic activity: agriculture, industry, and trade.

Moreover, while developing countries have made progress in all areas, the results have been disappointing for the agricultural sector. For the

Third World as a whole, per capita agricultural production has scarcely advanced; for the poorest countries it has presumably decreased. This situation is particularly alarming because most Third World people depend on agriculture as their principal means of subsistence.

An important consequence of the divergent development of the Third World is its increasing heterogeneity. The relative gap, measured by per capita income, is now three times greater between Bangladesh and Singapore (not to mention countries like Saudi Arabia and Kuwait) than between the developing and the developed world.[17] In the fifties, the first development economists could embark on the quest for *one* model, *one* strategy, for the Third World. Today it is clear that no single model exists; the problems of Mali, for instance, call for measures different from those appropriate for Korea or Iraq.

However useful they may be, macroeconomic indicators do not tell everything, and we are well aware that growth and development are not always synonymous. We must now put aside these indicators and leave the narrow context of the national accounts to see how the economic changes have affected the living conditions of the people in the Third World.

2
CHANGES IN LIVING CONDITIONS

In my attempt to describe the changes that have taken place in the developing countries since the Second World War, I have thus far resorted mainly to macroeconomic indicators: GDP, sectoral value added, GDP per capita. The explanatory power of these indicators is limited, however. One of the many slogans that appeared on the walls of the Sorbonne in 1968 was: "Nobody falls in love with a growth rate." It typified the spirit of protest that shook the developed countries throughout the sixties. After two decades of unprecedented economic growth, these countries were questioning the ultimate aim of progress and concluding that increases in GDP and improvement in the quality of life were not always synonymous.

This interrogation did not remain confined to the developed world. Inside the Third World itself, the development strategies that had been pursued since the war were increasingly challenged, from the end of the sixties onward. Arguing that twenty years of economic growth had scarcely bettered the lot of the majority of the people, the critics contrasted the idea of economic growth, mere evolution of statistical indicators, with the idea of the development of the whole human being. I shall deal with this debate in more detail in Chapters 8 and 9; meanwhile I shall attempt to clarify it by examining the changes that have occurred in the living conditions of Third World populations during recent decades. Two specific questions are important here. First, to what extent have the basic needs (nutrition, literacy, health, etc.) of the people been satisfied? Second, how have the profits of growth been shared and the additional incomes been distributed?

To begin with, however, I must sound a note of warning. In the vast majority of the developing countries the statistics concerning income and, in general, all the "social" indicators are never completely reliable — which, of course, does not necessarily mean that the data of the national accounts, of the type used in the previous chapter, are completely above suspicion either. It thus appears advisable to handle these statistics cautiously and to refrain from blind faith. Moreover, in certain countries such statistics do not even exist. If follows that the replies to our two questions will be closer to conjectures than to firm and definitive answers.

SATISFACTION OF BASIC NEEDS

Even though no definitive list of basic needs exists, these would presumably include food, shelter, health, and education. I shall first endeavor to assess the extent to which these fundamental needs have been fulfilled in the Third World during recent decades, before examining whether there is any direct link between the fulfillment of these needs and the average per capita income in a given country.

Food and nutrition

In the case of nutrition the problems evoked at the beginning of this chapter are compounded by another one: the lack of a universally accepted definition of minimum nutritional requirements. Nutritionists continue to argue about the respective importance of deficiency in proteins and in calories (not to mention specific deficiencies in vitamins or in minerals). Thus, in the sixties it was claimed that protein deficiency was particularly important. Today the majority of nutritionists believe that every individual spontaneously chooses a diet in which the proteins represent 10 to 12 percent of the total food energy, so that if food energy consumption falls below requirements, the person is simultaneously exposed to a protein deficiency. The two types of deficiency are therefore closely linked, and consequently specialists now pay more attention to deficiency in calories. This does not solve our problem, however, since the same specialists do not always agree about the number of calories that constitute the minimum energy requirements.

In these circumstances it is presumably better to admit honestly that we do not know how many malnourished people there are in the world today. The United Nations, for instance, estimates that the number was 415 million in the middle of the seventies. On the other hand, a World Bank report which takes into account the effects of income distribution estimates that the real figure is over one billion; certain authors quote two billion.[1] While there is no agreement concerning the exact number of people suffering from malnutrition, all the surveys do agree that the number has increased since the sixties.[2]

Between 1960 and 1975 average per capita consumption of calories increased in the Third World; this increase was nevertheless slower in the poorest countries.[3] Moreover, the advances varied from one region to

TABLE 2.1 Evolution of Life Expectancy and Infant Mortality

Country group	Life expectancy at birth (number of years)			Infant mortality (per 1,000)	
	1950	1960	1979	1960	1975
Low-income developing countries	37.0	42.0	51.0	142	122
Middle-income developing countries	48.6	53.0	61.0	72	46
Developed market economies	66.0	70.0	74.0	25	15
Developed planned economies	62.4	69.0	72.0	. . .	. . .

SOURCES: World Bank, *World Development Report,* 1978 and 1981.

another. While progress was substantial in Latin America, North Africa, the Middle East, and China, per capita calorie consumption did not change in the other Asian countries, and it dwindled in sub-Saharan Africa.

Whichever estimate we use concerning the number of malnourished people, their proportion in the total population of the Third World is quite large, between 20 and 50 percent. This does not mean that the corresponding food deficit is especially high, however. Several studies have tried to estimate the quantity of cereals that would be required to make up this deficit. The figures vary, of course — just as do the estimates concerning the number of malnourished — ranging from 25 million to 50 million tons. Nevertheless, such tonnage corresponds to only 2 to 4 percent of the world grain production, or less than 10 percent of the production of the developing countries. The actual volume required is therefore relatively small. Unfortunately this does not mean that it would be easy to rid the world of the scourge of hunger. As I shall attempt to show in Chapter 7, solving the problem of malnutrition demands more than a mere increase in the production or imports of cereals.

Health

Taking into account the unreliability of existing data, life expectancy and infant mortality are presumably the best indicators available for the health sector. Both show that during recent decades health conditions notably improved throughout the Third World (see Table 2.1). Moreover, the rate of improvement has been exceptionally rapid: in two or three decades these countries have attained a level of life expectancy that the developed countries obtained only after a whole century. In the early sixties the average life expectancy in the Third World was 50 years, a figure which the European countries did not reach until the beginning of the twentieth century.

The advances achieved in the health sector are in fact the best indication we have that the improvement of living conditions in the Third World has been widespread, rather than limited to a small minority. These advances also lead us to believe that even though malnutrition may have increased during recent decades, it has probably not done so dramatically, since this would hardly tally with the general improvement in the health sector.

This improvement is mainly due to the extension of available health services. The number of doctors, nurses, and hospital beds per thousand inhabitants has increased throughout the Third World, though there has been the only-too-familiar lag on the part of the poorest countries: in 1977 in the countries with GDPs per capita below $360, there was still 9,900 inhabitants per doctor as against 4,300 per doctor in the other developing nations. The remarkable results achieved in the fight against infectious diseases furnish the most striking example of this improvement in health conditions. The epidemics of yesterday have been virtually wiped out. Malaria and cholera, for instance, kill infinitely fewer people today than they did thirty years ago, while the plague and smallpox have practically disappeared.

Education

The developing countries have also made notable advances in the area of education. (See Table 2.2.) Since 1960 the number of pupils in primary schools has multiplied by 2.4, in secondary schools by 4.6, and in higher education by 6.3. Between 1950 and 1980 the proportion of literate adults increased from one-third to one-half.

The results vary a great deal, however, depending on the region. In ten years, from 1960 to 1970, the rate of literacy increased from 65 to 75 percent in Latin America, from 45 to 53 percent in Asia, but only from 20 to 26 percent in Africa. Similar differences appear among the various groups of countries.

The rapid progress in education should not make us forget the numerous problems which plague this sector in the Third World. Faced with a rapid increase in the size of classes, these countries have substantially enlarged their teaching staff. Nevertheless, the number of pupils per teacher still remains high even today (more than one and a half times what it is in the developed countries); it has in fact hardly varied since 1960. Equally important are the drop-out rates, which have improved only very slowly: even at the end of the sixties nearly half the pupils left school before they had reached fourth grade.

Although it cannot be expressed in quantitative terms, a much more serious problem is the adaptation of education to needs. The complaint that education is almost exclusively modeled on the instruction given in the developed countries and is consequently unsuited to local needs has been heard for a long time (in some instances for more than a century); this criticism has, however, recently intensified.[4] Primary education has been accused of encouraging the rural exodus instead of teaching the villagers

TABLE 2.2   Growth of Education in Developing Countries, 1960–1975
(median values)

Country group	% of primary school age children in school		% of secondary school age children in school		% of adults who are literate	
	1960	1975	1960	1975	1960	1975
Low-income countries	30	52	2	8	29	38
Middle-income countries	79	97	12	35	54	71

SOURCES: World Bank, *World Development Report,* 1978 and 1980.

the practical knowledge they would require, and higher education, of producing unemployed graduates whose training is also unrelated to the needs
of the country. Of course, this type of accusation is not confined to the
developing countries; we have heard it voiced in the developed countries
too. Yet such criticism does indicate that in assessing the progress of
education in the Third World we cannot refer solely to the statistics on
school attendance and to the number of graduates.

Housing

The inadequacy of existing data on housing allows only some very
limited speculation in this field. It does seem, nonetheless, that there has
been certain progress since 1960.[5] In many countries the number of people
per room has decreased, while the number of dwellings with running
water, sewerage, or electricity has increased. These improvements have
generally affected only the urban areas, however; traditional habitation in
the rural sector has changed very little on the whole.

Income per capita and standard of living

As I mentioned at the beginning of this chapter, during the last fifteen
years the very purpose of economic growth has been called into question.
In this debate economic progress has frequently been opposed to well-
being, and increases in per capita income have been set against improvement in the standard of living. An innate difficulty in this sort of discussion is that while we are able to define and measure economic growth or
income per capita, we do not yet have a universally accepted definition of
well-being or standard of living — any more than we have one of happi-
ness.

We can nevertheless attempt to restate the problem by inquiring
whether a connection exists between income per capita and the satisfaction
of certain basic needs. In more precise terms, is there a direct relation in
the developing countries between the average income per capita and the

degree of fulfillment of needs in such areas as food, education, and housing?

We have seen in Tables 2.1 and 2.2 that with regard to health and education a direct relation does exist, at least if we study the situation at the country group level: in general, in the low-income countries, health and education indicators are less satisfactory. Can we generalize and say that the per capita income of a country determines the extent to which the needs of the population are fulfilled? This question seems highly pertinent, because, after all, if the answer were affirmative, we could tell the contenders that they are mistaken in putting economic growth on trial, since obtaining a high GDP per capita is the necessary and sufficient condition for fulfilling the needs of the population.

Attempting to answer this question, Morawetz regressed each of sixteen indicators of satisfaction of basic needs on GNP per capita and on the growth rate of this GNP per capita.[6] He thereby demonstrated that a significant relationship does exist between GNP per capita and virtually all the indicators, but that on the whole this relationship is weak. Furthermore, for the majority of these indicators there is no significant relationship between the *growth* of GNP per capita between 1960 and 1970 and the *variation* of each indicator during the same period. To repeat Morawetz's own conclusions, it therefore seems that per capita GNP (or its growth) does not enable us to measure the degree of satisfaction of basic needs (or the improvement in this degree). In other words, knowing the per capita GNP of a country does not really enlighten us about the extent to which the needs of the population are fulfilled.

We can approach the question another way by looking at the Physical Quality of Life Index (PQLI) for different countries.[7] This index is in fact a simple arithmetic average of three indicators – life expectancy, infant mortality, and literacy – which have been expressed on a scale of 1 to 100. Although this index presents certain theoretical difficulties, such as the appropriateness of the weighting of the indicators, it nevertheless has the advantage of simplicity and will enable us to reply in part to the question we have raised.

If we arrange the countries by income groups and calculate for each group the GNP per capita and average PQLI, we see (Table 2.3) that the PQLI varies monotonically with the per capita GDP. This would seem to confirm that the GDP per capita does "determine" the quality of life. If we compare these indexes for different countries, however, we perceive substantial divergences. For Sri Lanka, for instance, the PQLI is higher than it is for Mexico, even though the GDP per capita is five times higher in the latter country. For Algeria the PQLI is as low as it is for India, even though India is much poorer; and for the Indian state of Kerala, where per capita GDP is lower than in the rest of the country, the PQLI is much higher!

TABLE 2.3   Economic and Social Indicators of Selected Countries

	Per capita GNP, 1976 ($)	PQLI	Life expectancy at birth (years)	Infant mortality per 1,000 births	Literacy (%)
Low-income countries	*166*	*40*	*48*	*135*	*34*
Bangladesh	110	32	46	153	22
India	150	41	49	129	34
Kerala, India	110	69	60	66	69
Mali	100	14	38	188	5
Sri Lanka	200	82	68	47	81
Lower middle-income countries	*429*	*67*	*62*	*76*	*59*
Angola	330	16	38	203	10–15
China (PRC)	410	71	65	65	50–70
Korea, Rep. of	670	82	65	47	88
Zambia	440	38	44	159	47
Upper middle-income countries	*1,215*	*68*	*62*	*85*	*66*
Algeria	990	41	53	145	26
Cuba	860	85	70	27	78
Iran	1,930	52	57	104	37
Mexico	1,090	75	65	66	74
Taiwan (ROC)	1,070	87	70	25	85
High-income countries	*4,976*	*93*	*71*	*20*	*97*
Czechoslovakia	3,840	93	70	21	100
Kuwait	15,480	75	69	44	55
Netherlands	6,200	96	74	11	98
United States	7,890	95	73	15	99

SOURCE: Overseas Development Council, *The United States and World Development: Agenda 1979* (New York: Praeger, 1979).

In sum, the level of a country's per capita GDP is not a reliable index of the extent to which the needs of its population are fulfilled; at most, GDP per capita can indicate what *potential* the country has for satisfying these needs. There is therefore no automatic relation between economic growth and improvement in living conditions: in fact, at comparable levels of GDP per capita the differences in degrees of satisfaction of needs are mainly the outcome of the policies pursued by the governments.

The above discussion does not exhaust the subject of the relation between growth and basic needs. Most important, it has not broached the controversial question of whether a policy oriented toward the satisfaction of basic needs can be followed only at the expense of growth. I shall deal with this problem in Chapter 9.

SHARING THE PIE

The development strategies of certain Third World countries have been attacked because, according to their critics, they would not lead to the satisfaction of the basic needs of the people. They have also been contested because they allegedly neglect, even impoverish, certain social categories. These two criticisms are evidently connected, though they do not exactly coincide. An improvement in average living conditions could in fact be accompanied by a deterioration, absolute or relative, in the situation of certain social minority groups. In order to examine the latter criticism in the light of the facts, we must thus study the changes in income distribution that have taken place in these countries during recent decades.

The study of the degree of satisfaction of basic needs was hazardous enough, but the present undertaking is even more so, owing to the scarcity and unreliability of income statistics. Moreover, while the relation between growth and income distribution is one of the oldest themes of economic theory, its statistical analysis is much more recent. In the developing countries it was only during the seventies that political leaders and economists began to be seriously concerned with this subject. With rare exceptions (India being one of the most remarkable), income data have not been collected for a long enough period and with sufficient care to permit a reliable analysis of the changes in distribution since, let us say, the fifties.

In the absence of time series concerning a specific country, statisticians have used series concerning various countries at different levels of development (cross-country series) in an attempt to find out what is happening in one country with regard to income distribution as the GDP or the average income increases. Although it may be useful as an aid to thought, the latter method unquestionably presents certain theoretical shortcomings. I shall therefore postpone using it until Chapter 8 and try now to study the changes in income, utilizing the existing time series.

The controversies about the evolution of income generally concern the fate of those in the poorest categories; unfortunately, these debates are often complicated by the confusion of two conceptually distinct questions:

— Have the poor (let us say the category formed by the poorest 20 or 40 percent of the population classified according to income) become *relatively* richer or poorer over time (has their share of the national income increased or decreased)?
— Have the poor become richer or poorer in *absolute* terms (has their average income, in constant dollars or pesos, increased or diminished)?

For the sake of clarity — insofar as that is possible — I shall deal with these two problems separately.

Relative impoverishment . . . ?

During recent decades, what has been the evolution of the share of the national income going to the poorest strata in the developing countries? For a great number, if not for the majority, of these countries we know nothing. For many others this share seems to have grown or at least to have remained constant: one can cite, in no particular order, China, South Korea, Taiwan, the Ivory Coast, Iran, Israel, Singapore, Costa Rica, El Salvador, and perhaps Colombia and Puerto Rico.[8] This list includes countries that have been explicitly concerned with the distribution of income and others less worried about it; fast-growing countries and slow-growing ones; countries that are outward-looking and others more inward-looking.

Among the fast-growing countries, South Korea and Taiwan are outstanding examples. In South Korea, income distribution has improved since the early sixties; today it is probably one of the least inegalitarian of the Third World.[9] The situation in Taiwan is even more remarkable; its rapid growth since 1950 has been accompanied by a continuous increase in the share of national income going to the poorest inhabitants, a rare exception to "Kuznets' law," according to which, during the course of a country's development, this share must first decrease before it increases (see Chapter 8). Communist China has followed a very different model from the one pursued in these two countries but with results that are just as exceptional. The land reform which ended in 1952 had already involved important redistribution of wealth and incomes in the rural areas (which account for over four-fifths of the population); the collectivization of land and a deliberate policy of income equalization after the Cultural Revolution have further improved the distribution of income. Today the share of the poorest 20 percent of the rural population is probably at least double what it was in the thirties.[10]

For another group of countries the share of national income going to the poorest has diminished. This group includes countries of the three continents of the Third World: Latin America (Argentina, Brazil, Mexico, Panama, Peru), Asia (India, Malaysia, Philippines), and Africa (Kenya, Tanzania, Ghana).[11] In this case too, it is impossible to establish a direct link between deterioration in income distribution and external economic policies or rapidity of growth.

Mexico and Brazil are no doubt the most quoted examples among these countries presumably because their particularly rapid economic growth has apparently mainly served to enrich the wealthy classes. From 1960 to 1970 the share of the total income received by the wealthiest 5 percent of the population rose from 23 percent to 27 percent in Brazil and from 29 percent to 36 percent in Mexico. The changes in income distribution have been most thoroughly studied in India. These studies are not always conclusive and sometimes even contradictory, but this is often due to differences in the time series analyzed or in the population samples used. In any event, we apparently find in this country the juxtaposition of a process of impoverishment, relative or even absolute, in certain states (Assam and West Bengal?) side by side with an improvement in income distribution in others (Andhra-Pradesh and Tamil Nadu?). Moreover, taking the country as a whole, the income distribution has in all likelihood deteriorated during recent decades.[12]

Or absolute poverty?

A slight reduction in the *share* of national income that goes to the poorest categories may well be compatible with stagnation, or even with growth, of their *absolute* income, provided the total national income increases sufficiently. Thus, in spite of their *relative* impoverishment, the income of the Mexican poor has probably not decreased and may even have increased somewhat over the recent decades. But are there countries where the poor have experienced an absolute fall in income?

In this case too, continuing to leave aside the speculation based on cross-country series, we find some contradiction in the available evidence. It has even happened that, for the same country and from the same statistical series, two researchers have reached opposite conclusions.

With regard to the large countries, only for China and Mexico is it reasonably certain that the poorest strata did not experience any fall in their absolute real income. Let us now see, region by region, what we can learn from the studies carried out on the evolution of poverty. In these regional surveys we must pay particular attention to Asia and especially to its rural population: according to the World Bank three-quarters of the world's "absolute poor" inhabit this region, and over four-fifths of them live in the rural areas. Our evaluation of the results of the fight against poverty in recent decades will therefore depend essentially on our conclusion with regard to the evolution of the living conditions of this continent's rural poor.

The International Labor Office (ILO) recently made a study of the evolution of rural poverty in six Asian countries (Bangladesh, Indonesia, Malaysia, Pakistan, the Philippines, and Sri Lanka) and four Indian states (Uttar Pradesh, Bihar, Tamil Nadu, and Punjab).[13] The conclusions of this study, which give no cause for optimism, are as follows. First, in all instances, there has been an increase in the proportion of the population whose income is below the poverty line (Table 2.4).[14] Second, the real income of the poorest 10 or 20 percent of the rural population has fallen. Finally, where information is available, the real wages of agricultural workers appear to have stagnated.

The results of this study therefore point to a general deterioration in the living conditions of the rural poor in the above countries. This conclusion is so appalling that we should not accept it without first checking these results carefully; we should also avoid any hasty generalizations. For instance, the results obtained for Pakistan and Sri Lanka appear to contradict the conclusions of other surveys; moreover, we cannot generalize to

TABLE 2.4 Percentage of the Rural Population below the Poverty Line in Selected Asian Countries

Country or state	Year	Rural population in poverty
Pakistan	1963–64	72
	1971–72	74
Punjab, India	1960–61	18.4
	1970–71	23.3
Uttar Pradesh, India	1960–61	41.6
	1970–71	63.6
Bihar, India	1960–61	41
	1970–71	59
Tamil Nadu, India	1957–58	74.1
	1960–61	69.8
	1969–70	74.0
Bangladesh	1963–64	40.2
	1975	61.8
Malaysia	1957	30.0
	1970	36.5
Philippines	1956–57	10.4
	1970–71	12.7

SOURCE: Data from Keith Griffin and Azizur Khan, coordinators, *Poverty and Landlessness in Rural Asia* (Geneva: International Labor Office, 1977).

the whole of the Indian Union the evolution observed in four states.[15] But these limited reservations cannot explain away all the above results, and it seems difficult to avoid the conclusion that in several countries the situation of the rural poor has deteriorated during recent decades.

Other surveys confirm the general pessimism of the ILO study. An extremely comprehensive study by the Asian Development Bank concludes: "There is a general consensus in the literature that the rural poverty problem has worsened considerably in the [Asian Development Bank] region in the past decade."[16] The report supports this assertion by pointing out that during the seventies the number of underemployed or unemployed in the rural sector increased, and that the real wages of the agricultural workers decreased in most countries of the region. Furthermore, in several countries the number of landless workers increased, as did their proportion in the agricultural population: this proportion rose, for instance, from 22 percent in 1961 to 38 percent in 1973 in Bangladesh, and from 25 percent in 1961 to 38 percent in 1971 in India.

On the whole, the major surveys made in the seventies reach identical results, and even when all due caution has been taken, it is hard to avoid their general conclusions. The verdict is disastrous. During recent decades the situation of the rural masses of non-Communist Asia has at best stagnated and at worst has deteriorated. Whatever assumption we retain, there is a striking contrast between the present picture and the euphoria created fifteen years ago by the beginnings of the Green Revolution![17]

Like South Asia, sub-Saharan Africa is one of the regions of the world where poverty is the most widespread. In this instance the virtually total lack of reliable statistics makes it even more difficult for us to form an opinion with regard to the evolution of poverty. We have seen that the situation of the poor has improved, in absolute terms, in the Ivory Coast. On the other hand, it seems to have worsened in Kenya and Tanzania.[18] Moreover, in the Sahelian countries that were affected by drought in the seventies, the situation of the majority of the population has unquestionably suffered serious deterioration. In the case of sub-Saharan Africa, then, while the lack of statistics makes it advisable to refrain from hasty generalizations, the indications that we do possess are scarcely encouraging.

Finally, in Latin America it seems that while the proportion of the population living in poverty has diminished, the absolute numbers remain more or less the same. The Economic Commission for Latin America (ECLA) of the United Nations estimates that in 1960 half the population of the region was living in poverty and about a quarter in extreme poverty. In 1970 these proportions had become, respectively, 40 percent and 19 percent, but the absolute figures (110 million people living in poverty, 55 million in extreme poverty) had remained approximately the same.[19]

It is even more difficult to present a picture of the evolution of the living conditions in the Third World during recent decades than it is to assess its economic growth. In the literature devoted to this subject, incomplete or contradictory statistics are often accompanied by interpretations that are at best subjective and at worst prejudiced. This chapter is doubtless not an exception, and its conclusions could always be challenged. The situation is such that each reader must decide for himself whether the glass is half full or half empty.

Unquestionably, some advances have been made in the satisfaction of the basic needs of the Third World population. Thus, for example, health conditions have improved and education has progressed in virtually all the countries; in these two sectors the gap between developed and developing countries (measured, for instance, by life expectancy or literacy rates) has diminished. Moreover, the situation (relative or absolute) of the poorest classes has improved in several of the developing countries.

Yet we cannot close this chapter on an optimistic note. Even if we do not possess irrefutable proof, too many indications lead us to believe that the situation of the poorest has scarcely improved during recent decades. This is true even for certain regions or countries which, like Brazil, have experienced rapid economic growth.

Above all it is true for the poorest countries. These nations have progressed only slowly in the health and education sectors, for instance. But it is with regard to the living conditions of their most destitute peoples that we have true cause for alarm. For hundreds of millions of human beings in sub-Saharan Africa and South Asia, life has apparently not improved since the last war. In fact, it may even be optimistic to say that their situation has not worsened. The results of three decades of efforts by the international community offer no occasion for congratulations.

3
THE TURNING POINT OF THE 1970s

In many respects the 1970s — more precisely the first half of the decade — constituted a turning point in the history of postwar international economic relations. After two decades of rapid economic growth, in the countries of the "North" as well as in those of the "South," the signs of disorder multiplied to culminate in a series of crises between 1971 and 1975. Since then continuous efforts have been made to recover an economic dynamism that has apparently vanished and to establish a new international economic order. At the same time, in the Third World countries, a general attack was being launched against the current models of development.

ECONOMIC TURMOIL

When specialists in economic history perform an autopsy on the crises of the years 1971 to 1975, they will no doubt be able to perceive how the premonitory signs had multiplied from the end of the sixties onward. The importance of the population explosion in the Third World was more clearly understood at the beginning of the 1960s, when the results of the censuses carried out at that time were published. The isolated forecasts of certain experts who then announced the imminent danger of famine in the Third World appeared to be abruptly confirmed when, in 1965–1966 and in 1966–1967, two inadequate monsoons brought India to the brink of famine; only a massive international effort saved the country from disaster. During this period the energy dependence of the developed countries increased; for instance, the energy imports of the United States rose from 7 percent of its consumption in 1960 to 14 percent in 1972. Inflation, which had apparently been overcome in the industrialized countries of the OECD, began to accelerate at the end of the sixties; the gold exchange standard, which had reigned supreme since 1945, received a first blow in 1968 with the creation of the double market for gold. Finally, also at the end of the sixties, the first signs appeared of a slowdown in the growth of productivity in North America.

Apart from a few specialists, however, few people worried about these discordant notes. With regard to future decades, economists anticipated the continuation of the rapid growth of the previous years, in the developed as well as in the developing countries.[1]

During the first half of the seventies a rapid series of events undermined this confidence. In the financial field, the doubling of international reserves between 1969 and 1972 contributed to the acceleration of inflation. The attacks against the dollar led to the suppression of its convertibility and to a series of devaluations in 1971 and 1973. Subsequently, realignment followed by general floating of the currencies signaled the explicit abandonment of the system of fixed parities which had prevailed since the end of the war. Reinforced by the upsurge in raw material prices between 1972 and 1974, inflation reached record, double-digit rates in 1974 and 1975. Although this inflation later fell slightly in the industrial countries (before rising again at the end of the decade), it showed no sign of declining in the developing countries.

The world food situation seemed to have improved since the crisis of 1965-1967; the hope created by the Green Revolution had been accompanied by a reconstitution of the world grain reserves. In 1972, however, the Soviet government's decision to abandon its policy of "self-sufficiency" and to compensate for an inadequate cereal harvest with purchases abroad caused an at once important and unexpected puncture on the international cereal market. In India, a series of poor monsoons brought the cereal harvests, from 1973 to 1975, below the record levels of 1971 and 1972. The ensuing rise in cereal imports further diminished the world grain reserves. In 1974, when the World Food Conference opened in Rome, these reserves corresponded to scarcely more than the amount required for one month of world consumption; at the beginning of the sixties they had corresponded to nearly three times as much. Meanwhile, the price of wheat on the world market, which had slightly decreased since 1950, tripled from 1972 to 1974.

What happened in the field of energy is no doubt even better known. Oil prices, which had remained practically constant since the beginning of the fifties, started increasing at the beginning of the seventies as the producers began to organize. Following the Yom Kippur War in October 1973, these prices quadrupled. Subsequently, they rose quite slowly between 1975 and 1978 (and even fell by 9 percent in real terms) before doubling again between 1978 and 1980 (corresponding to a rise of 83 percent in real prices). Although the increase in prices of other primary products was less spectacular, it was just as significant. Between the end of 1972, when the prices of these products began to soar, and 1974, when they attained a peak, they multiplied by two or three. This rise in prices was not limited to specific products, since the price indexes of all categories (metals, agricultural raw materials, food products, beverages) at least doubled during this period.

The economies of the developed as well as of the developing countries very soon experienced the consequences of this series of shocks. In 1974 and 1975 the developed countries suffered from the most serious recession they had known since the last war; the hesitant recovery which followed this crisis did not enable them to regain the dynamism of the fifties and sixties. Their average annual rate of growth, which had been over 4 percent from 1950 to 1960 and over 5 percent from 1960 to 1973, fell to 0.2 percent in 1974, 0.9 percent in 1975, and on average, scarcely reached 3 percent during the seventies. Unprecedentedly, the recession of 1974–1975 was accompanied by high inflation, which resisted the usual Keynesian remedies and has continued unabated since then. The second oil price shock, at the end of the decade, was less severe than the first; it corresponded to a price rise which, in percentage terms, was only half as high as the 1973–1974 increase. By 1979, however, oil represented a larger share in total spending; consequently the "oil transfer" due to the increased energy bill amounted to some 2 percent of the developed countries' GDP on both occasions. Nevertheless, the industrial economies appear to have supported the 1979–1980 shock better than the first one. Their growth rate fell but remained positive (1.2 percent in 1980 and in 1981), their investments did not decline as much, and their current account deficit did not widen as much as on the first occasion.

The impact on the developing countries of these external shocks and of the international economic crisis has been somewhat less damaging than was expected in the mid-seventies. The average growth rate of the oil-importing developing countries declined but remained relatively high (5.1 percent per year between 1970 and 1980; see Table 3.1). Of course the poorest among these countries suffered most; their growth rate fell by almost one-third between the sixties and the seventies. Even in this case, however, income per capita increased on average during the last decade, and only a few countries experienced the severe deterioration that had been predicted.

Yet, the oil-importing developing countries had been directly hit by the crises at the beginning of the seventies. The rise in the prices of oil and cereals, as well as of fertilizers and capital goods, led to a considerable increase in their import bills. Moreover, their exports suffered from the impact of the crisis in the developed countries (to which two-thirds of their exports go). In the developed countries, the slowdown in growth had been

TABLE 3.1 Annual Growth Rates of Gross Domestic Product in
Developing Countries

(percentages)

	1960–70	1970–80
Oil importers	*5.7*	*5.1*
Low-income oil importers	4.2	3.0
Sub-Saharan Africa	4.0	2.4
Asia	4.3	3.2
Middle-income oil importers	6.2	5.6
Sub-Saharan Africa[a]	4.1	3.5
East Asia and Pacific	7.9	8.2
Latin America/Caribbean	5.3	6.0
Middle East, North Africa	4.1	4.9
Southern Europe	7.0	4.6
Oil exporters	*6.5*	*5.2*
All developing countries	*5.9*	*5.1*

SOURCE: World Bank, *World Development Report,* 1981.
  [a] Excludes South Africa.

accompanied by a decrease in the demand for imports and, more alarming still, by an increase in protectionist tendencies; furthermore, the decrease in the demand for raw materials exported by the Third World had led to a fall in the prices of those materials. Cornered between the increase in imports and the decrease in exports, the oil-importing developing countries experienced an exceptional deficit in current account balances in 1974 and 1975. After a temporary improvement in 1976 and 1977 that deficit began to worsen again in 1978. The second oil price shock in 1979–1980 compounded this new deterioration. In 1981 the current account deficit of these countries reached $68 billion (more than five times the 1977 figure), and it will probably be around the same level in 1982 and 1983 (see Table 3.2).

Faced with this deterioration in their current accounts, the countries concerned only had two alternatives. The first was to reduce considerably their imports of consumption and capital goods, thereby sacrificing the well-being of their population and their possibilities of growth. The second was to resort to massive external financing. It is, in fact, thanks to important inflows of public or private foreign capital that these countries were able to avoid dramatic cuts in their imports. As a result, of course, the share of external financing in the gross investment of these countries substantially increased; it rose from 15 percent in 1970 to 28 percent in 1975. This increase has been particularly high for the low-income African countries, where it rose from 20 percent to 59 percent.

The type of financing received differed according to the category of countries. Virtually forbidden access to the private capital market because of the very fact of their extreme poverty, the low-income countries had to

TABLE 3.2   Balance of Payments of Oil-Importing Developing Countries
(in billions of dollars)

	1975	1976	1977
Exports, fob	88	108	130
Imports, fob	117	123	142
Trade balance	− 28	− 15	− 12
Services and private transfers, net	− 9	− 9	− 7
Official transfers, net (ODA)	7	7	7
Current balance	− 30	− 17	− 12
Capital balance	27.0	27.0	25.0
Net transactions of monetary authorities	− 2.9	9.6	12.4
Other official financing	1.8	2.0	− 0.4
Changes in official reserves	− 1.1	11.6	12.0

SOURCE: Organization for Economic Cooperation and Development (OECD), *Economic Outlook,* Paris, December 1981.

depend essentially on development assistance. Today this assistance still comes mainly from OECD countries, in spite of a substantial increase in the aid from OPEC countries. Thus, in 1980, official development assistance from OECD nations reached $26.8 billion, while $7.0 billion came from the OPEC group and $1.8 billion from socialist countries.

Expressed in constant dollars, public aid from OECD countries increased by approximately 44 percent since 1970.[2] Expressed as a percentage of the gross national product (GNP) of the contributing nations, it stagnated during this decade, going from 0.34 percent in 1970 to 0.36 percent in 1975 to 0.35 percent in 1981: we are far from the 0.70 percent target set by the International Development Strategy for the seventies. In spite of the feeble increase in the total volume of aid, there has nevertheless been a tendency to redistribute it in favor of the poorest countries, as is shown in Table 3.3. For instance, the 31 least developed countries, which had received 8.0 percent of public aid in 1970, received 19.3 percent in 1980. As we can see in Table 3.3, in 1975 public aid from the OECD countries represented 3.0 percent of the GDP for the low-income oil-importing countries, against 2.0 percent for the intermediary nations and 0.5 percent for the richest ones. Yet the poorest countries still received less per inhabitant ($4.75) than the two other categories (respectively $9.18 and $5.78). Even in 1980 the per capita assistance received by the low-income nations from the OECD and OPEC governments was less than half the corresponding receipts of the middle-income countries. The redistribution of public aid to the neediest countries has been anything but spectacular.

For their part, the middle- and high-income developing countries increasingly resorted to nonconcessional financing offered on market

1978	1979	1980	1981	1982	1983
149	192	241	248	268	297
170	225	289	303	325	354
− 21	− 33	− 48	− 54	− 57	− 57
− 9	− 15	− 23	− 26	− 28	− 28
7	10	11	13	15	16
− 23	− 38	− 60	− 68	− 70	− 69
38.7	48.0	57.5	65	66	67
15.2	10.2	− 2.5	− 3	− 4	− 2
− 0.2	1.4	4.3	5	7	7
15.0	11.6	1.8	2	3	5

terms. In the seventies the inflow of this type of financing increased much more rapidly than the official financial transfers on concessional terms. From 1970 to 1980 the transfers at market rates to the developing countries quintupled (from $11 billion to $55 billion), rising from 57 percent to 62 percent of the total external financing of these countries. The biggest share of these nonconcessional flows has been private bank credit; during this period it rose from $3.0 billion to $18.0 billion. Today these private loans form about one-fifth of the financial flows received by the developing countries, while in 1960 they represented less than 2 percent. Similarly, private and public export credits have increased very rapidly, rising from $2.7 billion in 1970 to $14.7 billion in 1980.[3]

The bulk of the nonconcessional flows went to the least poor among the Third World countries. In 1978 oil-importing developing countries with an income per capita above $450 received 41 percent of total development aid but 87 percent of all other forms of financial inflows. In particular, private bank credits mostly went to countries whose economic situation looked more secure: in 1978 and 1979 a score of countries (eleven of which were OPEC countries with balance of payment surpluses) received some 80 percent of the new credits.

In recent years, however, the unprecedented growth of financial flows to developing countries has caused some concern because of the ensuing indebtedness of these countries. The total debt level of the Third World did indeed grow rapidly during the decade: between 1971 and 1981 it increased sixfold, rising from $87 billion to $525 billion. The build-up of nominal debt accelerated markedly during the first oil price crisis and remained high in 1976–1978, when it was accompanied by large increases

TABLE 3.3   Official Development Assistance from OECD Countries to
Oil-Importing Developing Countries

Country group	Net inflow as a percentage of GDP		Net inflow per capita ($)	
	1970	1975	1970	1975
Countries with 1970 GDP per capita below $200	2.08	2.98	2.24	4.75
Countries with 1970 GDP per capita of $200–$400	2.35	2.00	5.84	9.18
Countries with 1970 GDP per capita above $400	0.41	0.49	2.56	5.78
All developing countries	1.35	1.54	2.79	5.53

SOURCE: "Development Trends since 1960 and Their Implications for a New International Development Strategy," *United Nations Journal of Development Planning* (New York), no. 13 (1979).

in foreign exchange reserves (see Table 3.2). In more than half of the oil-importing developing countries the total debt grew two and a half times as fast as export earnings between 1973 and 1978. In 1979–1980, however, the debt increase decelerated somewhat, and the reserve build-up almost ceased in 1980 and 1981. As a proportion of their GNP, the debt level increased during the decade, rising from 12.3 percent in 1970 to 17.8 percent in 1979. Apart from fears arising from the high level of the developing countries' debt, doubts were also recently voiced about the feasibility of commercial banks' increasing their loans to these countries, because of the banks' own regulations (such as existing limits on the ratio of loans to capital) and because of their overexposure in certain countries.

All the same, we should not exaggerate the extent of these problems. The service of the debt still represents an acceptable part of the exports of the Third World (8.9 percent in 1970, 12.6 percent in 1979), thereby indicating that these countries' ability to repay has not been seriously jeopardized. Furthermore, a substantial part of the developing countries' debt has served to finance a build-up of foreign exchange reserves. In any event, the private debt is concentrated in a small number of countries, so that while repayment may present serious difficulties in certain cases, it should not lead to widespread problems. Similarly, constraints due to credit regulations or overexposure seem to be limited to a few banks which could be, and in some instances have been, replaced by other lending institutions willing to expand their operations in developing countries. Nevertheless, in the end, these countries' ability to repay — and consequently their ability to gain the confidence of potential lenders — will depend on their ability to increase their export earnings at the necessary pace. In this respect a decline in the exports from the developing to the developed countries could lead to a critical situation for certain of the former countries.

In conclusion, it seems that if the developing countries have been less severely affected by the shocks of the seventies than was initially feared, it is mainly due to a considerable increase in private loans received by the middle-income countries and to a redistribution of official assistance towards the poorest countries. In spite of its immediate advantages, this solution is nonetheless fraught with danger for the coming years, since the future stability of the system depends upon the maintenance of both the indebted countries' export capacity and the financial intermediaries' ability to carry out the necessary capital transfers. The foreseeable increase for the eighties in the current account deficit of the oil-importing Third World countries – a deficit arising inter alia from the increase in energy import bills – will compound the problem. It might be imprudent to expect that, in the financial field, the next decade will be as problem-free as the last one.[4]

THE QUEST FOR A NEW
INTERNATIONAL ECONOMIC ORDER

From a political and economic standpoint, the decolonization of the Third World in the aftermath of World War II is perhaps one of the most important events of modern history. From the economic viewpoint, which is the aspect that interests us here, one of the results of these political upheavals has been the dispersion of the decision-making centers of the international economy. Economic policies concerning India or Senegal are no longer defined in London or Paris but – in principle – in New Delhi or Dakar; international problems of trade or finance are dealt with by over a hundred independent countries and no longer by a handful of nations north of the Tropic of Cancer.

At the time when a growing number of countries were reaching political independence, economic interdependence was increasing. The rapid post-war economic development was accompanied by a growing interpenetration of the national economies throughout the world. Today there is probably not a single country which is not economically dependent on others. Maybe we already understood this when we saw how the economic crisis at the beginning of the seventies affected virtually all the nations. In this respect perhaps this period of economic turmoil is the first one which really deserves to be described as a *world* crisis.

No doubt these two factors – multiplication of national centers of economic decision and increasing interdependence of the economies – explain the intensification of international economic negotiations since the war. For the Third World countries, preoccupied with their development, many of these negotiations offer above all an opportunity to try to obtain from other governments, in particular from those of the developed nations, certain conditions favorable to their own growth. This series of negotiations, commonly known as the North-South dialogue, has intensified considerably since the beginning of the seventies.

It would be a mistake, however, to trace the beginning of this dialogue back to the oil crisis. In the sixties the organization of the Third World, which had first been undertaken as a search for political independence vis-à-vis the two blocs, had started to concentrate on economic demands, when détente and the emergence of a multipolar world made political nonalignment lose its claim to priority. The first United Nations Conference on Trade and Development (UNCTAD) in 1964 and the organization at the United Nations of "the group of 77" emphasized the trend toward a situation where the tensions between North and South would aggravate the confrontation between East and West.

All the same, we have to recognize that the dialogue between North and South progressed extremely slowly until 1973. Of course a few steps had been taken. In 1968, at the second UNCTAD, the industrial countries had agreed to the principle of establishing generalized systems of preferences for imports from the developing countries; Europe was already associated with a certain number of African countries through the Yaoundé agreements. On the whole, however, the developed countries did not appear very interested in these negotiations.

For various reasons the pace of the negotiations changed after the events of the fall of 1973. One reason was doubtless the new political weight of the developing countries, which they owed to their alliance with the OPEC countries. Another was that all nations eventually realized the extent of the crisis and understood that only collaborative action would permit them to master this new situation. As the secretary general of the United Nations said in 1975, "The international system of economic and trade relations which was devised thirty years ago is now manifestly inadequate for the needs of the world community as a whole. The charge against that order in the past was that it worked well for the affluent and against the poor. It cannot now even be said that it works well for the affluent."

At the beginning of 1974 a Special Session of the United Nations General Assembly on Raw Materials and Development (Sixth Special Session) adopted a motion to found a New International Economic Order. In September 1975 the Seventh Special Session passed a resolution on the development of international cooperation. Meanwhile, the Convention of Lomé, which linked Europe to some fifty associated states, had been signed, and the president of France had proposed a conference on energy, which later became the Conference on International Economic Cooperation (CIEC). In 1976, the fourth UNCTAD concluded an agreement to set up an "Integrated Program for Commodities" in order to stabilize the prices of these products. The CIEC ended in 1977 with an agreement to set up a Common Fund for the financing of these commodity agreements and to provide, as a "special action," an additional $1 billion to the poorest developing countries. In March 1977 it was agreed at an UNCTAD conference that the debt of the least developed and poorest countries should be cancelled; in November 1979 the Lomé Convention was renewed.

What have been the concrete results of this feverish activity and these innumerable resolutions? They are not particularly impressive. In spite of the creation of special new funds and the replenishment of old ones, development assistance from the developed countries remains, today as in 1970, at half the agreed target (0.70 percent of GNP). With regard to trade, the situation worsened during the seventies because of the "neoprotectionism" which spread in the industrialized countries in the wake of the crisis. The Common Fund has still not begun to function, and the Integrated Program has scarcely progressed since the initial propositions. Moreover, since the end of the 1970s the dialogue between the developed countries and the developing countries has been bogged down in routine. In May 1979 a few results of limited scope saved the fifth UNCTAD from being called a complete failure; nine months later, however, nothing saved the third UNIDO Conference from total disaster. In August 1980 a Special Session of the U.N. General Assembly on Economic Issues, assembled in New York to adopt an International Development Strategy for the eighties, could agree only on a text which was nothing short of an ineffectual compromise, and it failed in its second aim, the initiation of Global Negotiations. Three years after having been conceived, the latter have still not been started and already appear to be moribund. Eight years after its promulgation the New International Economic Order remains buried under an avalanche of ministerial perorations and a heap of international resolutions.

Although the scant results of the dialogue between North and South can hardly be called encouraging, it nevertheless has a more positive aspect which we should not overlook. The emergence of the Third World on the international economic stage is not a passing phenomenon; neither is it merely an accidental result of the energy crisis. On the contrary, it constitutes a permanent factor in international relations because it is the manifestation of a planetary interdependence which goes far beyond the mere question of energy. No doubt one of the rare beneficial consequences of a decade of economic turmoil is that we understand better today than we did ten years ago the extent to which the economies of North and South are linked in every sector. In 1970 the developed countries could still afford to neglect the Third World as a trade partner or as a source of raw materials, energy, or capital. They can no longer do so today, and therein lies perhaps the best assurance that the dialogue between North and South will continue.

THE DISILLUSIONS OF PROGRESS

The political leaders and economists of the Third World who assumed the responsibility of developing their young nations in the aftermath of the Second World War did not have at their disposal an established collection of theories of economic growth. Although the problems of economic development were the chief concern of the classical school from Adam Smith to Karl Marx, they had not been given serious attention from the last quarter of the nineteenth century onward. Around 1950 the theories which dominated economic thought in the developed countries — where these new leaders of the Third World had been trained, after all — were essentially the neoclassical and especially the Keynesian theories.

In these circumstances it is not surprising that the economic philosophy and practice of the nonsocialist developing countries have been markedly influenced by these two theories. The Keynesian theory, which had essentially served to explain the cyclical instabilities of the capitalist economies, was adapted to take into account the new preoccupations concerning growth, while neoclassical marginalism permitted some sophisticated fine-tuning in the research of optimal combinations of production factors. Using one or the other of these theories, economists could build intricate models in which adequate doses of "capital" and "labor" would miraculously lead to the desired growth rate. Thanks to the techniques of national accounting — another by-product of Keynesian concepts — the results of the recommended policies could be evaluated by measuring the evolution of the gross domestic product and of the principal macroeconomic aggregates.

In both the neoclassical and the Keynesian schools, the problems of income distribution and employment nevertheless remained . . . marginal. They were even more so in the minds of the planners and leaders, who were concerned primarily with the growth of production. In the early fifties Arthur Lewis, whose writings were to influence considerably the evolution of thought in this field, set the tone in *The Theory of Economic Growth:* "First it should be noted that our subject matter is growth, and not distribution." [5]

This exclusive attention to the problems of growth went hand in hand with a marked predilection for industry. After all, was not development synonymous with industrialization? The main role of agriculture was to supply industry with the labor, the capital, and the cheap food necessary for its development — a function similar to the role this sector was supposed to have played in the developed countries when they were at a comparable stage of development. As a potential source of foreign exchange for the financing of industry, export crops received some attention, but the food production sector was, by and large, not considered worthy of such solicitude. While it may not always have been as explicit, the idea often was that growth of food production would "naturally" accompany any increase in the population: in the battle for development, the food wagon was in the rear guard.

Although the above picture is obviously rather oversimplified, for there have been exceptions in various countries, it nevertheless does represent the general trend that prevailed until the seventies in the majority of the nonsocialist developing countries. Until that time, in fact, criticism of the situation was relatively rare. The few critics (for instance, Raùl Prebisch with the Latin American school of *dependencia* or, in a different way, René Dumont) could generally be dismissed as "nonobjective" or, worse, "leftists." Because of the lack of statistics concerning income and employment, it was in any case difficult to measure objectively the evolution of the population's living conditions. Since, after all, the aim of development was growth of the GDP, there was no cause to criticize a theory and a practice which enabled certain countries to attain record growth rates. Even the food crisis of the years 1966–1967 did not really shake the confidence of Third World leaders; they knew that in case of need the breadbasket of the U.S. Middle West was at hand to help countries in difficulty.[6]

Paradoxically, criticism of these strategies grew at a time when the impressive results in GDP growth during the First Development Decade were being confirmed. We can trace a few stages of this campaign. At the end of the sixties Gunnar Myrdal launched a comprehensive attack against the ongoing policies of the South Asian countries in his monumental work *Asian Drama.*[7] In 1971 Professor Dandekar published his statistical survey *Poverty in India,* in which he showed that the per capita income of 40 to 50 percent of the Indian population was not sufficient to assure them adequate food and established that the situation had scarcely improved after two decades of effort.[8] In Brazil, there was growing evidence that the exceptional growth rate of the sixties had not really improved the lot of the poorest. Similarly in Pakistan, rapid economic growth was accompanied by an increase in underemployment and in the disparities between the east and the west of the country, as well as by a growing concentration of wealth, a dangerous situation which was not appreciated until it exploded at the end of the sixties.

The world food crisis in 1973–1974 shook the governments of the Third World, who then learned that they could not count on American and Australian cereals' being always available whenever they needed them. The message was particularly clear for India, which was suffering from poor harvests at the time, and for the Sahel, which was experiencing one of its longest droughts. At the same time, the world learned about the extent of malnutrition: in 1974 the United Nations announced that there were 400 million malnourished people in the Third World, and two years later the World Bank asserted that the real figure was closer to one billion.

The universities woke up in turn and started asking questions. What had two decades of development meant for the poorest? Statistical or theoretical studies on income distribution became fashionable. In 1974 a comparative study of different countries concluded that "development is accompanied by an absolute as well as a relative decline in the average income of the very poor. Indeed, an initial spurt of dualistic growth may cause such a decline for as much as 60 percent of the population."[9] Although this study was criticized on account of its questionable logic and less-than-reliable data, its controversial findings aroused considerable interest and caused researchers to pay more attention to the distribution of the profits of growth. Subsequently other studies confirmed that in several countries the lot of the poor had scarcely improved since the middle of the century (see Chapters 2 and 8).

The criticism of the development strategies pursued so far was accompanied by the quest for strategies which would be better able to satisfy people's basic needs. The experiences of certain countries that had endeavored to fight poverty directly were carefully studied. Particular attention was paid to Communist China, whose spectacular results in the fight against poverty were beginning to be known beyond her borders. Toward the middle of the seventies the critics of current development strategies had gathered convincing proofs to support their argument. The ranks of these critics had grown, and their heresy was about to become the new orthodoxy. In June 1976 the World Conference on Employment assembled under the auspices of the International Labor Office and adopted a program of action, declaring that "strategies and national development plans and policies should include explicitly as a priority objective the promotion of employment and the satisfaction of the basic needs of each country's population."[10] The strategy of basic needs was thereby officially enthroned.

The nice unanimity of this conference did not prevail for long, however. The rather awkward enthusiasm of the developed countries aroused the suspicion of certain leaders of the Third World. Could it be that the promotion of basic needs was a stratagem devised to maintain the Third World countries in their rural condition of underdevelopment and to deny them access to modern technology? Was it not also a means for the developed countries to escape their financial responsibilities (by promoting a "second-rate" development in the countries of the South) and their political responsibilities (by diverting attention from the changes required to create a New International Economic Order)? The very words "basic needs" soon provoked mistrust among Third World diplomats, and the phrase quickly became taboo at international conferences.

Of course this did not imply a simple return to previous development strategies. Evidence of their insufficiencies continued to accumulate, and far from the diplomatic jousts of the North-South dialogue the quest for alternative models was going on. While it is generally admitted today that the former strategies have frequently failed, there is still no agreement as to what could replace them. Thus, the very idea of a basic needs strategy still awaits a concrete and above all operational formulation. We shall return to this subject in Chapter 9.

For the Third World countries, as indeed for all nations, the seventies were marked by significant upheavals. In the field of development many habits and dogmas were challenged. The optimism of the sixties, which resulted from several decades of exceptional growth, gave way to concern, even pessimism, with regard to the future; at the same time, the ultimate aims of growth and the established economic order were being impugned. Today, the models of the past can no longer be accepted, but the quest for other development strategies and for a new international economic order still has not reached any concrete results.

For thirty years the Third World experienced unprecedented economic growth: its gross domestic product increased fivefold, and the average income per capita more than doubled. The new countries set up their administration, built their infrastructure, and developed their natural resources. There was marked progress in health, education, and housing.

At the close of this period of exceptional growth, however, a number of flaws are clearly visible. The gap between developed and developing countries is wider than ever, and gaps within the Third World itself have also increased. While a great number of developing countries have given proof of an unexpected dynamism, a minority have not succeeded in breaking the vicious circle of poverty. Even in the fast-growing countries, the situation of the poorest strata has scarcely improved in some instances.

In coming decades the evolution of this core of poverty will constitute the real challenge of the Third World, and the most vital development issues will concern the condition of these one billion men and women imprisoned in the most degrading poverty. In its recent report the Brandt Commission emphasizes the prime importance of this question and declares: "Priority must be given to the needs of the poorest countries and regions. We call for a major initiative in favor of the poverty belts of Africa and Asia."[11] Today it is clear that current development strategies will not solve this problem because three decades of efforts have resulted in, at best, virtual stagnation and, at worst, deterioration of over half the population of the Third World.

It is perhaps paradoxical that at the time when it has become unquestionably necessary to change the content of growth, the very possibility of its continuation appears uncertain. The confidence that marked the fifties and sixties has not resisted the shocks of the seventies. Today neither the South nor the North feels optimistic with regard to the decade which has just begun. The uncertainties weighing on the future of energy, of course, but more generally the challenges of the end of the century, too long ignored, will now have to be confronted.

2
THE PROBLEMS OF THE END
OF THE CENTURY

4
GROWTH IN THE DEVELOPED WORLD

For better and for worse the economies of the developing world are now linked with those of the developed countries; the growth of the one group is tied to the fortune of the other. We can illustrate this interdependence by recalling how in 1974–1975 loans obtained from financial institutions of the developed countries enabled the Third World to maintain a high growth rate. This growth, in turn, brought about an increase in imports from the developed countries, whose economies thereby received a particularly welcome support in difficult circumstances. In fact, it has been estimated that if the non-OPEC developing countries had reduced their manufactured imports to compensate for the oil price rise of 1973–1974, there would have been an additional three million unemployed in the OECD countries. Similarly, in the coming years, the economic situation in each group of countries will influence developments in the other, and consequently, we can not consider the future of the Third World economies without first assessing the prospects for growth in the developed countries.

DIMENSIONS OF INTERDEPENDENCE
At once cause and effect of the rapid world economic growth during the last few decades, interdependence itself is now an economic phenomenon of worldwide significance. The links among the developed capitalist economies were made only too clear during the crisis of the thirties. Perhaps a crisis of comparable dimensions was required for us to understand the complexity of the relations that today link our economies and those of the Third World. It may be useful, however, to examine here some aspects of this interdependence: the main ones concern energy, raw materials, trade, finance, and labor migration.

The developed countries' dependence on the Third World for energy is sufficiently clear today that it is not necessary to dwell on it here. (In Chapter 6 I shall deal with the similar dependence of certain of the *developing* countries.) In addition, all industrial countries depend to one degree or another on imports for obtaining the raw materials their economies require; this dependence is particularly acute for Japan and the European countries. Almost all tropical agricultural products as well as a considerable share of the minerals required for industry have to be imported. Neither the European Community nor Japan produces more than 25 percent of any of the minerals that are vital for its economy, and even the United States produces less than 50 percent.[1] From the developing countries originate imports of all tropical products and a substantial proportion of other raw materials. Over one-third of the European Community's mineral imports come from Third World countries, while the United States relies on them for over one-half its supplies of tin, rubber, and manganese. In fact, approximately 60 percent of the world imports of the main raw materials other than oil come from the developing countries.

For the developed economies, Third World countries also represent an increasingly important market: during recent years the proportion of their exports going to these countries has grown considerably. Today, Japan, the United States, and the European Community send over one-third of their exports to the developing countries. The United States exports more to the Third World than to Europe, China, and the Soviet Union combined; similarly the European Community sells more to the Third World than to the United States, Japan, and the socialist countries.

Symmetrically, the Third World economies depend on the developed countries in numerous areas. Trade with industrial countries is responsible for over 70 percent of the developing countries' exports and constitutes their main source of foreign exchange. The growth of these exports was considerably stimulated in the fifties and sixties by the policies of trade liberalization adopted by the developed countries: in the early seventies, after implementation of the tariff reductions of the Kennedy Round, these countries' trade regulations were less restrictive than they had ever been since 1914. We have nevertheless seen, since 1974, how a deterioration in the industrial countries' economic situation can affect the developing countries through the channel of trade. The recession of 1974–1975 led to a decrease in demand for imports by the developed economies and consequently to a decline in Third World exports and a reduction in the prices of raw material exports. In addition, protectionism increased in the industrial countries, mostly in a nontariff guise: "voluntary" export restraints, countervailing duties, import quotas, subsidies, and so on. These "neoprotectionist" tendencies have been resisted by the industrial countries themselves, however, and the recent conclusion of the Tokyo Round should support their efforts. (We should note nevertheless that the tariff reductions agreed upon during this Round are on the whole smaller for the products that are most important for the developing countries.)[2] In any case, the experience of the sixties and the seventies clearly indicates that for better or for worse the evolution of the developed economies will directly affect Third World exports during the coming years.

Even if the exports of the non-oil developing countries were to increase substantially in the coming years, the financial needs of these countries would persist. The purchase of capital goods required to implement their development programs, the imports of energy to satisfy rapidly growing needs and of food to make up a widening deficit, are going to weigh heavily on their trade balances. According to the World Bank, during the next decade the deficit (expressed in constant prices) of these countries' current accounts will remain close to the record level reached in 1980.[3]

In these circumstances only huge financial transfers will enable the oil-importing developing countries to balance their current accounts without sacrificing their import programs. The poorest countries, which do not have access to private capital, will have to continue to rely on official aid for the bulk of these transfers. Since OPEC countries already devote a large proportion of their GNP to this development aid, it seems unlikely that their contribution will increase significantly in the future.[4] Even in the desirable, but unfortunately improbable, event of a considerable increase in aid from the socialist countries, the developing countries would undoubtedly continue to depend mainly on the capitalist developed countries for their financing on concessional terms.[5]

For the middle-income developing countries, private financing will no doubt continue to play the vital role that it filled in the seventies, though – to repeat an important point – it may not be able to do so as effectively as before. In any event, the banking institutions of the developed countries will contribute to this financing by recycling the oil countries' surpluses and by transferring funds originating in the developed economies.

Public financing as well as transfers of private capital will be affected by the developed countries' economic situation. All too often a discouraging economic outlook becomes for these countries a convenient pretext for not fulfilling their aid commitments. Similarly, the transfers of private capital depend on the cooperation – or at least on the nonobstruction – of governmental authorities in the industrial countries; their goodwill, in turn, will probably depend on the state of these countries' balance of payments. In this area too, therefore, the economic situation of the developed countries will have repercussions on the Third World economies.

Labor migration is a last example of the way in which the health of the developed economies can influence the growth of developing countries.

Although this phenomenon is economically less important than commercial or financial flows between North and South, it is no doubt more immediately visible. Today some five million immigrants work in Western Europe, and six million in the United States. The funds sent by these workers to their native countries increased considerably during the seventies: for the developing countries as a whole, they rose from $3.5 billion in 1970 to $24 billion in 1980. For the countries of origin themselves these returns often represent a substantial support: for instance, Pakistan obtains as much foreign exchange from the transfers made by its migrant workers as from its exports. As we saw during the last decade, the reception extended to these migrant workers depends considerably on the economic situation of the host country: for instance, the number of foreign workers in Europe has declined by one million since the beginning of the 1974–1975 crisis. Similarly, in the coming years the economic evolution of the developed countries will directly affect the labor force of the neighboring developing countries.

In different ways and to different degrees the economic development of the Third World has been and will be increasingly affected by the growth of the developed countries. We could, of course, envisage instead the alternative solution of a radical break, with the developing countries entrenching themselves in a "Southern fortress." Whatever view we take of the long-term advantages of such a scenario, its short- and medium-term economic costs would be enormous, for the developed countries as well as for the Third World, because of the multiplicity and solidity of the economic links now existing between these two groups of countries. In any case, the political evolution of the last few years indicates that no such sudden "delinking" is likely in the immediate future.[6] In these circumstances the present interdependence among the different countries and regions can only continue and intensify, with the result that the economic evolution of the Third World will be increasingly affected by the situation in the developed countries.

THE FUTURE OF THE DEVELOPED ECONOMIES

What, then, are the prospects for growth in the industrial countries during the next few decades? While we cannot become involved in a discussion of this vexed subject here, we cannot really afford to ignore it either, since, as we have seen, it will have direct implications for the development of the Third World countries. Until 1972–1973 the public at large in the developed countries scarcely entertained any doubts with regard to the future of growth. As for the economists, anesthetized by twenty-five years of rapid economic development and lulled by the illusion that the Keynesian kit would always enable governments to control growth and inflation, the majority of them also envisaged continuing high growth, at least for the next decade or two.

Yet the reception given to the first report of the Club of Rome in 1972 is an indication that under this apparent calm some anxiety existed.[7] In the previous decade certain tensions had already appeared in the functioning of the world economy, while the student revolts had challenged the very content of growth. In spite of this, and even though *The Limits to Growth* had been a subject of intense discussion and an object of considerable criticism in certain spheres, this report presumably barely affected the thoughts and expectations of the man in the street.

At the time, the tidal wave of the years 1972 to 1975 could very well have appeared an immediate confirmation of the catastrophic predictions of this report. The abrupt rise in the prices of all raw materials seemed, in fact, to indicate that the physical limits to growth would very soon be reached. The recession of 1974–1975, however, brought about a fall in demand and, consequently, in the prices of raw materials as well as a decrease in the real prices of energy. With the beginning of a recovery in 1976 a return to normalcy seemed possible. Yet this recovery proceeded slowly and irregularly and was accompanied by persistent unemployment and inflation, until it was thoroughly shaken at the end of the decade by the "second oil price shock."

Until then, it was nevertheless tempting to believe that the past shocks only represented a cyclical recession similar to – though more brutal than – the recessions we had experienced and to some extent overcome since the last war. Inasmuch as the fundamental state of the world economy had remained the same, nothing hindered a return to high growth rates, full employment, and price stability. In a way, in 1976 as in 1932, prosperity always seemed to be "just around the corner." Even in 1977 a report made by OECD experts – bearing the characteristic title *Towards Full Employment and Price Stability* – stated that "the immediate causes of the severe problems of 1971–1975 can largely be understood in terms of conventional economic analysis . . . the most important feature [of recent history] was an unusual bunching of unfortunate disturbances unlikely to be repeated on the same scale, the impact of which was compounded by some avoidable errors in economic policy."[8] The report stressed the possibility of a return to a period of rapid economic growth accompanied by the resumption of full employment and the stabilization of prices: for the period 1976–1980 an annual growth rate of 5.5 percent for real GNP could be envisaged. We know what actually happened. During this period the average annual growth rate of the industrial countries did not attain 4 percent, and growth slowed down at the end of the decade; as for full employment and price stability, they appear further away today than ever before.

The failure of traditional economic tools and the apparent impossibility of obtaining the desired return to normal have gradually created the suspicion that structural changes have taken place in the international economy and that, rather than a passing crisis, the years 1972 to 1975 have marked a turning point in postwar economic history.

Since 1977 various studies have shown — with hindsight — why the rapid growth of the 1948–1973 period could not last and how in the coming years the developed countries will be faced with slower growth and a less stable economic situation. This is not a confirmation of the apocalyptic notes sounded in *The Limits to Growth,* however. In fact, this report based its argument primarily on the existence of physical limits to growth, and the more comprehensive studies which have been undertaken since then (by the Club of Rome inter alia) all but invalidate this thesis.[9] Mankind does not appear to be confronted with any limit to its physical resources but with the problems of organizing and implementing appropriate policies for a rapidly changing world.

In the case of energy, for instance, it is hardly contestable that the finite nature of oil and gas resources imposes limits to their production. Consequently, the problem is to assure the smoothest possible transition toward the utilization of less scarce resources (coal, nuclear fission) and, eventually, of renewable energies (solar, nuclear fusion). With regard to raw materials, existing reserves make very unlikely any overall physical scarcity, but the investment policies necessary for their obtainment will have to be implemented in time. Similarly, the preservation of the environment seems to be possible at a nonprohibitive economic cost.

In most of the studies made during the last four or five years we thus find the idea that the problems of the recent years and of the forthcoming decades do not revolve around the exhaustion of physical resources but around the unsuitability, or the lack, of policies concerned with the exploitation of these resources. Without entering into a discussion not central to our concerns, I shall simply outline here some of the principal arguments advanced to this effect.

Reviving the Russian economist Kondratieff's largely forgotten theory of long-term cycles, Rostow argues that capitalist economies are subject to cycles lasting from forty to fifty years around an equilibrium path.[10] These cycles are caused by changes in the relative prices of raw materials (including energy and food) and industrial products. During an upswing of a Kondratieff cycle, for instance, the prices of raw materials are high and their supply is limited because of the lead time inherent in the implementation of investment projects; eventually, however, additional investments will bring about a fall in prices, corresponding to the cycle's downswing. According to Rostow the world economy entered a "kondratieff" upswing at the beginning of the seventies (the fifth since 1790). To accelerate the return to equilibrium it would now be necessary to invest in energy and food production, as well as in environmental protection and raw material production.

Even Herman Kahn has apparently been contaminated by doubts concerning the prospects for growth, although this futurist had for a long time been its unabashed sycophant.[11] While supporting Rostow's argument, Kahn gives more importance to the "social" limits to growth. According to him, the counterculture and the (unfounded) fear of the physical limits to growth have deeply affected — Kahn seems to think "infected" — Western values, which no longer give the same priority to the work ethic. More than technical difficulties, which can be overcome, it is this change of spirit that will turn the coming decades into an "epoque de malaise."[12] During this period the "super-industrial" economies of the West will be looking for their second wind, and their growth rates will not exceed 3 to 4 percent per year. At the end of this period, however, these countries will have overcome these problems of transition and will enter into the era of "post-industrial economies," a new Golden Age whose delights Kahn unfortunately does not describe.

The most comprehensive study concerning the future of the developed countries was made for the OECD by the Interfutures team.[13] This study also concludes that during the next few decades the developed countries will experience more moderate growth. Apart from the causes already mentioned (the problem of energy transition, difficulty of access to raw materials, change of values), other elements will contribute to this decline. Uncertainties regarding external factors (emergence of a multipolar world, instability of the monetary system) and internal characteristics (institutional sclerosis, governmental incapacity to master the complex data of their policies, decline in the expected profitability of investments, sensitivity to inflation) will prevent the return to the high growth of the fifties and sixties. During the next two decades the average annual growth of GNP should be about 3 to 4 percent. This rate will probably not suffice to bring about full employment during the eighties, but with the foreseen reduction in the growth of the active population, the situation could change during the following decade. For all countries, developed or developing, the main challenge of the coming decades will be to assure the energy transition; the situation of the world economy will remain precarious as long as the contribution of oil to the world energy supply is not reduced.

There are, of course, other reports on the economic prospects of the different countries or regions (for instance, the U.S. *Global 2000 Report* or the World Bank's *World Development Reports*).[14] Without describing their analyses here, I shall simply note that on the whole their forecasts tend to be broadly convergent. Different analysts may emphasize different factors, but there is remarkable agreement in their conclusions. In all likelihood the developed countries are heading towards a period of slow and irregular growth. Various uncertainties, especially that of the energy transition, are likely to make of the coming decades a period of turbulence and instability, while the current inflation and underemployment will persist, at least in the medium term.

If these are the prospects for the developed economies, what are their implications for the developing countries? Speaking in October 1979 to the board of governors of the World Bank, its president declared: "Without [a major recovery of the momentum of growth in developed countries] the prospects of the developing countries themselves are severely limited. The truth of the matter is that the economic fortunes of the developed and developing countries are more and more intertwined in our increasingly interdependent world." Unfortunately, as we have seen, there is little likelihood of a substantial recovery in developed countries. Under such conditions, the future for the developing countries does indeed look bleak.

Let us not indulge in any illusions: if the prospects for the developed countries during the next decades look mediocre, the outlook for the developing countries is undoubtedly bad. The links between these two groups of countries are now so numerous and solid that the difficulties of the developed economies are bound to affect the Third World countries. In these circumstances, only a sustained effort by the international community would be able to save the developing countries – in particular, the poorest of them – from a grave deterioratioin in their situation. Unfortunately it is all too clear that the industrial countries, preoccupied by their own problems, are no more inclined towards such action today than they have been in the recent past.

5
DEMOGRAPHIC TRANSITION

The rate of population growth in the Third World countries during the last three decades has been unprecedented in their history. During this period, the imbalance created by the reduction in mortality has caused a doubling of their population, and the other demographic indicators have also changed rapidly, albeit with a certain lag. In this regard, World War II appears as a watershed, since postwar trends differ radically from historical precedents. In these circumstances of continuous upheaval it becomes extremely risky to venture long-term projections.

Before they even try to make any forecasts, demographers must first endeavor to apprehend the ongoing evolution, making the best possible use of frequently limited and unreliable data. In a rapidly changing situation this endeavor is in itself particularly hazardous. It becomes even more so when we go from interpretation to explanation and attempt to link the observed phenomena with their underlying causes. And yet only such an attempt at explanation might eventually enable us to discern more clearly the future trends and the policies required.

This should lead us to feel a certain sympathy for demographers, whose job, never easy, is especially hard in these uncertain times. But it should also cause us to handle statistics, explanations, and above all, demographic forecasts with the greatest of prudence. This general advice applies, of course, to the particular case of the present chapter.

RECENT TRENDS
Because of the inevitable time lag between demographic phenomena and their expression in statistics, experts are perhaps condemned, during a time of rapid change, to deal always with problems that are already partly obsolete. Thus in the fifties, demographers studying the Third World

situation focused mostly on the problem of mortality, though mortality was already falling at an unprecedented rate. When the growth of population due to this rapid decline was better understood, experts began to concern themselves, in the sixties, with the question of fertility. The latter, in turn, was beginning to decline at this time, but it was only during the following decade that this phenomenon was actually perceived by the statisticians.

Between the early sixties and the late seventies the mortality rate of the developing countries (including China) continued to decrease, falling from 17 to 12 per thousand. At the same time the birthrate fell even more, from 40 to 34 per thousand. Consequently the rate of population growth also declined, going from 2.3 percent to 2.2 percent. Table 5.1 shows how the birthrate has actually declined in all regions of the Third World since 1960. This general fall in birthrates is in itself an encouraging sign. Even more promising is the fact that this reduction appears to have accelerated in every region during the last two decades. For the whole Third World the birthrate declined by 1 point from 1960 to 1965, by 1.7 points from 1965 to 1970, and by 2.9 points from 1970 to 1974. (We must note, however, that in Africa this rate is higher and declines more slowly than in the other regions.) This reduction in the birthrate appears — according to the fragmentary state of present information — to be general, since it has occurred in 77 of the 88 countries for which data are available.

This reduction was more marked and presumably began earlier in the smallest countries. In 14 out of 66 Third World countries with fewer than 15 million inhabitants and for which statistics are reliable, the fall in birthrates between 1965 and 1975 exceeded 20 percent.[1] A certain number of medium-sized countries also experienced considerable reductions. In South Korea, Thailand, Turkey, Colombia, and Egypt birthrates fell by 25 percent or more between 1955 and 1974. For the eight largest countries, however, the trend is less evident, since between 1955 and 1974 only China, India, Indonesia, and Mexico experienced reductions above 10 percent.[2] Even though comparatively little is still known about China, it is certainly an exceptional case. There, fertility has declined abruptly, and today the birthrate is in all likelihood below 30 per thousand, perhaps even 25. This rate, which is close to that of certain European countries, has been achieved in a socioeconomic structure that is still essentially agricultural, thereby making the Chinese case unprecedented in history. Together with Korea and Thailand, China experienced in the ten years from 1965 to 1975 a fall of more than 20 percent in the fertility rate — a more rapid decline than the fall that occurred in Europe during the second half of the nineteenth century.

At the regional level, Asia is doubtless the most remarkable example of the decline in birth and fertility rates. In the countries where Chinese

TABLE 5.1   Crude Birthrate Trends in Developing and Developed Countries

Region	No. of countries	1975 pop. (millions)	Crude birthrates (per thousand)				
			1955	1960	1965	1970	1974
Africa	38	366	48.5	48.3	47.9	47.1	46.2
Latin America	21	289	43.0	42.2	40.8	39.4	37.6
Asia[a]	34	1,318	44.6	44.8	43.5	41.9	38.1
All developing countries[a]	93	1,973	45.1	45.1	44.1	42.4	39.5
All developed countries	35	1,124	22.3	21.3	18.9	17.3	16.6

SOURCE: Robert S. McNamara, *Address to the Massachusetts Institute of Technology* (Washington, D.C.: World Bank, 1977).
[a] Excludes People's Republic of China.

culture prevails, the fall has generally been particularly rapid. On the other hand, in India, opposition to the forced sterilization policies of the mid-seventies has brought about the discredit of population policies and a subsequent rise in the birthrate. In Latin America, Colombia achieved remarkable results; its fertility fell by 25 percent between 1965 and 1975. More recently Mexico and Brazil also experienced notable declines in fertility. These three examples may indicate a general trend in the Latin American continent which would have been considered improbable twenty years ago because of the influence exerted by the Catholic Church. Africa is the only Third World continent that did not experience an important fall in its fertility rate during the 1970s. Since mortality declined during the same period, its population growth rate consequently increased; today this growth rate is higher than in any other region.

Mortality continued to decline in the Third World during the last decade, but not as quickly as it did during the previous twenty years. Perhaps the food crises of the early seventies in part explain this slowdown in Bangladesh or in the Sahel. The low mortality which many countries had already attained by 1960 presumably also explains why progress was slower during the following years.

In the areas of mortality and fertility, indications of the ongoing evolutions are fragmentary and fragile. We shall have to wait for the results of the censuses that are to be made during the eighties to understand better the extent of these evolutions. In any event, the evidence accumulated throughout the seventies now permits us to state that, with the exception of Africa, the Third World has entered a phase of demographic transition. After a rapid fall in mortality following World War II, many developing countries are now experiencing a decline in fertility that should eventually lead to a new state of stationary population. While the actuality of this transition phase is now clearly established, its rapidity and duration are still matters for speculation.

TABLE 5.2   World and Regional Population, 1950 and 1975, and Medium Projections, 1980 and 2000

Area	Population (millions)				Percentage increase		Percentage distribution	
	1950	1975	1980	2000	1950–1975	1975–2000	1975	2000
World	2,513	4,033	4,415	6,199	60.5	53.7	100.0	100.0
More developed regions	832	1,093	1,131	1,272	31.4	16.4	27.1	20.5
Less developed regions	1,681	2,940	3,284	4,927	74.9	67.6	72.9	79.5
Africa	219	406	469	828	85.3	104.0	10.1	13.4
Latin America	164	323	368	608	97.1	88.5	8.0	9.8
North America	166	236	246	290	42.3	22.5	5.9	4.7
East Asia	673	1,063	1,136	1,406	58.0	32.2	26.4	22.7
South Asia	706	1,255	1,422	2,205	77.7	75.7	31.1	35.6
Europe	392	474	484	520	21.0	9.7	11.8	8.4
Oceania	13	21	23	30	67.3	40.0	0.5	0.5
U.S.S.R.	180	254	267	312	41.3	22.6	6.3	5.0

SOURCE: *World Population Trends and Prospects by Country, 1950–2000: Summary Report of the 1978 Assessment* (United Nations publication, ST/ESA/SER.R/33).

LONG-TERM PROSPECTS

The uncertainty regarding the present demographic evolution of the Third World makes long-term forecasting particularly hazardous. In these countries the fall in birth and fertility rates has been relatively rapid – at any rate more rapid than was foreseen by demographers as recently as twenty years ago. It is hard to predict, even for the next decade or two, what the future evolution of these variables and of the mortality rate will be.

It is not surprising, therefore, that estimates of world population at the end of the century differ, depending upon the sources used: 6 billion according to the World Bank, 6.2 according to the United Nations, 6.35 according to the Bureau of the Census. As can be seen, however, these differences are slight. Similarly, if we look at the estimates made by the United Nations, the gap between the medium projection and the high and low projections is not very large (±7 percent). The smallness of this margin of error implies that, whatever the efficacy of the population policies implemented between now and the end of the century, the size of the world population in the year 2000 will scarcely be changed. (See Table 5.2.)

By contrast, the uncertainty of demographic forecasts as well as the potential impact of population policies can be more easily recognized when we examine long-term projections.

As we have seen, the majority of Third World countries have now entered a phase of demographic transition; it thus seems almost certain that the world should complete its transition and reach a state of stationary

TABLE 5.3 World Population Projections under Various Assumptions
Concerning the Decline in the Net Reproduction Rate

Projections	Net reproduction rate = 1	Stabilization period	Stable population (millions)	Index (P 1 = 100)
P 1	1970-1975	2095-2100	5,690	100
P 2	1980-1985	2095-2100	6,417	113
P 3	2000-2005	2095-2100	8,389	147
P 4	2020-2025	2120-2125	11,172	196
P 5	2040-2045	2145-2150	15,148	266

SOURCE: Based on Tomas Frejka, *The Future of Population Growth: Alternative Paths to Equilibrium* Population Council (New York: John Wiley, 1973).

NOTE: The second column (Net reproduction rate = 1) shows different periods when an average net reproduction rate of 1 is assumed to be reached. The third column gives the corresponding period when world population will subsequently stabilize, and the fourth indicates the level of stable population. The last column is an index of these eventual population levels based upon P 1 stable population.

population during the coming century. The main questions, of course, are when this stationary level will be reached and what the world population will be at that time.

In this case also the estimates differ. To quote a few examples, the World Bank estimates that the stationary state could be reached with a population of 10 billion. Interfutures places this stabilized level between 11 and 12 billion, while the United Nations forecasts 12.3 billion (medium assumption), 9.5 billion (low assumption), and 15.8 billion (high assumption). This time the margin of error is thus larger (from −23 percent to +28 percent), which clearly indicates the uncertainty concerning population changes over the long term. This very fact underscores the decisive importance that population policies may have on this final level of world population.

By accelerating the current fertility decline in the Third World, these population policies could indeed advance the moment when a net reproduction rate of 1 will be attained.[3] This advance, in turn, would permit reaching the final stationary level at an earlier time, and more importantly, would considerably decrease the size of this steady-state population. As can be seen in Table 5.3, each decade of delay in obtaining a net reproduction rate of 1 increases by approximately 15 percent the size of the final world population (when the stationary state will have been reached). If this rate of 1 were reached around the year 2020, the final population would be some 11.2 billion — the assumption made by Interfutures. If this date could be advanced by two decades, the final level would be 2.8 billion smaller. If, on the other hand, this date were postponed by twenty years, the level would be larger by some 4 billion — the equivalent of the present world population.

TABLE 5.4   Population Projections during the Period 1980–2100 According to the Medium Variant of the United Nations (millions)

	1980	2000	2025	2050	2075	2100
Total	4,415	6,407	9,051	11,081	12,048	12,257
All developed countries	1,131	1,368	1,510	1,563	1,572	1,570
All developing countries	3,284	5,039	7,541	9,518	10,476	10,687
Africa	469	834	1,438	2,005	2,344	2,435
Latin America	368	625	963	1,204	1,300	1,308
North America	246	296	332	339	339	339
East Asia	1,136	1,373	1,650	1,761	1,775	1,776
South Asia	1,422	2,384	3,679	4,739	5,247	5,358
Europe	484	540	580	592	591	589
South Sea Islands	23	33	43	50	52	52
U.S.S.R.	267	321	367	391	398	399

SOURCES: Leon Tabah, "The Changing Demographic Balance," *Populi* (Journal of the U.N. Fund for Population Activities, New York), no. 2 (1979), and United Nations, *The World Population Situation in 1979* (New York, 1980).

The importance of hastening the date when the net reproduction rate will be equal to 1 is all the more considerable for the countries now experiencing rapid population growth. For instance, if India reaches this rate in 2000, her population will stabilize 70 years later, at about 1.4 billion. If this rate is not reached until 2040, the final population will be 2.9 billion, twice as large. For Mexico, a similar delay would lead to an increase of 140 percent (from 175 to 420 million) in the size of the stationary population; for Bangladesh it would be 170 percent (from 245 to 660 million).[4] We recall that these countries, especially the last two, are in fact among those where birthrates have scarcely declined during the last thirty years. Of course, the eventuality that Bangladesh will ever have 660 million inhabitants seems — fortunately — highly unlikely. Nevertheless, the above figures do give us a disturbing idea of what a delay in the fall of fertility rates implies.

According to the "base case" what would the map of world population be in the stationary state? Table 5.4 shows the projections of the world population up to 2100, according to the United Nations' "medium" assumption. Of course, we do not know which countries will be "developed" and which will be "developing" in 120 years' time. Nevertheless, we see that today's developed countries, which now account for one-quarter of the world's population, will not represent more than one-eighth at the end of the twenty-first century, while the developing countries' population will treble during this period. As compared to 1980, the population of East Asia will have increased by more than half, and the populations of Latin America and of South Asia will be over three times larger. The most startling projections, however, concern Africa, whose population will increase fivefold in a century and reach 2.4 billion in the year 2100 – a figure which corresponds to the population of the *whole* Third World (China included) at the end of the sixties.

These forecasts cannot but leave us with a feeling of incredulity. Anybody familiar with the Indian subcontinent cannot conceive of its population exceeding five billion people in the future. Similarly, it is hard to believe that within a century the African continent could have a population surpassing two billion.

Projected changes for Third World cities confound the imagination even more, however. Forecasts for the year 2000 announce a Calcutta with 16 million inhabitants and a Shanghai with 23 million; São Paulo would reach 26 million, and Mexico City would exceed 31 million. For the big cities of the Third World, with their already unprecedented levels of crowding, noise, and pollution, such projections imply an almost incomprehensible situation. And what will the situation be like at the end of the twenty-first century, when total Third World population will be twice as large as in 2000? We have to admit that we really do not know, but the prospects are certainly alarming.

ACCELERATING THE DEMOGRAPHIC TRANSITION?

Since the Third World has finally begun a transition phase which should lead it to population stability during the next century, can we now stop worrying and relax our efforts? Does not this fact confirm that the apprehensions aroused by demographic growth were groundless or at least exaggerated? It may be worthwhile recalling and briefly discussing here some of these fears.

When the world heard about the "population explosion" in the sixties, the specter of Malthus reappeared. Set off on an exponential race, world population could not but sooner or later exceed the planet's food production capacities. At the beginning of the seventies, further fear was aroused by the idea of the "limits to growth." With pollution increasing in step with population while resources of fossil fuels and raw materials remained limited, it seemed clear that mankind was heading towards catastrophe.

Of course, all that was a bit simplistic, and the now apparent signs of a decline in the Third World's population growth confirm the demographers' predictions. Moreover, today the implications of population growth for the consumption of world resources are certainly better understood.

The pressure exerted on the finite resources (essentially fossil fuels and mineral products) of our planet is more a result of economic growth than population growth. To adopt the terms of the Brandt Commission: "So far the bulk of the depletion of non-renewable resources and the pressure on the oceans and the atmosphere have been caused by the spectacular industrial growth of the developed countries where only one-fifth of the world's people live." [5] The developing countries (excluding China) account for 52 percent of the world population but represent only 18 percent of the world GDP; on the other hand, the developed countries with market economies comprise 16 percent of the world population and contribute 65 percent of the world GDP. Insofar as the utilization of scarce resources is proportionate to GDP, it can be seen that the developed countries consume nearly four times more of these resources than the developing countries.

Even if we take into account the fact that the population growth rate is three times higher in the developing than in the developed countries, the pressure exerted on resources by the *increase* in population is still less important for the former than for the latter, because of the differences in income and consumption per capita. This does not mean, of course, that Third World population growth has only a negligible influence on the demand for scarce resources. Nevertheless, the preceding discussion does enable us to understand that, when the developing countries are reproached with hastening the exhaustion of the planet's resources through their irresponsible population growth, they are justified in protesting that the fault in fact lies with the developed countries' consumption.

In any event, the problem of nonrenewable resources seems to be of vital importance only in the field of energy, because, as recent reports have shown, a global exhaustion of mineral products is not likely to occur within the foreseeable future. [6] Consequently it would seem either that the initial fears provoked by Third World population growth were not well-founded (in the case of raw materials) or that the accusation of excessive consumption was not leveled against the main culprit (in the case of energy, where the rich countries' consumption is in fact much more to blame).

Does this mean that all the debates concerning the dangers of population growth were, in fact, much ado about nothing? Not exactly, for while this growth does not represent an immediate danger for the resources of the *planet,* it nevertheless does constitute a significant check to the economic progress of the individual *countries.* Various factors contribute to make excessive population growth a serious obstacle to economic development. These include the increase in family or government expenditures due to the larger number of economically dependent people and the worsening of the problems of unemployment, urban explosion, and food.

The rapid increase in the number of economically dependent people is in fact one of the most immediately perceptible consequences of population growth. During recent decades all developing countries have experienced a rapid decline in infant mortality while their birthrates have remained high. Consequently, today about 40 percent of the Third World population is less than 15 years old, while the corresponding proportion is only 25 percent for the developed countries (see Table 5.5). The dependence ratio — the number of people below 15 or above 65 divided by the

TABLE 5.5   Age Structure of Population, 1970 and 1975, and
Medium Projections, 2000

| Area | Year | Percentage of population | | | | "Dependent" age groups per 100 of 15–64 years | |
		Total	Under 15 years	15–64 years	65 years and over	Under 15 years	65 years and over
World	1970	100.0	36.6	57.9	5.5	63	9
	1975	100.0	36.4	58.0	5.6	63	10
	2000	100.0	31.8	61.9	6.3	51	10
More developed regions	1970	100.0	27.1	63.4	9.5	43	15
	1975	100.0	24.8	64.6	10.6	38	16
	2000	100.0	21.5	65.3	13.2	33	20
Less developed regions	1970	100.0	40.7	55.6	3.7	73	7
	1975	100.0	40.6	55.6	3.8	73	7
	2000	100.0	34.4	61.0	4.6	56	8

SOURCE: United Nations, *The World Population Situation in 1979* (New York, 1980).

number of people between these two ages — is approximately 80 percent in the developing countries, against 54 percent in the developed countries. This means that in the developing countries the income earned by the active population will be divided among a greater number of people than in the developed countries. Since for the first ten or fifteen years of life, children add to total consumption without contributing to production, a fall in the birthrate would immediately lead to higher average incomes.

Of course, it can be argued that when these children become adolescents they will join the country's labor force and contribute to production growth. But in countries where unemployment and underemployment are already severe, an increase in the labor force is liable to create more problems than it will solve. In this respect there is a definite danger that the situation will worsen during the coming decades, when the adolescents born during the sixties and seventies enter the labor market. Between now and the end of the century the Third World labor force will increase by more than 50 percent. In Latin America, as a result of the particularly high population growth of recent years, it will increase by 75 percent. We can appreciate how vast the problem is when we realize that, in order to provide employment for the newcomers in the labor market, the developing countries will have to create, between 1980 and 2000, a number of additional jobs equivalent to the size of their *total* active population in 1950. It thus seems likely that underemployment will persist or even increase in most developing countries during the coming years. Of course the implementation today of measures aiming to reduce the birthrate will affect the labor market only in fifteen years' time at the earliest — all the more reason for beginning as soon as possible!

Unemployment and underemployment in the rural areas are among the principal causes of the rural exodus and the explosive growth of Third World cities. The developing countries' urban population approximated 250 million inhabitants thirty years ago. Between 1950 and 1980 this population more than tripled, and it will double again within the next two decades! We have seen how enormous certain Third World cities will be by the end of the century. A few exceptions apart, it has proved impossible to control the growth of these anthills; rather than real cities, they are, indeed, vast urban agglomerations, where most of the people live in shantytowns and suffer from overcrowding and hazardous sanitary conditions. Of course the overall population growth is not the only reason for the rural exodus and the growth of the cities, but it is certain that a slowdown in population growth would help check an urban explosion which today proceeds in a most anarchic fashion.

In many countries, population growth has outrun the governments' capacity to provide the necessary public services in education, health, utilities, transport, and other areas. For example, while the *percentage* of children enrolled in primary schools increased between 1960 and 1975 (rising from 46 percent to 62 percent), the *number* of children out of school has nevertheless grown (from 110 million to 121 million).[7] Several governments that were formerly open supporters of universal education have had to abandon their declared objectives discreetly for lack of sufficient administrative and financial means.

I shall not dwell here on the problems population growth has caused in agriculture and nutrition as well as in the environmental field; these questions are dealt with in detail in Chapters 6 and 7. Let me note, however, that in all Third World regions with the exception of Latin America, the agricultural labor force increased faster from 1961–1965 to 1975 than the area under cultivation. Consequently the number of acres per agricultural worker declined, increasing unemployment and checking income growth. The growing density of the population also led to or accelerated the incompletely understood but certainly serious phenomena of deforestation, increasing soil salinity, desertification, and erosion. This ecological deterioration is all the more alarming because, for technical and economic reasons, it is often no longer possible to reestablish the preexisting conditions; the most one can hope for is to check current degradation by emergency measures. Unfortunately, in coming decades the rapid increase in population density will often stymie such measures, however limited their objectives.

POPULATION POLICIES

In August 1974, the World Population Conference opened in Bucharest. Taking place shortly after the Sixth Special Session of the U.N. General Assembly and the proclamation of a New International Economic

Order, this conference was the scene of acrimonious debates between developed and developing countries. The developed nations, borrowing from Malthus, claimed that overpopulation was the main cause of poverty, and most of them argued that a slowdown in population growth was a prerequisite of economic development. Reacting against this attitude, practically all the developing countries upheld the Marxian position that the real cause of poverty is the unequal distribution of wealth and that overpopulation is a symptom, and not a cause, of underdevelopment. While the arguments were often distorted by the inevitable rhetoric, the debate nevertheless revolved around an important and as yet unsolved question: for the reduction of birthrates, is the improvement in living conditions more, or less, effective than direct policies of birth control?

Whatever the positions taken in Bucharest, the opinions and policies of Third World governments have changed considerably during the last decade. The surveys made by the Secretariat of the United Nations show, in fact, that at present 81 percent of the Third World population live in countries whose governments consider a slower rate of population growth desirable for the success of their development policies. Moreover, the countries that do want a reduction in this growth rate have indicated a marked preference for direct methods of intervention, albeit without ruling out indirect ones. Indeed, recent years have seen both a real flowering of new population policies and a reinforcement of those already existing.

It is tempting to see in this expansion of direct action programs the main cause of the fall in fertility which has occurred during this period in several Third World countries. There is certainly some truth in this assumption. With the exception of India, Pakistan, and Bangladesh, where long-standing population programs have been poorly administered, all the developing countries with important family planning programs have experienced rapid declines in fertility. From 1970 to 1976, the crude birthrate in Java and Bali, where an important family planning program is being carried out, fell from 41 to 33 per 1,000. In Taiwan, the percentage of illiterate women using contraceptives rose from 19 percent to 78 percent between 1965 and 1976, the period when a vigorous program was being implemented.[8] It is clear today that well-organized birth control programs can be effective in substantially reducing birthrates.

In spite of the proved effectiveness of the direct action methods and notwithstanding the interest they have elicited in Third World governments, family planning programs are still not sufficiently large and effective. In most countries they receive less than 1 percent of the government budget; moreover, they are usually poorly administered. This is partly the reason why, in several countries where such a program functions, the number of people using contraceptives scarcely varied during the seventies.

This could lead us to believe that there is more to the general fall in birth and fertility rates than the simple result of the implementation of family planning programs. In this respect, the evidence gathered with regard to the effectiveness of these programs has not yet concluded the debate between the partisans of direct methods and the advocates of indirect action through the improvement in living conditions. This debate will probably never end, because in attempting to explain changes in birthrates it is extremely difficult to distinguish the respective influence of each one of these factors. But there is considerable evidence proving the importance of economic and social conditions for the decrease in fertility. Recent studies, for instance, have shown how, in the countries where fertility has recently declined, this fall is probably due more to the changes in the economic and social environment than to the use of birth control methods.[9]

Although causality cannot really be proved, a link does seem to exist between crude birthrates and different indicators of socioeconomic development in the areas of health, education, urbanization, nutrition, and income distribution (see Table 5.6).[10] A particularly important factor in the evolution of birthrates seems to be whether the profits of economic and social development are divided in an egalitarian way: this factor is apparently much more important than, for instance, average indicators such as GDP per capita. Thus Sri Lanka and the state of Kerala in India have experienced rapid falls in birthrate in spite of very low levels of GDP per capita. In both cases, however, income distribution within the country is relatively egalitarian; moreover, infant mortality is low, and the literacy level high (see Table 2.3).

In this respect it is interesting to compare the experiences of Mexico and South Korea. Both have experienced considerable growth in GDP; in 1973 Mexico's GDP per capita was $890, more than twice Korea's ($400). Yet income distribution was and has remained more egalitarian in Korea than in Mexico: in 1969 the poorest 40 percent of the Korean families received 21 percent of the total income; in Mexico the same group received only 10 percent. Infant mortality was much lower in Korea: in 1970 it was 38 per 1,000, as against 61 per 1,000 in Mexico. Finally, the level of literacy was higher in Korea (91 percent) than in Mexico (84 percent). It is not a coincidence that in 1970 the crude birthrate had fallen to 29 per 1,000 in Korea while in Mexico it was still 45.

Nor could this difference be explained by the simple fact that Korea started a family planning program as early as 1964, while Mexico remained hostile to the idea of governmental intervention in this area until the early seventies. In fact, the birthrate in Korea began to fall before the implementation of any population program; it declined from 45 per 1,000 in 1958 to 38 in 1964, seven points in six years. It is estimated, moreover, that the program subsequently adopted accounted for, at most, one-third of the rapid decline in the birthrate during the sixties. In Mexico, by contrast, the

TABLE 5.6 Correspondence in 1970 between Crude Birthrates (CBR) and Selected Development Indicators

Indicators	No. of countries	CBR over 45	CBR 40 to 44	CBR 30 to 39	CBR less than 30
Health					
Infant mortality					
(rate per thousand)	34	128	84	61	20
Life expectancy (years)	43	46	57	64	68
Education					
Literacy (% of population over					
15 years of age)	39	33	57	78	80
Urbanization					
Adult male labor in agriculture					
(% of total male labor)	46	77	64	45	15

SOURCE: See Table 5.1.

NOTE: The values shown for the development indicators at each level of CBR are median values for the countries in the sample.

birthrate fell by only two points between 1958 and 1970, and the progress made during the last decade was more marked in the regions that were economically and socially more developed.[11]

Nothing, then, that has happened since 1974 has settled the dispute between the partisans of direct action to limit birthrates and the advocates of indirect action through socioeconomic improvement. There has at least been progress in the debate, however, since considerable evidence now exists regarding the effectiveness of each type of intervention. The idea of integrating these two types of action had already been discussed, at least on a fairly theoretical level, at length in Bucharest. The changes in positions adopted by many Third World governments since then should now facilitate the implementation of integrated population policies incorporating both of these elements.

The seventies represented an important turning point in the evolution and the understanding of the Third World's population problems. During the fifties, demographers confined themselves mainly to the mortality aspect of these problems. During the following decade, specialists "discovered" the population explosion in these countries and shifted their attention to the problems of fertility. In the seventies most developing countries accepted the idea of government action in the area of family planning. While appropriate policies were being implemented, the first signs appeared of a decline in fertility and birth rates. Moreover, understanding of the links between direct population programs and other forms of intervention improved during the decade. We may now hope that in the eighties these population programs will be expanded while they are fully integrated in the socioeconomic development plans.

The Third World demographic transition is now well under way. Far from inciting governments to relax their efforts, this should, on the contrary, encourage them to intensify their action. The population programs implemented between now and the end of the century will probably not notably modify the world of the year 2000, but they can considerably change the world of the twenty-first century. As things stand, this century already seems condemned to suffer from a sufficient number of problems; it thus seems all the more necessary to do the maximum now to limit the additional burden which unprecedented population growth is bound to create.

6
ENERGY CRISES

Ever since the fourfold increase in oil prices at the end of 1973, energy has become a subject of unquestionable importance for the developed countries. The acute crisis of 1974–1975, the ensuing sluggish recovery, the persistence of unemployment, and high inflation have all been attributed — at times incorrectly — to the energy situation. Preoccupied with its own problems, the Western world often tends to consider energy preeminently a North-South issue and to blame the developing countries for its present economic misfortune. The political solidarity which the non–oil-producing developing countries have maintained with the OPEC group should not make us forget, however, that these countries also have been affected by the "oil price shocks" of the last decade. In the coming years the energy problem will continue to plague the oil-importing countries, be they developed or developing.

ENERGY TRANSITION
It is doubtful whether any economic question has been as thoroughly studied during the last decade as the energy problem. In this instance too the fear aroused by the "limits to growth" and apparently confirmed by the oil price shock of 1973 has been replaced by a more balanced approach to the problem. At the same time, the doubts as to the reality of the "energy crisis" — doubts which had been triggered by the fall in real oil prices between 1975 and 1978 — disappeared after the new price rise of 1979–1980. The majority of governments have now reached a clearer understanding both of the reality of the crisis and of the policies required to bring it to an end.

Fairly broad agreement emerges from all the studies which have recently been devoted to this subject.[1] World energy resources should enable us to meet, over the long term, levels of world consumption far exceeding today's. But this will require a transition from the present energy system, mainly based on oil, towards other energies, new or traditional, characterized by higher costs. Because of the inertia of energy systems, the transition period will be long (half a century at least); moreover, this period will be marked by considerable instability and high risk of crises.

It may be worthwhile comparing present energy consumption, as well as future consumption (as it is forecast today), with the estimated resources of different types of energy. In 1980 world consumption of commercial energy amounted to some 7 MMTOE (billion tons of oil equivalent), and it is expected to have approximately doubled by the year 2000 (13.5 MMTOE). The following figures from the Interfutures report are resource estimates of the main commercial energies; they can thus be taken as measures of the remaining "stocks" of each energy type.[2]

oil	173–750 MMTOE
natural gas	200–500 MMTOE
coal	6,750 MMTOE
heavy crudes and tar sands	300 MMTOE
oil shales	420 MMTOE
uranium and thorium (without breeder reactors)	100 MMTOE

Although these resources far exceed present energy consumption, they cannot alone provide a long-term solution. The situation is different, however, with regard to new and renewable energies, whose potential supplies are as follows:

uranium and thorium (with breeder reactors)	125×10^6 MMTOE
nuclear fusion	250×10^6 MMTOE
solar energy	?
hydraulic energy	9 MMTOE per year
geothermic resources	125,000 MMTOE

Of course, with the exception of hydraulic energy, the other new technologies are not quite operational yet. But with regard to the breeder reactor, nuclear fusion, and solar energies, it now seems very likely that commercially viable technologies will eventually be forthcoming.

In the very long term, therefore, energy production should not be limited by resource availability, provided we move towards a system based on nuclear energy (with breeder reactor fission or fusion) and on solar energy. But this optimistic conclusion should not lead us to overlook the problems posed by this transition.

First of all, as we have seen, this transition period will be long. It is estimated that the share of oil in world energy consumption, which was about 43 percent in 1980, will still be around 30 percent in the year 2000. During the same period, the share of coal will remain at about 30 percent, while the percentage of nuclear energy will rise from 1 percent to 7 percent. As for the new energies, they will meet less than 3 percent of world demand at the end of the century. In the past, a period of between half a century and a century has always been required for a new primary energy to take over half the world market; the transition that has now begun is unlikely to prove an exception to this rule.

Moreover, we know that the development of certain types of energy may cause serious ecological problems (effects on the climate of the carbon dioxide produced by the burning of fossil fuels, effects on the environment of coal mining, danger of contamination from nuclear energy) as well as difficult security problems (nuclear energy again).

Finally, the development of new energy sources will be costly; in particular, it will require a high level of capital expenditures. These new energies themselves will be more expensive, and consequently the transition period of the coming decades will be accompanied by a rise in energy prices. It is now all but certain that the cost (in real terms) of energy will increase again before the end of the century; with regard to oil, the pace of this price rise will depend on future increases in world demand, the policies of the exporting countries, and the agreements (or lack of agreement) between producing and consuming countries.

Of all economic sectors, energy is presumably the one where the interdependence of countries is most evident. It would therefore be difficult to study the developing countries' energy prospects without first saying something about the other groups of countries. The situation of the industrial countries of the OECD is doubtless the best known. In 1980 these countries were responsible for 37 percent of world production and 52 percent of world consumption of commercial energy. Their energy consumption grew rapidly until 1973; since then it has increased more slowly and will no doubt continue to do so in the future. Less rapid economic growth has in fact slowed down — and will continue to slow down — the increase in demand for energy; in addition, conservation policies have also contributed to check this demand.[3] In spite of this leveling of their energy consumption, these countries should still account for nearly half the world energy demand in the year 2000. Present per capita consumption in the developed countries is ten times higher than in the middle-income developing countries and a hundred times higher than in the low-income countries; today an American consumes twenty times more commercial energy than a Malaysian and a thousand times more than a Nepalese.

The OPEC countries contribute about one-fifth of the world energy supply. Their oil production, like that of the rest of the world, will increase less rapidly during the coming years, in particular because of the exhaustion of certain oilfields and the determination of several of these countries to preserve their potential wealth.[4]

The socialist countries (excluding China) account for about one-third of the world energy production and a somewhat smaller share of its consumption. The Soviet Union plays an important role in this group because of its oil production; this country is the first world producer and, after Saudi Arabia, the second exporter. Uncertainty as to the exact amount of its reserves precludes any reliable forecasting; however, it is likely that its oil production will increase more slowly during the coming years, while its natural gas production will accelerate. On the whole, the energy production of the socialist bloc should increase less rapidly in the future, but this group will probably remain a marginal exporter, at least through the eighties.[5]

In 1980 the developing countries (China and OPEC included) accounted for 31 percent of world production of commercial energy, but their share of world consumption was only half as much. The increase in their consumption was nevertheless rapid: from 1960 to 1976, while the developed countries' consumption doubled, the Third World's tripled. Although the rate of increase has declined since 1973, it nonetheless remains higher than in the developed countries. Moreover, the Third World countries rely on oil for their energy supply even more than the industrial countries do: their oil consumption increased annually by about 7 percent from 1965 to 1975, and today oil accounts for about 57 percent of their commercial energy supply.[6] Their remaining energy needs are covered by solid fuels (19 percent of the supply), natural gas (12 percent), the last 12 percent being assured mainly by hydroelectric power.

For various reasons, commercial energy consumption will increase rapidly in the Third World during the coming decades. The total energy demand of these countries will grow considerably because of the requirements of economic development, industrialization, and urbanization. In addition, commercial energy will presumably continue to replace the "noncommercial" or traditional forms of energy: wood, charcoal, residues (see the last section of this chapter). For instance, Interfutures forecasts a doubling of the OECD countries' energy consumption between 1976 and 2000; for the developing countries the multipliers will be between five and seven. In spite of this, an inhabitant of the developed countries (East or West) will still consume seven times as much commercial energy at the end of the century as an inhabitant of the Third World.

PROSPECTS FOR COMMERCIAL ENERGY IN THE THIRD WORLD

The energy situation of the developing countries varies enormously; a United Nations survey of 96 developing countries reveals the inequality of their positions in this area. A first group of 31 countries, including the

OPEC producers, includes all countries exporting energy or importing less than 25 percent of their commercial energy consumption. This group possesses virtually all the developing countries' oil reserves, 90 percent of their natural gas reserves, and more than half their coal reserves. A second group includes the countries (eight only) importing between 25 and 75 percent of their consumption; on the whole, these countries are well endowed with energy resources. A last group includes 57 countries whose imports meet 75 percent or more of their energy consumption requirements. It is alarming to note that these countries are the ones that appear to have the least promising energy resources (with the exception of a limited hydro-electrical potential).

It is therefore not surprising that during the last decade the increases in energy prices acutely affected the vast majority of the Third World countries. In 1973 the quadrupling of oil prices led to a $10 billion increase in the import bill of the oil-importing developing countries. In 1974–1975 this additional burden, together with the effects of the industrial world's economic situation, made for an unprecedented deficit in their current account balance (see Chapter 3). Although it is difficult to separate the different causes of this deterioration, it is estimated that 40 to 60 percent of the increase in these countries' debt during this period was due to the rise in oil prices. The increases of 1979 and 1980 further worsened the situation. Altogether, the cost of these countries' oil imports was multiplied by twenty during the seventies, from about 3.7 billion dollars at the beginning of the decade to 74 billion in 1980. As a proportion of their total import bill, oil imports rose from 8.6 percent in 1970 to 26.3 percent ten years later; in fact these countries had to devote over 40 percent of the substantial increase in their export revenues to the payment of their inflated oil import bill.[7]

For the oil-importing developing countries the events of the seventies doubtless sufficed to prove the importance of implementing policies aimed at reducing imports and developing domestic energy resources. These resources had been largely neglected until 1974, mainly because imported oil prices made their exploitation uneconomical. From 1955 to 1970 *real* prices of crude petroleum (free on board at the Persian Gulf) had declined by approximately 60 percent. At the beginning of the seventies, the cost of crude oil production in the non-OPEC countries was between $2.80 and $5.00 per barrel, while OPEC oil could be bought for $1.80 free on board Persian Gulf — or less than $3.00 (including cost, insurance, and freight) in the importing countries. It is therefore not surprising that oil companies and importing countries (developed or developing) neglected to exploit energy resources which did not appear to be profitable.

The situation has, of course, changed during recent years, and present oil prices should provide sufficient incentive for all countries to develop their energy resources. Unfortunately, however, the developing countries' governments – a few exceptions apart – have not yet implemented the required policies. Only a few of them have allocated a substantial proportion of their investible funds to energy development: the developed countries are not alone in reacting slowly to the energy crisis. Even the exploration and evaluation of energy resources have very often remained inadequate; consequently it is still difficult today to have a clear idea of the energy potential of the oil-importing developing countries.

Yet in the case of oil and natural gas, this potential appears far from insignificant. The Third World (OPEC included) provides 55 percent of world production of crude oil, and its share in the international energy trade (of which oil constitutes 90 percent) is still higher. Although the oil-importing developing countries own only 2 percent of the world's proven oil reserves, they might possess 15 percent of the ultimately recoverable resources.[8] The Bureau d'études industrielles et de coopération, the consulting arm of the French Petroleum Institute, has carried out a survey of the oil potential of 70 developing countries, mostly energy importers. According to this survey the level of potential resources is high (above 750 million barrels) in 23 countries, fair (100–750 million barrels) in 15, and low (less than 100 million barrels) in only 32. Moreover, natural gas is always underused in these countries. A large proportion of the gas obtained with oil is flared; the World Bank estimates that the resulting energy waste was equivalent to nine million barrels of oil per day in 1977 – approximately the oil production of Saudi Arabia!

In spite of these relatively promising results and of the urgency of the problem, the developing countries have not significantly stepped up exploration and investment in the oil sector since 1974. Thus, according to the French Petroleum Institute survey, the research efforts were adequate in only 10 of the 70 countries. In 1975–1976 exploratory drilling in the oil-importing developing countries was lower than in 1972–1973 and amounted to only 5 percent of the world total. The drilling density – the number of wells drilled per thousand square miles of potential area – was 5 for these countries against 20 for the OPEC nations and 190 for the industrial ones.

Several factors have contributed to create this apparently paradoxical situation. First of all, oil exploration costs are high (about 25 percent of the total investment cost) and rising.[9] Moreover, exploration involves high risks (on average, only one drilling operation out of ten proves successful). Finally, the developing countries often lack both the necessary data base for an oil exploration campaign and the skilled personnel capable of analyzing these data or of cooperating with foreign oil companies.

The Third World is relatively less well endowed with regard to coal. The whole of its recoverable reserves amounts to only 10 percent of the world total; and of that 10 percent, India alone possesses more than half, while

Yugoslavia and Brazil together account for another quarter. The Third World's share of ultimately recoverable resources is even smaller (2.28 percent). There is, however, a vast potential for increasing coal production in the developing countries, since their current production (176 million tons in 1977) represents only 0.3 percent of their recoverable reserves. About twenty developing countries have no — or virtually no — coal production at present, even though they possess reserves that could be exploited under financially viable conditions. As in the case of oil, several reasons explain this apparent paradox.

First, while exploration may be less expensive for coal than for oil, it nevertheless involves important financial risks. This is no doubt one of the main reasons that many countries have never evaluated their coal potential. Second, the weaknesses of the local transport systems cause delay in the development of coal resources: even India, which has one of the largest railroad systems in the world and a century-old coal industry, has difficulties in this respect. Thirdly, the investment cost for a mine and its infrastructure is high (from $20 to $150 per ton of annual production), and its financing is not without problems.[10] Finally, the demand (in the home or the foreign market) is often too limited or insufficiently known to justify the exploitation of existing resources.

For all these reasons, rapid growth of coal production in developing countries appears unlikely in the near future. In many countries, coal resources would first have to be assessed before their exploitation could even begin. Consequently, in the next decade increases in coal production will occur mainly in developing countries already producing today.

There is a significant potential for hydropower development in many Third World countries. Africa has about 22 percent of the world's hydroelectric resources, but only 2 percent of these have been developed. In Latin America and in Asia the proportions of hydropower resources under exploitation are, respectively, 6 percent and 12 percent of the potential resources. The latter figures can serve only as a guide, however, since certain potential sites have a capacity far exceeding local needs, so that the cost per kilowatt-hour becomes prohibitive. One possibility would be to locate energy-intensive industries close to these sites; another would be to export electricity to neighboring countries.[11] In the past, the development of hydroelectric power was checked by the lack of geologic and hydraulic surveys of the potential sites and, consequently, by the lack of adequately prepared projects. Moreover, the high capital cost also discouraged this development until recently.[12]

The developing countries have only a limited share of the world uranium resources (18 percent), with Niger owning over half these countries' reserves. In most cases, however, uranium cannot be used by the producing countries, since they have neither the technical capacity to process it nor, in some instances, an electric network large enough to absorb the power of a nuclear plant. In fact, the majority of developing countries that already have nuclear power installations (Argentina, India, and Pakistan) or are in the process of building one (Korea, Brazil, Iran, Iraq, and Mexico) are not themselves uranium producers. Apart from security and environmental problems, nuclear energy also presents the drawback of having a high capital cost.[13] In addition, in the long term, it still remains possible that increases in demand will raise uranium prices. For all these reasons the utilization of nuclear energy will probably remain confined to a small number of large, middle-income developing countries. The International Atomic Energy Agency estimates that in 1990 only eleven Third World countries will operate nuclear installations.

The exploitation of oil shales will also probably remain of marginal importance during the next decade in the developed as well as in the developing countries. Yet in the long term, when exploitation technologies have been perfected and production costs have become more competitive because of increases in imported oil prices, these shales could play an important role.[14] The main potential Third World producers are Zaire, Morocco, Brazil, Thailand, and China.

Like oil shales, and for the same reasons, tar sands will not constitute an important energy resource over the short or medium term. World reserves are not precisely known, but they are no doubt quite large. Only Canada has undertaken their commercial exploitation, at a very high cost (the investment required comes to some $30,000 per barrel of daily production). Ultimately, however, Ecuador, Peru, Venezuela, Madagascar, and the Ivory Coast may be able to find important energy resources in their sands.

Peat could form a convenient energy resource for many developing countries. The extent of peat reserves is, however, practically unknown. Exploitable deposits have been identified in Cuba, Jamaica, Rwanda, and Burundi. For the Third World countries, peat exploitation presents the additional advantage of requiring little capital but a great deal of labor.

Finally, to close this inventory, I should mention geothermal power. Though its present development is very limited, several developing countries (Indonesia, Philippines, Mexico, El Salvador) are using this energy to produce electricity. About twenty other Third World countries may have a certain geothermal potential, but it is unlikely to be exploited until this new technology has further progressed.

This rapid survey of the Third World's potential energy resources shows that important reserves do exist. Yet these reserves are distributed very unequally among the countries, many of which are singularly deprived. For reasons of cost their exploitation had been neglected for a long time; because of the recent changes in imported energy prices, however, it has now become urgent to undertake their development.[15] For the developing countries, the delays inherent in the implementation of investment programs in this sector will be aggravated by problems of financial, administrative, and technical capacity. Almost ten years have passed since the first oil price shock jolted the energy-importing countries; in the South as in the North, very little has been done since then to respond to this warning signal. The consequences of this procrastination are clearly dangerous for all consuming countries; for the poorest among them — which are also those having the greatest difficulty in reacting — these consequences could eventually prove little short of disastrous.

PROBLEMS OF NONCOMMERCIAL ENERGIES

The commercial energies briefly surveyed above represent only a part of the developing countries' energy resources. The forms of energy used by the traditional sectors (sometimes called "noncommercial" energies, though they are often bought and sold) include wood, charcoal, and plant and animal residues, to which wind and water power are occasionally added.

The contribution of these noncommercial energies to the total energy balance of the Third World is not exactly known; it is estimated at close to one-quarter of the developing countries' energy consumption, or a little less than 5 percent of world consumption. The proportions vary, however, according to the region or country. In Africa these energies contribute to about two-thirds of the total energy production, and in certain countries (Nepal, Mali, Tanzania) this proportion exceeds 90 percent.[16]

Even today half the world population uses noncommercial energy for preparing food. It is, of course, mostly the rural population that uses these forms of energy: in Africa, for instance, it is estimated that the rural dwellers (90 percent of the total population) account for only 5 percent of the consumption of commercial energy.

Because of the importance of traditional energies in Third World consumption, we might think that their population is partly protected from the energy crisis which affects the "modern" economic sectors. Unfortunately, serious difficulties also exist with regard to the noncommercial energy supplies. Although less known, this "other energy crisis" is no doubt more dramatic, and its long-term consequences may be more threatening.

Wood is currently the most important of the noncommercial energies, accounting for 85 percent of the consumption of these energies; it has no doubt been thus ever since mankind succeeded in mastering fire several hundred thousand years ago. Because of the intensive deforestation of recent decades, however, a large number of Third World countries are now experiencing supply difficulties and even actual scarcities.

In view of the lack of adequate information concerning the extent of this phenomenon and its consequences, we should beware of hasty generalizations or unjustified alarmism. Deforestation, after all, is not a new phenomenon: Plato deplored the disappearance of the forests of Attica, and the Emperor Hadrian strove — in vain, as we know — to preserve the cedars of Lebanon from destruction.[17] Whatever the reality and the extent of deforestation throughout history, however, it is unfortunately certain that this phenomenon has accelerated recently in the developing countries.

These countries' forests are gradually being destroyed by the collection of fuel wood (which represents 90 percent of wood consumption) and by the extension of cultivated land. Between 1900 and 1965 half the developing countries' wooded area was cleared to make way for agriculture. At the current pace of deforestation (15 to 20 million hectares, an area half the size of California, destroyed every year), these countries' forests would disappear in 80 years at the maximum. In fact, since population growth may lead to an increase in the present pace, the time required for this destruction to be completed could be much shorter. According to the *Global 2000 Report,* "By 2020, virtually all the physically accessible forest in the less developed countries is expected to have been cut."[18] Current afforestation efforts are dramatically insufficient, not even reaching one-tenth of what these countries require in order to be approximately self-sufficient in fuel wood by the year 2000.

This trend is general, affecting all regions, and practically all countries, in the Third World. As an immediate consequence, a great number of these countries suffer from fuel-wood scarcity. For this reason, their people sometimes spend up to one-quarter of their time or income obtaining the wood they need just for cooking. Until recently, Bamako, in Mali, was getting its wood from forests less than fifty kilometers away; now the distance is double that. A generation ago, villagers in the Nepalese hills, at the foot of the Himalayas, had to walk one or two hours to collect their wood; now an entire day is necessary.

The ecological consequences of this deforestation are perhaps even more serious than their immediate human cost. As in Attica 2,500 years ago, the destruction of the forest cover provokes a deep erosion of the soil, which loses its fertility. Nepal is probably the best known and most tragic case of these ecological disasters: at the present rate its hills will be laid completely bare within fifteen years. It is estimated that every year, 240 million cubic meters of earth are carried away by this country's rivers towards India. Moreover, because of the lack of forest protection, these rivers' floods are more frequent and violent, causing uncontrollable destruction for the downstream population in India and Bangladesh.[19] The same problem exists from the Ethiopian highlands to the Bolivian Altiplano, from Haiti to the mountains of Pakistan. In many regions the degradation of the soil has reached a point of no return, and no hope remains of maintaining, much less reestablishing, the fertility of the soil.

Fuel-wood scarcity has led to an increasing use of other fuels, which in the rural areas consist mainly of animal (dung) or crop residues. (Latin America, where kerosene is widely used, is an exception.) In India, for instance, for lack of wood many villagers have had to use cow dung as fuel. But cow dung used for this purpose can no longer serve to fertilize the fields, and as a consequence, the crop yields are adversely affected. It is estimated that the cow dung used as an energy source in India represents the equivalent of six million tons of nitrogen fertilizer every year, more than this country's annual consumption of fertilizer. Similarly, the utilization of crop residues for fuel occurs at the expense of soil fertilization or cattle feeding. In the whole Third World, every year, 400 million tons of animal or plant residues are burned, residues which could have served to regenerate the soil; used as fertilizer they would have permitted an additional production of 20 million tons of cereals — enough for more than 100 million people.

The reforestation programs launched by a number of countries have often proved unsuccessful. It is generally difficult to enlist the cooperation of the population even though they would eventually benefit from such measures. The very reasons which caused deforestation in the first place — population pressures, fuel scarcity — lead the villagers, when the necessity arises, to fell the trees prematurely, even when they are aware of the disastrous consequences. Even China, at the beginning of its vast reforestation programs, experienced difficulties of this kind (though its problems now appear to have been overcome). As a rule, such large-scale programs will be successful only insofar as appropriate forms of decentralization are devised to assure the active participation of the future beneficiaries.

As we have seen, deforestation is not a recent phenomenon, but postwar population growth has acutely accelerated it. The recent commercial energy price rises can only further worsen the situation, as they will encourage energy users to return to traditional energies — to wood, that is. Before 1973, scientists who were alarmed by the deforestation of the developing world were hoping that "modernization" of the rural areas would ultimately lead to the use of kerosene as a replacement for wood. It is now feared, however, that to a certain extent the opposite process will occur as the oil crisis accelerates the destruction of the forests.

As in the case of commercial energies, the crisis in traditional energies calls for a significant effort in research and development; during recent years, in fact, research has been intensified to improve the efficiency of these noncommercial energies. This research has a pragmatic, down-to-earth aspect which stands in striking contrast to the abstraction and sophistication of research in the "new energies." Thus, improved stoves built with earth and old tin cans have already led to substantial savings in wood consumption. Solar ovens and solar distillers have also been made, but they are still too expensive to be used on a wide scale. In many Asian countries, biogas installations are used to produce a mixture of fuel gases from plant or animal residues; one advantage of these plants is that after utilization, the cow dung can still be used as fertilizer. Much has been expected from this original technology, but in many countries there are insufficient residues to permit the production of a significant volume of gas. The production of alcohol (methanol or ethanol) from organic residues or plants is another possibility. So far, Brazil is the only developing country to have started such a program on a large scale; ultimately, however, the development of similar programs could raise the problem of competition with other crops (see the following chapter). Finally, photovoltaic cells are of evident interest for the tropical countries, but their present cost is still too high to permit their widespread utilization.[20]

While all these technologies are of vital interest for countries still depending on noncommercial energies, none has received sufficient attention so far. Priority in research has always gone to the more sophisticated and glamorous energies — which happen to be more directly relevant to the needs of the developed countries. Yet it is very likely that these small-scale, humble technologies could contribute more than the others to the solution of the energy problems of the Third World population.

The developing countries are faced with a double energy crisis whose two components reinforce each other. Because of the magnitude of these problems and the difficulties inherent in solving them, the implications of this crisis are even more dangerous for these countries than for the industrial ones.

Everything indicates that during the coming years the demand for energy will continue to grow at a rapid pace in the Third World. As in the past, the demand for traditional energy, particularly for fuel, will increase scarcely more slowly than population. Commercial energy consumption will probably increase even faster, at a pace equal or superior to the rate of growth of these countries' GNP. In both cases, because of the lead time and difficulties inherent in energy production programs, it is most unlikely that production will increase as rapidly as demand. As a result, the situation is bound to deteriorate over the short term, even if decisive steps were taken today. (This does not mean, of course, that such measures would not serve any purpose but, on the contrary, that their adoption and implementation are particularly urgent.)

There is no end to the debate as to which of the two energy crises is the more serious and the more difficult to solve. According to the Brandt

Commission, "the energy crisis of the poor is in some respects less intractable than that of the rich," because trees, unlike oil, are a renewable resource and can always be planted. Technically, of course, this does not seem to pose great difficulties, but the political, administrative, and social problems are enormous, as the experience of most developing countries indicates. As the Commission pointed out, "Experience in China has shown that the combination of a strong political commitment at the top with broad public participation and shared benefits at the bottom can provide a basis for rapid reforestation." [21] But how many developing countries have displayed such a "strong political commitment at the top," not to mention "broad public participation and shared benefits at the bottom"?

Be that as it may, there is little hope that a rapid solution to the technical problem of commercial energy could provide an alternative source of inexpensive energy and thereby improve the situation in the traditional energy sector. As we have seen, the transition toward new commercial energies will last half a century at least, and the new energies will not be cheap. This half-century time span also corresponds to the life left to the Third World forests, at the present rate of deforestation. This means that these forests could well disappear — and we can imagine the ecologic and human disasters such a disappearance would cause — before any new commercial energy could contribute to their preservation. However rough the above calculation, it may serve to illustrate the complexity and urgency of the energy problems which assail the Third World.

7
A HUNGRY FUTURE?

For the public at large the most important and evocative aspect of underdevelopment is widespread hunger. Ever since we became aware twenty years ago of the Third World population explosion, Malthus's predictions have returned to haunt us; there is presumably no other aspect of the relationship between population growth and underdevelopment that has been as widely discussed as the food problem. Unfortunately, this discussion, like others, has generated more heat than light. The same statistics can give rise to optimistic interpretations or alarmist forecasts. Short-term variations are presented as long-term trends; claims of victory and reports of failure alternate every other year. The day before yesterday the Green Revolution was hailed as the miracle bringing abundance to the hungry countries, but yesterday it was denounced as being socially unjust as well as ineffective during drought periods; today we learn that India, having accumulated embarrassing cereal surpluses, has joined the club of food aid donors!

The man in the street, bombarded by contradictory information, will have considerable difficulty in arriving at a reasonably clear idea of the problem. In view of this, let us try to relocate recent events within the broader context of the last few decades before we examine the prospects for the future.

THE FOOD EQUATION SINCE WORLD WAR II

World food production has increased at an unprecedented pace since the last war. From 1950 to 1980, for instance, world production of cereals more than doubled, going from 685 million to 1,437 million tons. This rapid growth was by no means limited to the industrial countries; in fact,

TABLE 7.1   Food Production Index (1961–65 = 100)

Country group	Total				Per Capita			
	1950	1960	1965	1975	1950	1960	1965	1975
Developed countries	72	95	104	129	84	99	102	115
Developing countries	63	91	104	144	85	98	101	107
Low-income	68	95	100	137	88	102	96	104
Middle-income	60	89	107	148	84	97	101	107

SOURCE: Economic Research Service, U.S. Department of Agriculture.

as Table 7.1 shows, production increased more rapidly in the developing than in the developed countries. We also see in Table 7.1 that in the area of food production, as in all the sectors of economic activity, progress has been slower in the poorest than in the middle-income countries.

But as Figure 7.1 shows, in a more immediately visible way, because of population growth food production per capita has practically stagnated in the Third World during recent decades. In the developed countries, by contrast, this production per capita has increased notably during the same period. From 1960 to 1980 the developing countries' food production increased at an annual average rate of 2.8 percent, while population grew at an annual rate of 2.4 percent: production per capita thus increased by only 10 percent in twenty years. The progress of the poorest nations was still more limited during this period, and the last decade was even marked by a decline. These countries' annual growth rate of total food production went from 2.5 percent in the sixties to 2.0 percent in the seventies; for the latter decade this corresponds to a *fall* at an annual rate of 0.4 percent in food production per capita. Africa was particularly affected because of the drought in the Sahel region at the beginning of the seventies: for the whole of the continent, production per capita declined by about 10 percent during this decade.

Yet, while the Third World's food production has grown scarcely faster than its population, its total consumption has increased more rapidly because of a rise in per capita income. Since 1960 food demand has increased by approximately 3.5 percent per year on average, while production has grown at less than 3.0 percent per year: the gap between food production and consumption has been filled by imports, which have consisted mainly of cereals.

Discussions about the world food problem have focused on cereals. These provide over 60 percent of the calories consumed by the Third World population (70 percent in the poorest countries) and also constitute the major component of international trade in food products. The importance of cereals in food consumption varies, however, according to the region: while they play a particularly significant role in human consump-

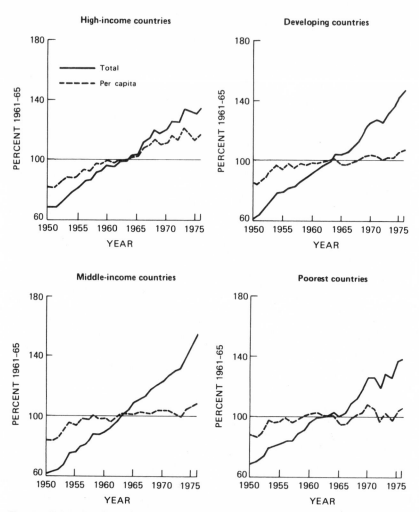

FIGURE 7.1.   Food production indices, total and per capita, 1950–1976
(1961–65 = 100). From National Research Council, *World Food and Nutrition
Study: The Potential Contributions of Research* (Washington, D.C., 1977), p. 37.

tion in Asia and the Middle East, they account for only half the calorie
intake in sub-Saharan Africa.

The increase in food imports by the Third World countries has meant a
deterioration in the balance of their cereal trade. While the three continents of the Third World exported nearly 10 million tons of cereals in the
thirties and were still practically self-sufficient at the beginning of the fifties, their *gross* imports reached 40 million tons at the beginning of the
seventies and, in 1980–1981, amounted to approximately 96 million tons

(about 70 million tons in *net* imports).[1] Today, food products account for about 9 percent of the middle-income countries' total imports (17 percent in the case of the poorest countries).

As Table 7.2 indicates, the developing countries now increasingly depend on North America for their cereal imports (which consist mainly of wheat). In 1978, approximately 78 percent of the world wheat exports came from the United States and Canada; the rest was divided between Australia (18 percent) and Argentina (4 percent). Today, grain exports from North America approximately equal the consumption of the 660 million inhabitants of India.

The growing dependence of the Third World — and of virtually all the rest of the world for that matter — on North America presents an unquestionably high risk. We have recently seen that cereals can serve as an additional weapon in the American arsenal. Without even going into this political problem, variations in the North American climate could in themselves constitute a worldwide danger. A prolonged drought or a premature frost in this region could cause a fall in cereal stocks and an upsurge in world prices, with serious consequences for the poorest countries. While the grain-importing developed countries would no doubt manage to find the dollars required for payment of their imports, the low-income countries would have extreme difficulties in obtaining the required foreign exchange. At a time when we appear to be entering a period of greater climatic instability there is thus in this dependence a serious and too often overlooked risk for world food security.

American agriculture has thus become of prime importance for the food security of the world in general and of the developing countries in particular. During recent years the world has had two main food reserves: the cereal stocks maintained by the exporting countries and the land kept fallow in the United States by federal price-support programs. During the sixties and the beginning of the seventies about 15 percent of this country's arable land (approximately 50 million acres, nearly the area of Kansas) were thus kept out of production. In case of need these land reserves could be put into production within a year: this is what actually happened, for instance, at the time of the 1973–1974 food crisis.

If we want to estimate the food reserves available in case of crisis, we must therefore take into account not only the existing cereal stocks but also the capacity of this idle but potentially productive land. Defined in these terms, world food reserves corresponded to three months of consumption at the end of the sixties; today they represent less than two (see Table 7.3).

The deterioration that has thus occurred in the level of food reserves during the seventies is in fact a new and lasting phenomenon. Even during the worst years of the previous decade (after India's massive imports of

TABLE 7.2   Net Grain Imports (−) and Exports (+) by Region
(annual averages in millions of tons)

Year	Western Europe (1)	Eastern Europe (2)	Soviet Union (3)	North America (4)
1934–38	− 23.1	+ 2.7	+ 1.3	+ 5.3
1948–52	− 21.9	+ 0.5	+ 1.7	+ 22.4
1952–56	− 21.9	− 1.4	+ 2.0	+ 24.2
1956–60	− 23.3	− 5.4	+ 5.3	+ 31.0
1961–65	− 26.2	− 6.5	+ 2.1	+ 49.2
1966–70	− 23.0	− 4.4	+ 2.9	+ 52.0
1971–75	− 21.5	− 7.1	− 7.1	+ 78.7
1976–77	− 25.2	− 11.7	− 13.1	+ 94.8

SOURCE: Food and Agriculture Organization (FAO).
   a Excluding Japan.

cereals following the two insufficient harvests of 1965–1966 and 1966–1967, for instance) these reserves had never fallen below the equivalent of 80 days of world consumption. Moreover, we can see that the situation improved only slightly after the 1973–1974 food crisis. Expressed in number of days of world consumption, the reserves went from 40 days in 1974 to 65 in 1978, then fell again to 51 days in 1979.

This new situation is particularly dangerous for the developing countries, which cannot take for granted that food aid from the rich countries will remain available in the event of a world crisis. The experience of the seventies substantiates such misgivings. World food aid had increased during the sixties, reaching nearly 13 million tons a year between 1969 and 1972. Yet in 1973–1974, because of the fall in their cereal surpluses, the developed countries decreased their aid by more than one-half, to less than 6 million tons. Since then, the slow reconstitution of reserves has apparently not led to excessive generosity, as this aid still remains below the target of 10 million tons per year.

However useful it might be, the above analysis of the evolution of the world food situation presents only one aspect of the problem. We may here draw a parallel with the energy problems, where a simple study of the commercial energy crisis would completely leave aside the often less apparent problems of noncommercial energies. Similarly, in the developing countries, a mere balance between food supply and demand is not sufficient to ensure that the nutritional needs of the entire population are satisfied. In fact, such a balance indicates only that the requirements of the solvent buyers are met, without telling us anything about the situation of the minority (or is it the majority?) of the population, which, for lack of sufficient income, cannot obtain the food it needs.

It is mainly these insolvent people who constitute the hundreds of millions of malnourished people of whom I spoke in Chapter 2. From this

Japan (5)	Oceania (6)	Latin America (7)	Asia[a] (8)	Africa (9)	(7 + 8 + 9)
− 1.9	+ 2.8	+ 9.0	+ 0.3	+ 0.6	+ 9.9
− 2.7	+ 3.4	+ 0.9	− 3.4	− 0.3	− 2.8
− 4.1	+ 3.1	+ 1.2	− 2.1	+ 0.1	− 0.8
− 4.2	+ 3.1	+ 1.6	− 7.5	− 0.9	− 6.8
− 7.2	+ 6.7	+ 2.1	− 14.9	− 2.4	− 15.2
− 12.6	+ 7.0	+ 3.3	− 19.7	− 3.9	− 20.3
− 17.2	+ 9.7	− 1.2	− 24.8	− 6.3	− 32.3
− 21.2	+ 11.2	+ 1.6	− 26.1	− 8.3	− 32.8

standpoint, the fact that the food required is physically available, in other producing countries or even at the local grocery, does not solve the problem. Growth of food production in the developing countries cannot be an end in itself: it is also necessary that this growth be accompanied − and it generally is not − by an increase in the incomes of the malnourished so as to enable them to obtain the necessary food.

In this respect the example of India in recent decades is particularly enlightening. After an exceptional harvest in 1971, this country experienced a series of setbacks, and it was only in 1976 that previous production levels were surpassed. Cereal stocks, which had fallen to less than three million tons in 1973, rose again to reach 19 million tons in 1979. In 1978 and 1979, the Indian government "lent" cereals to other Asian countries, and the experts started declaring again (as after every series of three successive good harvests) that the country had finally reached food self-sufficiency.

In fact, in 1979, a drought caused a fall in the harvest equal to two-thirds of the accumulated stocks, and all this buoyant optimism was abruptly called into question. But this is not where the paradox lies. It is in the fact that from 1975 to 1978, while India was accumulating unprecedented food reserves, the average per capita consumption was stagnating at an extremely low level. Per capita consumption for 1975–1977 was in fact lower than for 1970–1972, or even than for 1960–1962.[2] As a matter of fact, while an index of per capita consumption since 1950 shows important short-term fluctuations, it does not reveal any long-term trend, either upward or − fortunately − downward.

The food problem, be it in India or at the world level, is all too often approached exclusively from the production angle even though this approach alone cannot lead to an effective fight against malnutrition. Only when the two aspects of the problem − production *and* consump-

TABLE 7.3   Indicators of World Food Security, 1966–1979
(million metric tons and days)

Year	Reserve stocks of grain	Grain equivalent of idled U.S. cropland	Total world reserves	Reserves as days of annual grain consumption
		(million metric tons)		
1966	167	53	220	82
1967	189	60	249	89
1968	220	74	298	103
1969	206	71	277	92
1970	166	48	214	69
1971	183	65	248	78
1972	142	35	177	54
1973	147	3	150	44
1974	131	3	134	40
1975	138	3	141	42
1976	194	1	195	55
1977	191	24	215	59
1978	226	24	251	65
1979	200	0	200	51

SOURCE: Worldwatch Institute, Washington, D.C.

tion — are considered together will there be any possibility of real progress in this area.

LESSONS OF THE GREEN REVOLUTION

For experts on the Third World's food problems, few events have aroused as much hope, and perhaps as much criticism, as the Green Revolution. Since the middle of the sixties it has been at the center of the debates on the world food situation, and its future will in part determine the evolution of world hunger in the coming decades. Obviously no study of this problem would be complete without an analysis of the results and the potential of this technology.[3]

While the Green Revolution was popularized by the successes (and certain failures) that it met in South and East Asia, it was born in fact in Mexico, and its range of action has gone beyond Asia to reach most Third World countries cultivating wheat, rice, or corn. Sub-Saharan Africa, however, where these cereals are cultivated on a smaller scale, has been left relatively untouched.

At the beginning of the forties, food production in Mexico was stagnating while population was increasing rapidly. In 1943, the Mexican government, with the aid of the Rockefeller Foundation, embarked upon an agricultural research program; Norman Borlaug, who received the Nobel Peace Prize in 1970 for his work, was one of its first directors. The results were spectacular: in twenty years average national yields doubled for corn and quadrupled for wheat. In spite of a population growth rate exceeding 3 percent per year, Mexico was transformed from an importer of corn and wheat in 1944 to an exporter of these products in the sixties.[4] The particularly striking success obtained for wheat was due to the production of new varieties which responded remarkably well to fertilizer and whose short stalks did not lodge under the additional weight of the ears caused by the increased yield. Another exceptional characteristic of these new varieties was their lack of sensitivity to temperature change: unlike all other varieties previously cultivated, they could therefore adapt easily to various geographic conditions. Yet the Mexican success has an interesting epilogue. Because of high population growth, increase in per capita income and food consumption, and crop diversification away from food production, Mexico has now returned to a position of food deficit and every year must import part of the cereals required to feed its population.

In 1960, the Rockefeller Foundation, encouraged by the results of the Mexican wheat, joined with the Ford Foundation to found the International Rice Research Institute (IRRI) in the Philippines. IRRI's work rapidly led to the production of a rice variety (IR 8) which more than doubled the yield of most local rice varieties in Asia. Like the "miracle" varieties of wheat — and in contrast to the local rice varieties — IR 8 and its successors require substantial quantities of fertilizer as well as controlled and regular irrigation in order to realize their high-yield potential.

Because of their great adaptability, the new varieties of wheat and rice spread extremely rapidly. In the whole of North Africa and Asia only a few dozen hectares were planted with these varieties in 1965; in 1969, 12 million hectares were covered and in 1975, 41 million! The countries which have principally benefited from this development are in South Asia (India, Pakistan, Sri Lanka) and in East Asia (the Philippines, Indonesia, Malaysia), but the new strains have also been planted in Asia Minor (Turkey) and in Latin America (Colombia). In Asia and North Africa the areas covered with high-yield varieties are divided equally between rice and wheat. Nonetheless, the expansion of these new varieties has been more rapid in the case of wheat. In 1975, for instance, 38 percent of the areas under wheat cultivation were planted with high-yield varieties; the corresponding percentage for rice was only 26 percent. This is mainly because the areas devoted to wheat usually have better water control than do rice areas and are thus more suitable for these new varieties.

Thanks to these new seeds, the Philippines were able to attain self-sufficiency in rice at the end of the sixties, after having depended for half a century on imports to meet their requirements. (Yet here, as in Mexico, this situation could not be maintained.) Turkey began its green revolution in 1967 by importing Mexican wheat seeds; in seven years national production increased by more than one-half, rising from 9 million to 14 million tons. In Colombia, the International Center for Tropical Agriculture introduced IRRI varieties in 1971. By 1975 practically all of the irrigated rice areas had been planted with high-yield varieties; production had more than doubled compared to 1969, and yields had multiplied by 2.4 compared to 1965.

We can best measure the successes and limits of the Green Revolution by looking at its impact on the countries of the Indian subcontinent. These six countries (India, Bangladesh, Pakistan, Burma, Sri Lanka, and Nepal) produce about 200 million tons of cereal per year. Rice accounts for somewhat more than half this tonnage and wheat, for 25 percent; the rest is made up essentially of corn, millet, and sorghum. Wheat is Pakistan's main cereal; it also constitutes about 25 percent of India's grain production. Rice predominates in the northeast of the region (Burma, Bangladesh, the Indian state of West Bengal) and in Sri Lanka.

Examining the growth of cereal production since 1960, we notice a turning point around the years 1965–1967. A low annual growth rate (0.3 percent from 1960 to 1965) was followed by a much more rapid one (3.7 percent from 1965 to 1974). This acceleration of production is especially notable for wheat (from below 2 percent to over 10 percent).

Until 1965 growth in production was mainly due to the use of traditional methods: expansion of the cultivated areas, development of irrigation, preliminary use of fertilizers on local cereal varieties. In India, for instance, the increase in the cultivated area accounted for over half the growth of cereal production during this period (3 percent per year from 1950 to 1965). The two inadequate monsoons of 1965–1966 and 1966–1967 caused a fall in the cereal harvest and led the governments of the region to give more attention to agriculture. It so happened that at this time the first imports of high-yield varieties were arriving, and the rapid adoption of these seeds eventually led to substantial growth in cereal production. In fact, production growth since the mid-sixties is essentially a result of yield increases: in the case of India, for instance, these increases accounted for two-thirds of the growth of output (3.4 percent per year) between 1965 and 1979.

The Green Revolution has had a particularly pronounced impact on the two Punjabs (in India and Pakistan) and on the Indian state of Haryana, where it dramatically boosted wheat production and transformed the rural economies. In the other producing areas, however, its advance has been limited by the lack of irrigation facilities. In comparison, the Green Revolution seems to have had little effect on rice production. Since the first half of the sixties, Indian wheat production has tripled while rice production has increased by only one-third. Although two-thirds of this country's wheat areas are covered with high-yield varieties today, the proportion is only one-third for rice. In spite of the introduction of high-yield varieties, rice yields in South Asia still remain far below the yields in East and Southeast Asia. Finally, because of the demanding input requirements of the new wheat and rice seeds, the Green Revolution has completely bypassed farmers lacking irrigation systems. Its limits appear clearly enough when we consider that 80 percent of the cultivated area in India and 90 percent in Bangladesh do not have any irrigation facilities.

The Green Revolution has been accused of "making the rich richer and the poor poorer." Of course, the possibility of using this technology does not depend on farm size, and any farmer having at his disposal fertilizer, seeds, and water control can benefit from it. In practice, however, it is easier to organize irrigation on one large landholding than on a collection of small farms; moreover, the big farmers have easier access to the financial resources required for digging a well or buying seeds and fertilizer. In the Punjab, for instance, the large farms have been the first to use the new seeds. Furthermore, it has often happened that, lured by the prospect of substantial profit offered by the high-yield varieties, landowners have dismissed their sharecroppers — the latter often joining the growing ranks of landless workers — and have taken over the management of their own farms. Yet it would be a mistake to conclude that the social consequences of the Green Revolution have always been negative. This technology requires more labor for land preparation, fertilizer application, and harvesting. In the Punjab, for instance, the use of the new varieties led to an increase in the demand for labor and, consequently, to a rise in the wages of agricultural workers.[5]

On the whole, however, the situation of the rural population in the Indian subcontinent has not improved; in fact, it has presumably worsened (see Chapter 2). But this deterioration can be attributed more to the inequality of the economic and social structure (and of the land ownership in particular) and to the population explosion of the last decades than to the Green Revolution.

The end of the sixties was marked by exuberant confidence in the possibilities of the new technology. Some of its enthusiasts believed that the miracle seeds promised general prosperity in the medium term. These dreams of abundance were abruptly shaken by the cereal deficits of the beginning of the seventies, and it is now evident that, contrary to its zealots' hopes and in spite of unquestionable successes, the new technology has not led to a general improvement in living conditions.

In this respect it is worthwhile comparing the two comprehensive surveys made by the Asian Development Bank on the economic and social situation in rural Asia. The first, which was concluded in 1968, is relatively optimistic and foresees that the Green Revolution will lead to general and egalitarian development throughout the region. The second, which was carried out ten years later, is frankly pessimistic. I have mentioned its conclusions concerning the evolution of rural poverty; with regard to the food situation it states, in a somewhat disillusioned manner, that "overall, the most optimistic view which can be taken of the food situation is that the region is not much worse off now than at the time of the first Asian Agricultural Survey." [6]

Are we then to conclude that the Green Revolution has been a failure? No, since, after all, it led to a rapid growth of cereal production which in all likelihood would not have taken place without it. After the droughts of the mid-sixties, India was thus able to increase its cereal production by half in ten years: in this country, where uncultivated land is particularly scarce, such growth would have been impossible without the high yields of the new varieties. Similarly, other countries have been able to attain food self-sufficiency — at least temporarily — thanks to the potential of these varieties.

The fact that, in certain cases, this newly won self-sufficiency has been lost again only indicates that, while this new technology can save time, it cannot replace the necessary implementation of policies to limit population growth. Similarly, it was naive to hope that technology alone could correct the effects of an inequitable economic and social structure and could benefit equally all categories of the population. But let us not blame the Green Revolution for inequalities whose source is elsewhere!

SCOPE FOR PRODUCTION INCREASES

In the coming years increases in Third World food production will have to come partly from an expansion of the cultivated areas and partly from yield increases. The former can be obtained by bringing still virgin land under the plow or by expanding irrigation on already cultivated land (which, by permitting multiple cropping, would lead to a similar result). As for increasing yields, this will require the utilization of more effective cultivation methods, which in turn generally imply the use of modern inputs.

Expansion of cultivated areas

The possibility of increasing the cultivated areas will depend first of all on the availability of arable land. There have been various estimates of the arable area of the globe.[7] They largely agree in their conclusion that approximately one-quarter of the land not covered with ice has agricultural potential (around 3.4 billion hectares) and that about half this land is currently cultivated. The potentially arable land is unequally divided, however, among the regions and countries. Africa and Latin America still have considerable reserves of uncultivated arable land, while Asia has far more limited resources (see Table 7.4).

TABLE 7.4   Cultivated and Cultivable Land per Inhabitant in Developing Countries
(in hectares)

Country group	Cultivated area per inhabitant	Cultivable area per inhabitant
All developing countries	0.33	0.79
Africa	0.55	1.71
Far East	0.21	0.28
Latin America	0.52	1.79
Middle East	0.39	0.60
Low-income developing countries	0.29	0.61

SOURCE: FAO, *Agriculture: Towards 2000* (Rome, 1979).

Less than one-third of the potentially arable land is cultivated in Africa and Latin America, but more than two-thirds is cultivated in Asia. A country-by-country survey of existing reserves is useful, however, to qualify this first conclusion (see Table 7.5). It can be seen that 46 percent of the population of the 90 countries considered in Table 7.5 (these countries accounting for 98 percent of the Third World population) live in countries having less than 10 percent of land reserves. Even in Africa, 46 percent of the population live in countries having less than 30 percent of reserves, an insufficient amount to provide for the population increase of the next two decades.

Moreover, preparing potentially arable land for cultivation poses several problems. One is the level of investment required. The cost of developing land can be estimated at $80 to $1,200 per acre. For the developing countries, maintaining until the year 2000 a rate of growth in cultivated areas of 1 percent per year (approximately the rate realized during recent decades) would require an average annual investment of about $13 billion — a figure equivalent to the *total* cost of agricultural investment in developing countries in 1975.[8] Taking into account the other agricultural investments that will be required in the coming years, maintaining such a rate of growth in cultivated areas would therefore involve a significant increase in the total agricultural investment.

Furthermore, the land with the best potential and the lowest development costs has generally been the first to be cultivated. It is therefore very likely that, as more and more marginal land is brought under the plow, its development costs will increase while its productivity declines. Such a production decline has already been observed in countries where, because of population pressure, land of mediocre quality has been brought under cultivation. Finally, we should not underestimate the technical or ecological difficulties entailed by the development of new land, as the disappointing ventures of the Brazilian forest and the virgin land of Kazakhstan have shown.

TABLE 7.5   Distribution of the Ninety Largest Developing Countries
According to Level of Land Reserves, 1975

Level of land reserves[a]	Number of countries	Percentage of population living in countries with given level of land reserves				
		Africa	Far East	Latin America	Middle East	All 90 developing countries
10% or less	18	5	63	6	76	46
10% to 30%	24	41	12	7	14	16
30% to 60%	22	26	22	30	0	21
More than 60%	26	28	3	57	10	17
Total	90	100	100	100	100	100

SOURCE: See Table 7.4.

[a] Ratio (in percentage) of the area of arable but not yet cultivated land to the total arable area (including cultivated land).

In recent years, the area under irrigation in the Third World has considerably increased (at the rate of 2 percent per year between 1966 and 1975); today it represents 14 percent of the total arable area. It is doubtful, however, that such a growth rate can be maintained in the future. Investment costs have risen rapidly during recent years, and they will no doubt continue to do so as less and less suitable sites are developed. Furthermore, in certain regions (such as the Middle East) the potential water resources are already more limited, and consequently the future development of irrigation is bound to proceed at a slower pace.

Soil degradation

During the last decade the developed countries have been preoccupied with their "environment"; on the other hand the Third World countries, confronted with apparently more urgent problems, have not given much attention to such "problems of the rich." It is likely, however, that ultimately the most dangerous form of environmental deterioration is precisely the one now affecting many developing countries. In these countries the irreversible process of soil degradation could well compromise the population's capacity to produce their staple foods.[9] This deterioration, which seems to be due mainly to the increasing population pressure and the mounting pace of economic activity in recent years, constitutes even today a little-known and scarcely measured phenomenon. There are, however, a sufficient number of signs to indicate both the generality and the seriousness of this problem.

In the previous chapter I discussed some of the often disastrous consequences of deforestation and subsequent erosion. Other factors also contribute to soil erosion: cultivation of unsuitable land, reduction in the fallow period, cultivation of crops that give insufficient protection to the soil, and so on. About 20 percent of the land in Bangladesh, 77 percent in El Salvador, and 80 percent in Madagascar are affected by erosion. Haiti — whose name, ironically, means "Green Island" — is surely one of the most serious cases: according to the United Nations, erosion constitutes that country's number one problem.

A particular form of erosion — desertification — affects all three continents of the Third World. It has been estimated that the *annual* loss of soil due to this phenomenon amounts to 0.3 percent of the total land area of these regions — twice the size of Belgium. In 1977 a United Nations conference on this subject estimated that 20 percent of the land in South America, 30 percent in Asia, and 35 percent in Africa presented moderate to very high risks of desertification.

Finally, the increase in soil salinity or alkalinity due to irrigation causes an annual loss of 0.2 percent of the irrigated area in the Third World. In Pakistan in 1960, one-fifth of the cultivated land of the Indus valley was thus affected, and the land deteriorated at a rate of 40,000 hectares lost each year.

A common cause generally lies behind these different phenomena of degradation: inappropriate soil utilization. In most cases, the initial conditions are such that either the land should be cultivated with care, after certain investments have been made, or it should simply not be cultivated at all. Population pressure is generally responsible for this mismanagement of the land: even if the farmers are aware of the ultimate dangers of improper cultivation, they have no other choice if they want to survive than to cultivate marginal land or to accelerate the crop cycle by shortening the fallow period.

It is for this very reason that the fight against soil degradation is so difficult. The measures required are well known and free of technical difficulties; most of them can in fact be justified on the basis of strict economic criteria (to the extent that the discounted benefits usually exceed the costs). As for the governments, which ten years ago still generally underestimated the extent of this problem, they are now beginning to give it serious attention. Nevertheless, government efforts to combat the ongoing deterioration of the land have generally met with only limited success. As in the case of reforestation programs, the active cooperation of the population is required, but here also it has proved difficult to obtain. It is not of course for any lack of goodwill or intelligence that the farmers — who, after all, would be the first to benefit from these programs — do not cooperate in the desired manner. They do in fact quickly understand, if they did not already know, that shortening the fallow period or plowing unsuitable land will lead, in five or six years, to soil erosion and a fall in fertility. Yet what choice do they have if they do not have any other means to feed their families?

Finally, there is a last cause of the loss of arable land that we should not overlook: urbanization. At present the losses urbanization entails are perhaps larger in the industrial world (where they amount to an annual decrease of 0.1 to 0.8 percent in agricultural area), but the long-term implications of this phenomenon will be more important for the developing countries. Already, Egypt loses 26,000 hectares of its best land (on the banks of the Nile) every year because of the expansion of cities and their infrastructure. The Indian government estimates that the land area used for nonagricultural purposes should increase from 16 million hectares in 1970 to 26 by the year 2000. But this phenomenon is presumably even more difficult to control than the degradation and erosion of the soil, because this would require that the very process of urbanization be successfully checked.

The cumulative effect of all these processes on soil loss and degradation is certainly considerable. In fact, a recent report sponsored by several international organizations (including the United Nations Environment Program) concludes that, worldwide, 200 acres of arable land are lost every minute. (As a comparison, the area of virgin land brought under the plow in the Third World each minute amounts to less than 40 acres.) If soil degradation were to continue at this pace, nearly one-third of the world's arable area would be lost by the end of this century.[10]

Potential for yield increases

Until the middle of the present century, an increase in cultivated areas had been the main source of growth in world food production. Since then a substantial proportion of this production growth has been due to yield increases. The main reason for this change is the diminution in the reserves of arable land, which itself is the result of the previous expansion in the cultivated areas. Moreover, this change in the relative importance of the two factors contributing to production growth (cultivated area and yield) seems to be accelerating. From 1960 to 1966, the annual growth rate of the developing countries' cereal production had been about 2.1 percent: the cultivated area had expanded at 1.2 percent per year, while the yields had increased at an average rate of 0.9 percent. From 1966 to 1975, the production growth rate was higher (2.3 percent), but the cultivated area increased at an annual rate of only 0.7 percent, while the yields grew at a rate of 1.6 percent. New farmland brought under cultivation accounted for more than half the increase in food production at the beginning of the sixties, but for only one-third around 1970; it is estimated that this proportion will come down to one-fourth during the eighties.

For the reasons mentioned above, extending the area under cultivation will become more and more difficult in the future, and production increases will have to come mostly from yield improvements. As the above figures show, yields did improve significantly between 1966 and 1975 (the first years of the Green Revolution), and these encouraging results could lead us to believe that future yield increases might still be possible. In fact, these yields are still extremely low today in many developing nations. Third World countries produce 92 percent of the world rice production, but their average yields scarcely exceed 1.5 tons per hectare; in the developed countries, by contrast, these yields average about 5.5 tons per hectare. Corn yields in Latin America are two to four times lower than in the United States; rice yields in Burma are four times lower than in Taiwan. There is a reservoir of agricultural techniques not yet used by most farmers whose utilization could lead to substantial increases in yield. With regard to cereals, for instance, the high-yield varieties of the Green Revolution are not used everywhere in the most effective manner.

Yet there are reasons to believe that the Green Revolution has now entered a phase of decreasing marginal returns. The first and spectacular successes were achieved by the most progressive farmers and on the best land. It is now a question of convincing farmers who are more conservative or less able to finance the required expenditures; it is also necessary to use less suitable areas or land lacking reliable water supply. As we know, high-yield varieties have been obtained only for *irrigated* crops of corn, rice, and wheat, and, ultimately therefore, their expansion will be limited by the development of irrigation.

Moreover, results similar to those obtained, with the high-yield varieties, for these three cereals have not yet been attained for any other food crops. This failure partly explains the mediocre performance of the food sector in the countries or regions where plants other than cereals constitute the staple food. Sub-Saharan Africa, for instance, finds a substantial part of its calorie intake in root plants; yet until recently these plants had been all but neglected by agricultural research.[11]

With regard to long-term food prospects, it is alarming to note that the present state of agricultural research does not permit us to hope for a rapid breakthrough similar to that achieved by the high-yield varieties.[12] We should bear in mind that research on these varieties began in Mexico in the forties, twenty years before it resulted in the spectacular yield increases of the Green Revolution in Asia. Two particular subjects of current research could yet prove to have — if and when the research succeeds — a potential similar to that of the high-yield varieties. The first concerns the improvement of the photosynthetic efficiency of plants through genetic changes; the second regards the development of cereals which would fix their nitrogen directly. So far, however, there is no sign of a breakthrough in either of these areas; such an achievement will no doubt depend on the progress of basic biology in the coming years.

All modern agricultural practices — whose utilization will be necessary to obtain the required yield increases — use substantial quantities of fertilizers, insecticides, seeds, and water, as well as farm machinery in certain cases. It is an illusion to believe that a substantial augmentation in world food production would be possible without an increased use of fertilizers and insecticides.[13] With regard to the long-term development of modern agriculture, therefore, the two main questions concern the future availability of fertilizer on the one hand, and of energy on the other.

The utilization of fertilizers in developing countries has increased at an annual rate of 14 to 15 percent during the last fifteen years. At the beginning of the seventies, a temporary scarcity had slowed down this progression, but the rise resumed after 1975. Nearly half the fertilizers produced are used for cereal production, and in this respect, a future scarcity of fertilizer could seriously affect world food production. Fortunately, the availability of fertilizer in the Third World should not be a problem, at least until the end of the century, provided these countries continue to develop their productive capacity at the rapid rate of recent years.

Nor should there be any lack of the raw materials required for the production of these fertilizers. Existing reserves of phosphate and potassium appear sufficient for future production of nonnitrogen fertilizers. The production of nitrogen fertilizers, however, requires considerable energy, and this has given rise to the fear that a future oil scarcity could limit production. Yet this fear does not seem to be justified, at least for the next two decades. First of all, the production of fertilizer accounts for only 2 to 3 percent of present world oil consumption. Moreover, the energy required for this production could, in many cases, be obtained from the natural gas which is now, in general, uselessly flared (see Chapter 6).

This leads us to the more general problem of the impact of the energy crisis on food production. Modern agriculture's dependence on energy has aroused fears that the present energy crisis could aggravate the Third World's food problems during the coming decades. In this respect, the first question that arises concerns the extent to which limitations on energy supply could reduce the developing countries' food production. Several factors indicate that in this case also the risk should be quite limited, at least until the end of this century.

In the first place, commercial energy presently accounts for only 5 percent, on average, of the total energy used for agricultural production in the developing countries, the rest being provided by human and animal labor. This proportion varies, of course, according to the region and the degree of modernization of agriculture, but even in Latin America, where agriculture is more developed, this percentage does not attain 20 percent. Moreover, in case of a scarcity, this commercial energy can be replaced by animal or human energy in many agricultural operations.[14]

Finally, the share of the agricultural sector in the total consumption of commercial energy is extremely low in all countries: about 3.5 percent for the industrial countries, perhaps slightly more for the developing ones.[15] If we consider the whole food chain (processing, transport, marketing, cooking), this percentage presumably reaches about 12 percent in the developed countries (12.8 percent in the United States in 1970), but it should not exceed 8 to 9 percent in the developing countries. In these circumstances it should therefore be possible for Third World governments, in case of a disruption in energy supply, to allocate a sufficient ration to the priority needs of food production.

Another question concerns the impact of the rise in energy costs on food prices. This impact is also likely to be slight. In the industrial countries the cost of energy represents 5 to 15 percent of the production costs (at farm gates) and a still smaller proportion of the costs to the consumers.[16] In the developing countries the corresponding percentage is even smaller because of the more limited use of commercial energy. In these circumstances a rise in energy costs should cause only a very slight increase in the consumer prices of food.

At first glance, then, it seems that energy problems should not constitute an insurmountable obstacle to the future development of food production. It may be safer, however, not to overestimate governments' capacity to cope with difficulties in their energy supply. In 1973–1974, as a result of a supply disruption, the farmers of certain countries (India and Bangladesh among others) were unable to obtain the oil or electricity they needed for their irrigation pumps and consequently suffered substantial harvest losses. In the absence of any contingency planning, similar problems may very well occur in the future in the case of a crisis or simply in the event of an unexpected disruption in procurement.

There is still, however, another important aspect of the link between energy prices and food production that must be considered here: the expanding cultivation of "fuel crops" for distillation and alcohol production. As energy prices increased during the seventies, several countries turned to alcohol distilled from farm commodities as an additional source of fuel for automobiles, since car engines can, without any adjustment, burn a gasoline-alcohol mixture containing up to 10 percent alcohol. In the last few years, Brazil and the United States have both announced major programs to convert agricultural commodities into alcohol, and other countries have been considering similar projects. At present world oil prices, ethanol production from various crops (corn, wheat, sorghum, sugarcane) already appears financially attractive.

It thus seems likely that in the eighties several countries will start their own production of fuel crops or develop their existing programs. But this prospect raises the question of eventual competition between fuel crop production and food crop production. As a matter of fact, these two crops could possibly compete for scarce resources such as fertilizer, water, labor, credit, or land; in the case of land, in particular, such competition appears very likely.

For instance, in the case of Brazil, whose ambitious fuel crop program was one of the first launched, achievement of the stated government goal of 10.7 billion liters of alcohol by 1985 would require nearly three million hectares of sugarcane, the equivalent of 10 percent of this country's cropland; reaching the objective of automotive fuel self-sufficiency would require an area half the size of this total cropland. One could of course argue that Brazil's vast land resources should be sufficient for both food *and* fuel production. But this land potential has not prevented Brazil from being in an acute grain-deficit situation; nor has it solved this country's persistent and widespread nutrition problem. It thus appears likely that a marked expansion of Brazil's fuel crop program would be achieved at the expense of food production and nutritional improvement.

The possibility of competition between fuel and food is not limited to the developing world. In January 1980, President Carter set a goal of two billion gallons for ethanol production in the mid-eighties, an objective which would require some 20 million tons of corn or its equivalent. Of course, the United States is not a food importer and does not suffer from widespread malnutrition, but such a decrease in its food production would correspond to a reduction by one-fifth of the amount available for exports. In turn, such a sizable reduction in the volume of exportable corn would be translated into substantial increases in world grain prices and, consequently, in the developing countries' food import bills. In the future, therefore, fuel crop production is likely to have a negative impact on food production in developing countries and, directly or through their imports, on their food consumption.[17]

If we now try to weigh the various factors which will determine the future growth of food production, we have reason to conclude that there is still considerable potential for development. In particular, there seems to be no approaching physical barrier limiting growth possibilities. In fact, various studies have concluded that the world food production could be multiplied by a coefficient ranging from five to thirty.[18] Whatever the uncertainty about the maximum level of this production, it thus seems that this potential should enable us to face the projected population increases during this century and presumably the next one.

Encouraging as this result might be, it does not in itself solve our problem. However important the food production potential of our planet, the steps taken towards its realization have been unquestionably slow during recent decades. If the obstacles to production growth are not primarily physical, they are political, social, administrative, or financial — but they are just as real. Since the middle of the present century, the food situation of the Third World has scarcely improved. Have we any reason to believe that the prospects for the next few decades are any better?

FOOD PROSPECTS

Before we venture in forecasting the future evolution of the Third World's food situation, it may be useful to look back and compare the present outlook with the situation that existed at the beginning of the seventies.

It is difficult to avoid the conclusion that the situation is much less encouraging today than it was ten years ago. In the early seventies, the optimism created by the first successes of the Green Revolution still prevailed; the seriousness and complexity of the problems of soil degradation and malnutrition were not clearly perceived; energy supply did not appear to be a problem; and American cereal stocks were apparently sufficient to make up for any unexpected fall in Third World harvests. All that has changed considerably in a decade. Today, the prospects of rapid yield increases are much less certain, and because of the expansion of the cultivated areas, reserves of uncultivated land are more limited. Moreover, new doubts have arisen concerning energy resources, soil quality, and the availability of food surpluses in developed countries.

Perhaps the only positive development of the last decade is governments' growing awareness of the extent of the problems. The crises of the seventies jolted Third World leaders; in many countries a higher priority is now given to food production. But the risk unfortunately remains that the apparent and temporary improvement in the world food situation could now lead governments to relax their newly awakened attention.

If we take into account all of these elements, future growth rates of food production similar to those of recent decades appear to be the best we can expect. Of course, a more rapid pace is technically possible, and every effort should be made to achieve it, but the experience of three decades should keep us from excessive optimism regarding the possibilities of success. Consumption, in turn, is also likely to continue to increase at a pace comparable to that of the past. In these circumstances, the developing countries' food deficits can do nothing but grow in the coming years.

From 1962-1964 to 1980-1981 the developing countries' net cereal imports rose from 32 million to some 70 million tons. If past trends continue, the United Nations estimates that these countries' net cereal deficits will reach 90 million tons in 1990 and exceed 150 million tons in 2000. Other studies confirm the growing size of the deficits projected for these two dates.[19] As we see in Table 7.6, by 1990 food deficits could represent a substantial share of consumption in certain countries, particularly in Africa.

Food deficits of this volume will of course entail a considerable number

TABLE 7.6   Food Deficits for Various Developing Countries

	Actual 1975		Projected 1990	
	Million metric tons	% of consumption	Million metric tons	% of consumption
India	1.4	1	17.6–21.9	10–12
Nigeria	0.4	2	17.1–20.5	35–39
Bangladesh	1.0	7	6.4–8.0	30–35
Indonesia	2.1	8	6.0–7.7	14–17
Egypt	3.7	35	4.9	32
Sahel group	0.4	9	3.2–3.5	44–46
Ethiopia	0.1	2	2.1–2.3	26–28
Burma	(0.4)[a]	(7)[a]	1.9–2.4	21–25
Philippines	0.3	4	1.4–1.7	11–13
Afghanistan	. . .	. . .	1.3–1.5	19–22
Bolivia and Haiti	0.3	24	0.7–0.8	35–38

SOURCE: International Food Policy Research Institute (IFPRI), *Food Needs of Developing Countries* (Washington, D.C., 1977).
   [a] Surplus.

of problems. The first concerns the capacity of the "capitalist" developed countries to produce the surpluses required to make up such a deficit. In all likelihood this problem will be aggravated by the Soviet Union's import demand, which will be added to the Third World's requirements: if the ongoing evolution continues, this additional demand could reach above 25 million tons by 1985. It is obviously impossible to forecast accurately Western cereal surpluses a decade hence, not to mention at the end of the century. It seems certain, nonetheless, that the production of surpluses of such a magnitude will be far from easy.[20]

The financing of such a volume of cereal imports will also involve considerable difficulties.[21] The majority of the oil-exporting countries and a large number of middle-income countries will probably manage to obtain the foreign exchange required. But it is difficult to see how the poorest countries (those of South Asia and sub-Saharan Africa) will finance the desired purchases.

And the question of the balance between food supply and solvent demand is only one aspect of the problem, as we have already seen. Even if by 1990 or 2000 the developed countries were able to produce, and the developing countries able to finance, the tonnage of cereals required to meet the Third World's import needs, this would not in itself solve the problem of malnutrition. Solvent demand for food represents only a part of nutritional needs; growth of food production — or of food imports for that matter — will not improve the nutritional situation of the very poor unless it is accompanied by an increase in their incomes enabling them to obtain this food. As the United States Academy of Sciences declared: "Even doubling food production next year on present patterns would not materially change the status of the great majority who are hungry and malnourished today."[22] It is therefore not surprising that the United Nations forecasts that, if the present food production and consumption trends continue (which implies that, one way or another, the ensuing deficit between production and consumption could be made up), the number of malnourished will scarcely decrease between now and the year 2000, going from 415 to 390 million. Even under the most favorable assumption (corresponding to a growth rate of agricultural production over the period 1980–2000 nearly 50 percent higher than the one achieved during recent decades) the number of malnourished would decline by only 40 percent in twenty years. It would therefore be a mistake to hope that mere growth of agricultural production will enable us to rid the world of hunger between now and the year 2000.

It would be a similar mistake to hope that fishing and aquaculture or synthetic foods can make an effective contribution to the fight against hunger within the next two decades.[23] Because of the existing limits to world fishing resources, fishing production and aquaculture should increase, at the maximum, as quickly as world population. As for synthetic foods (such as single-cell proteins), whatever their future in the twenty-first century, they will probably not be sufficiently perfected for general consumption during the present century. Furthermore, the problem of satisfying the insolvent demand of the poorest will arise for these artificial food products just as it presently does for natural foods.[24]

During this last decade it has become increasingly evident that the reduction of malnutrition would require a simultaneous attack on the two problems of production and income. Only by augmenting both the availability of food and the incomes of the poorest will it be possible to improve nutritional levels. In this regard, the United Nations projections mentioned above provide an interesting illustration. As we have seen, even in the case of very rapid growth in agricultural production, the number of malnourished people in the year 2000 will still be several hundred million. Yet preliminary studies indicate that a moderate income redistribution could decrease this number by half and that a more radical restructuring could reduce it by five-sixths.[25] We should of course take these figures with a grain of salt, but as an order of magnitude they do indicate the profound impact an improvement in income distribution could have on the nutritional level of the Third World population.

In 1974, the World Food Conference adopted a resolution stating that all governments "should accept the goal that within a decade no child will go to bed hungry, that no family will fear for its next day's bread, and that no human being's future and capacities will be stunted by malnutrition."[26]

Ten years have not passed since then, but it is already clear that the goal will not be attained. Since this resolution was passed, very little has been accomplished in the way of food aid and food security, development of food production, income redistribution, or implementation of nutrition policies. Since then, however, the food dependence of the Third World has worsened; in all likelihood, the number of malnourished has not decreased; the population of the Third World has risen by 15 percent; and throughout the world perhaps 10 percent of the arable land has been destroyed.

In retrospect it is sadly evident that the goal set in Rome in 1974 was unattainable. More serious, however, this goal still appears out of reach, even by the end of the century. While the seventies may have brought us little to cheer about in this area, they have at least enabled us to lose a few comfortable illusions. It seems fairly well established today that in the coming decades the Third World food situation will be particularly precarious. In the absence of rapid action on the part of the whole international community, serious if not disastrous deterioration appears very likely. If we let this deterioration occur through our inaction, we will not be able to blame our ignorance. The most prestigious commissions have in fact repeatedly warned us. The executive group of the Global 2000 Study forecasts that over the next two decades "per capita consumption in South Asia, the Middle East, and the less developed countries of Africa will scarcely improve or will actually decline below present inadequate levels."[27] The Presidential Commission on World Hunger, also set up at President Carter's initiative, concludes that "a major crisis of global food supply — of even more serious dimensions than the present energy crisis — appears likely within the next twenty years unless steps are taken now to facilitate a significant increase in food production in the developing nations."[28] Recommending a similar action program, the Brandt Commission declares: "In the absence of these measures the 1980's and 1990's could witness even worse scenes of starvation than have occurred in the 1970's, and dramatic rises in cereal prices everywhere."[29] Indeed, it will be difficult to claim that we had not been forewarned.

8
POVERTY

Ten years ago, the very idea of considering poverty as a problem in itself, distinct from the problem of underdevelopment, would probably have called for some justification. After all, "poor countries" and "underdeveloped countries" were synonymous terms, and to fight poverty in the Third World also clearly meant accelerating these nations' growth.

As we have seen, this conventional wisdom has been challenged during the last decade. Considerable evidence indicates that since World War II the profits of growth have been most unequally distributed among different social categories. As stated in 1974 by a study published under the auspices of the World Bank, "It is now clear that a decade of rapid growth in underdeveloped countries has been of little or no benefit to perhaps a third of their population."[1] Because of the unreliability of existing statistics, it is of course always possible to contest certain figures or examples; yet the subject as a whole cannot be dismissed so easily. An increasing number of surveys have now confirmed that, however exceptional the developing countries' growth during the last few decades, this overall result cannot hide many failures and shortcomings.

As a result, of course, many accepted ideas concerning the automatic diffusion of the profits of growth among all social categories (the so-called "trickle-down" theory) have been called into question, and the theoretical and practical questions regarding the link between production growth and income distribution have been taken up with renewed interest. Enthusiastically — and at times naively — universities and international organizations have set off in search of new development strategies.

Before these alternative strategies could be defined, however, it was necessary to answer a number of important questions. Who are the poor? What are their economic activities, their social characteristics? Next, what do economic science and statistical observation tell us about the link between economic growth and the elimination of poverty? Is there an automatic connection between the average level of the gross national product (GNP) per capita and the incomes of the very poor? Finally, if there is nothing automatic in this connection, are there alternative policies that could improve the situation of the neediest?

With regard to all these questions, unfortunately, the relative novelty of the inquiry and the lack of reliable data have prevented any advance beyond the stage of preliminary indications. On the basis of these, nevertheless, the search continues for new orientations to development efforts.

WHO ARE THE POOR?

Poverty is certainly a complex concept, one that cannot be defined by a single indicator only. An attempt to define it should take into account several criteria: income, assets, education, nutrition, class or caste, access to certain public services, and so on. No studies (other than fragmentary ones) have actually been made of these subjects; indeed, in most countries the statistics which would be necessary to carry out such studies do not even exist. For want of anything better, economists generally make do with the income criterion — not that this criterion is conceptually better, but in this field at least some statistical data do exist. I cannot overemphasize, however, the relatively poor quality of these data and consequently the tentative character of the conclusions which can be based on them.

If we then agree to use the criterion of income per capita to define "the poor," the problem is not thereby solved. The question arises of income comparison among countries (an income of $100 purchases more basic goods in India than in the United States) and among the regions of a same country (for instance, because of differences in the cost of living, an identical income will not have the same purchasing power in the town as in the countryside). Furthermore, the income threshold defining poverty can only be arbitrary: shall we say that a person is poor if his annual income is below $50, $100, or $200? To express this level in terms of purchasing power (an income permitting food consumption of so many calories or the procurement of a given quantity of a vital good) only shifts the problem, without removing the arbitrary aspect of the choice of the threshold.

In these circumstances any attempt to estimate the number of "absolute poor" may seem futile. Since the poverty line is by definition completely arbitrary, what can be the meaning, for instance, of the figure of 800 million set forth by the World Bank as the number of absolute poor in the world? For various reasons, however, this estimate is not without significance. First, the very magnitude of the poverty problem becomes clear when we know the extremely low income threshold which was used to arrive at the World Bank's estimate: $50 to $75 per capita, in 1970 dollars.[2]

Second, and more importantly, these estimates are of special interest because of the intertemporal and interregional comparisons they permit. In particular, they enable us to locate more precisely the poverty pockets. Thus, the World Bank estimates that 80 percent of the absolute poor live in the poorest countries, which for the most part are the countries of sub-Saharan Africa and South Asia. This result, which is not in itself surprising, only confirms that poverty is to a great extent a regional phenomenon.

Moreover, it is noteworthy that all the studies conclude that poverty in the Third World is essentially a characteristic of the rural sector. While there is a dim general awareness of the Third World's rural poverty, the real extent of this destitution is seldom clearly perceived. Western travelers, shocked by the sight of Third World cities, tend to associate poverty with the shantytowns of Dakar or the slums of Calcutta. All too often the leaders of these countries and the "international experts" similarly confuse the problem of poverty with that of the urban misery which surrounds them.

Although overcrowding in Third World cities makes destitution more immediately visible there, the situation is generally much worse in the rural areas. This fact, familiar to all who have lived in these countries' villages, should not surprise even a casual observer. For what indeed could be the reason for the rural exodus and the explosive urbanization of these countries if not the fact that the cities, for all their squalid poverty, are still less poor than the surrounding countryside? As the Brandt Commission reminds us, "The fact that people still migrate to these cities only underlines the desperate situation which they have left behind." [3]

Whatever the criteria used, all the existing data confirm that poverty is mostly a rural phenomenon. Thus, incomes per capita are systematically lower in the countryside than in the towns (even if we take into account the difference in purchasing power). A careful look at the existing data for ten countries reveals that the ratio of average urban income to average rural income ranges from 1.3 in Pakistan to more than 9.0 in Zambia; on the whole, these gaps are presumably higher in the Third World countries today than they were in the now-developed countries when the latter were at a comparable stage of development. [4]

Considering these disparities and the fact that three-quarters of the Third World's population are country dwellers, it is not surprising that the majority of the poor live in rural areas. [5] As Table 8.1 indicates, whatever income threshold is adopted to define the "poor," 85 percent of them live in rural areas.

In addition to the available income data, all other indicators similarly confirm the extreme destitution of the countryside. With regard to health care, for instance, cities are generally better serviced (in clinics, doctors, hospitals, nurses) than the countryside; the examples shown in Table 8.2

TABLE 8.1   Estimates of Total Population and Rural Population in Poverty in Developing Countries

Region	Population 1969	Total population in poverty		Rural population in poverty	
		Below $50 per capita[a]	Below $75 per capita[a]	Below $50 per capita[a]	Below $75 per capita[a]
		(millions)			
Developing countries					
Africa	360	115	165	105	140
America	260	30	50	20	30
Asia	1,080	415	620	355	525
All developing countries	1,700	560	835	480	695
Four Asian countries [b]	765	350	510	295	435
Other countries	935	210	325	185	260
		(percentage)			
Share of developing countries					
Africa	21	21	20	22	20
America	15	5	6	4	4
Asia	64	74	74	74	76
Combined share, relative to total population	100	33	49	28	41
Share of four Asian countries [b]	45	63	61	62	63

SOURCE: World Bank, *Rural Development,* Sector Policy Paper (Washington, D.C., 1975).
   [a] 1969 prices.
   [b] Bangladesh, India, Indonesia, and Pakistan.

are in this respect representative of the situation in most Third World countries.

According to the World Water Conference, about 75 percent of the Third World's urban population, but only 20 percent of its rural population, have access to adequate water supplies. As can be seen in Table 8.3, irrespective of a country's per capita income, the water supply and excreta disposal services are much worse in the countryside than in the cities. Schools are usually less numerous in the countryside (in proportion to the population); they are also not as good as those in the towns.[6] As a rule, all surveys and data available on the differences in conditions between town and countryside show that, in all sectors, rural areas are less well endowed than cities. Whatever definition of poverty is adopted, it is clear that the great majority of the Third World's poor live in the countryside.

It should therefore not be surprising that agriculture is the main source of employment for the poorest. In Africa and Asia (where 95 percent of the Third World's poor live, as Table 8.1 shows us), agriculture is the main activity of 75 to 85 percent of the rural population; in fact, apart from the cases of a few more-advanced countries and of areas close to town, virtually all rural inhabitants depend to some extent on agriculture. If we now turn our attention from the whole rural population to the poorest among

TABLE 8.2   Population per Medical Doctor in Selected Developing Countries

Country	Year	Population per medical doctor		
		Nationwide	Urban	Rural
Pakistan	1970	7,400	3,700	24,200
Kenya	1969	12,140	800	50,000
Philippines	1971	3,900	1,500	10,000
Honduras	1968	3,860	1,190	7,140
Colombia	1970	2,160	1,000	6,400
Iran	1967–70	3,752	2,275	10,000
Panama	1969	1,790	930	3,000

SOURCE: World Bank, *Health,* Sector Policy Paper (Washington, D.C., 1975).

these country dwellers, we find that the statisical data regarding their means of existence are very sparse. The little information that does exist nonetheless indicates that agriculture is even more important as a source of income for these poor than for the whole rural population. For instance, in the more developed rural regions of Malaysia, agriculture remains a more important occupation for the poor than for the other people: it constitutes the main source of income for 82 percent of the poor against only 50 percent for the rest of the rural population.

If 85 percent of the poor live in rural areas and 80 to 90 percent of these rural poor find in agriculture their principal means of existence, it follows that this activity is the principal source of income for some three-quarters of the developing countries' poorest population. René Dumont has repeatedly stated that the Third World's farmers are the proletarians of modern times. We should no doubt qualify this statement to take into account the fact that certain big farmers are not exactly among the needy, but there is no doubt that, on the whole, the Third World's most destitute social group is the peasant population.

Our statistical information regarding the employment of the poorest practically comes to an end here. We do not know, for instance, what their principal sources of income are, outside of agriculture. Nor do we know how many of them are self-employed or how many are wage earners; it seems, however, that wage earners are in the minority. This is probably explained by the fact that the majority of the poor live in the rural areas and obtain most of their income in kind from small farms where they are tenants, sharecroppers, or landowners.

The fact that the majority of the poorest laborers are self-employed and not wage earners should have important implications for the definition of antipoverty policies. Traditionally, debates on income distribution and poverty (in the Third World and elsewhere) have focused upon the employment level and the share of income going to labor. This approach, well known to economists, is based on classical and neoclassical theories

TABLE 8.3   Access to Community Water Supply and Excreta Disposal Services for Selected Developing Countries, 1975
(% population served)

Selected countries by GNP per capita	Water Supply			Excreta Disposal		
	Urban	Rural	Total	Urban	Rural	Total
Less than $150						
India	80	18	31	87	2	20
Ethiopia	58	1	8	56	8	14
Zaire	38	12	19	65	6	22
$150 to $299						
Pakistan	75	5	25	21	. . .	6
Tanzania	59	36	38	100	4	10
Indonesia	41	4	11	60	5	15
$300 to $599						
El Salvador	89	28	53	71	17	39
Philippines	82	31	50	76	44	56
Ghana	86	14	35	95	40	56
$600 to $999						
Chile	78	28	70	36	11	32
Turkey	74	64	68	13	5	8
Malaysia	100	6	34	100	43	60
$1,000 to $1,499						
Uruguay	100	87	98	97	17	83
Iraq	100	11	66	75	1	47
Costa Rica	100	56	72	94	93	93

SOURCE: World Bank, *Health,* Sector Policy Paper (Washington, D.C., 1980).

and contrasts the owners of capital, who are self-employed and receive high earnings, and the wage earners, who work for other people and have only limited incomes. Thus it is not surprising that in their fight against poverty, Third World governments have often sought to help the wage earners, particularly in the towns where it was easier for them to act. If the majority of the poor are self-employed, however, policies concerning salaried employment alone will clearly be at best inadequate and at worst counterproductive.

A final characteristic of the poorest is of course their almost total lack of tangible capital. Exhaustive data regarding the distribution of wealth or capital in the developing countries unfortunately do not exist. Yet it is very likely that this distribution is even less equitable than that of income. In any case, while we do not have statistics on the distribution of total wealth, we do at least possess data concerning the distribution of agricultural land. Such data are invaluable for a study of poverty, since the latter is preeminently a rural phenomenon.

Table 8.4 shows the extreme concentration of land which prevails in several countries in Asia and, especially, Latin America.[7] Half the farms in India cover less than one-tenth of the total agricultural area; in Pakistan one-third of the farms account for 3.5 percent of the total area. The situa-

TABLE 8.4   Land Distribution in Asia and Latin America

A. Asia

Country	Year	% of farms under 1 hectare	% of total area covered by farms under 1 hectare
Bangladesh	1960	51.6	15.2
	1974	66.0	24.0
India	1961	39.8	6.8
	1970/71	50.6	9.0
Indonesia	1963	70.1	28.7
Korea	1963	73.3	45.0
	1974	67.0	58.3
Philippines	1960	11.5	1.6
	1970	13.6	1.9
Pakistan	1960	32.9	3.5
Malaysia (West)	1960	45.4	15.2
Thailand	1963	18.5	2.5

B. Latin America

Country	Subfamily farms[a]			Small holdings[b]		
	Year	% of total farms	% of total area	Av. size (ha.) 1960	Av. size (ha.) 1970	% change 1960–70
Argentina	1960	43.2	3.4	. . .	. . .	. . .
Brazil	1950	22.5	0.5	2.46	2.16	− 12.2
Chile	1960	36.9	0.2	1.40	1.67	+ 19.3
Colombia	1955	64.0	4.9	1.64	1.64	0
Ecuador	1954	89.9	16.6	1.72	1.50	− 12.8
Guatemala	1950	88.4	14.3	. . .	. . .	. . .
Peru	. . .	88.0	7.4	1.70	1.44	− 15.3
Uruguay		. . .	. . .	2.64	2.71	+ 2.6
Venezuela		. . .	. . .	2.17	2.24	+ 3.2
El Salvador		. . .	. . .	1.67	1.56	− 6.6
Nicaragua		. . .	. . .	3.10	2.36	− 23.9
Jamaica		. . .	. . .	1.54	1.25	− 18.8

SOURCE: International Labor Office (ILO), *Rural Poverty in the Third World,* Geneva, May 1979.

a "Subfamily farms" were defined as "farms large enough to provide employment for less than 2 people with the typical incomes, markets and levels of technology now prevailing in each region."

b "Small holdings" were defined as enterprises of less than 5 hectares except in El Salvador (less than 10 hectares) and Jamaica (less than 25 acres).

tion is even worse in Latin America: in Ecuador, Guatemala, and Peru, nine-tenths of the farms cover, respectively, some 17 percent, 15 percent, and 8 percent of the cultivated area. In addition, we can see that during recent years the proportion of small farms (less than one hectare) has increased in several Asian countries, while the average size of the agricultural small holdings has decreased in most Latin American countries.

Moreover, data on land distribution fail to reveal two negative characteristics of the small farmer's situation. First, his land is generally the poorest, and land development is more difficult for small holdings than for large farms (in the case of irrigation, for instance). Second, population growth is usually particularly high among the neediest social categories, which means that the fragmentation of land will generally be more rapid among the smallest farmers.

These few indications regarding the characteristics of the poorest are obviously too sketchy. This is partly a reflection of ignorance on the part of economists, sociologists, and governments in this area. Because poverty in the developing countries has long been considered as one aspect of a general state of underdevelopment and not as a separate problem, the identification of the poorest strata has been generally neglected. Obviously a great deal still has to be done if specific policies in favor of the poorest are now to be defined.

POVERTY AND GROWTH

For the moment we cannot really say a great deal about the socioeconomic characteristics of the poorest. Can we at least speak more confidently about the impact of economic growth on the conditions of life of these needy people? Can economic theory and statistical observation shed some light on the links between growth and poverty or, more generally, between economic growth and income distribution?

The least we can say is that economic theory has not yet provided definitive answers to this problem. In fact, economists have in the past held opposite views, often based on mere speculation and rarely backed by statistical data.[8] Without going into this debate here, I shall simply point out — in order to explain the priority given to theoretical speculation — that it is only recently that the collection and systematic analysis of statistical data have been undertaken with regard to income distribution.

In this area as in many others Kuznets was a pioneer. In 1955 he reached the conclusion (much more, incidentally, by theoretical reasoning than by empirical observation) that, in the course of economic growth, income distribution first becomes more inequitable before it subsequently improves.[9] Thus the share of the poorest categories (let us say the poorest 20 or 40 percent of the population) in total income must decline first and increase afterwards (beyond a certain development level) in accordance with a "U curve." Later Kuznets provided empirical evidence of this "law" through cross-country analysis.[10]

Since then, several statistical studies have confirmed the results of these first analyses.[11] These studies, which link development level (measured by GNP per capita) and income distribution (generally measured by the percentage of total income going to the poorest quintile[s]), have all been based on cross-country analyses. Yet this method presents difficulties of a theoretical sort; in particular, it is questionable to deduce, from comparison among countries, "laws" that would apply to the evolution of any one country in the course of its development. But apart from a few partial studies on the experience of certain developing countries during the last three decades, economists generally have only cross-country analyses to shed light on the relationship that may exist between growth and income distribution, and to deduce operational guidelines for defining development policies. It goes without saying that the present understanding remains limited and that the recommended policies are not always fully reliable.

Kuznets' "law" does not necessarily imply that the absolute income of the poorest must decrease in the first stages of economic development. All will depend, in fact, on how rapidly the *relative* share of total income going to the poorest decreases and on how fast the average income of the country increases. For instance, if in the course of a decade a country's average per capita income increases by 50 percent while the share of total income going to the poorest quintile falls from 10 to 8 percent, the absolute income per capita of the poorest will rise by 20 percent. In fact, calculations based on the actual coefficients of a U curve (such as can be established through cross-country analysis) indicate that, contrary to the alarm of certain scientists, a growth pattern following such an example of Kuznets' law would not, at any stage, entail a fall in the absolute income of the poorest.[12]

But the most important result of the studies carried out in recent years is probably this: while the development level (expressed by the GNP per capita, for instance) seems in part to determine the structure of income distribution, there is nothing automatic or absolute in this relation. There is no iron law which would set, for a given level (X) of GNP per capita the share (Y) of national income going to the poorest quintile of the population. Thus, for instance, Mexico and Taiwan have practically the same GNP per capita ($1,290 and $1,400, respectively, in 1978) but quite different patterns of income distribution. In Mexico the poorest 40 percent of the population share 10 percent of the national income, while in Taiwan the corresponding share is 22 percent; moreover, in proportion to its population, Mexico has three times more people living in a state of absolute poverty than Taiwan. In fact, the cross-country analyses mentioned above also reach an identical conclusion: GNP per capita is not the only determinant of income distribution.

It appears then that Kuznets' law represents more a tendency than a deterministic relationship. To a given level of GNP per capita would correspond an average structure of income distribution, and the difference between this "average" and the actual structure in individual countries would depend on other factors, such as the countries' particular characteristics and growth pattern. For economists it is especially important to find out what these other factors are. If the characteristics or policies of certain countries have improved (or worsened) their income distribution, perhaps identification of these causes would enable us to draw useful lessons for development policies. And eventually it might be possible thus to reconcile high growth with a relatively egalitarian income structure.

FACTORS INFLUENCING INCOME DISTRIBUTION

I shall make no attempt here to review the progress made by theoretical studies on the relationship between growth and income distribution. My objective is more limited. We have seen during recent decades that growth and the decline of poverty were not necessarily synonymous. We have also seen that countries with similar levels of per capita GNP may have quite different patterns of income distribution. Can we draw any lesson from a contrasted study of these experiences? In particular, can we recognize certain factors or policies that have played a determining role in these results?

The search for the factors "explaining" income distribution is interesting not only on account of the relationships that it eventually reveals but also on account of those that it fails to establish. Thus it is noteworthy that, in spite of what we might think, certain variables apparently have no direct bearing on income distribution, at least when these variables operate in isolation.

For instance, the growth rate of GNP or of GNP per capita does not appear to influence directly the distribution of income or its evolution. Among the countries with rapid growth we find some with an egalitarian income structure (Korea, Yugoslavia) and some with an inegalitarian one (Brazil, Turkey). We find countries where income distribution has improved in the course of growth (Taiwan, presumably the Ivory Coast) and others where it has deteriorated (Mexico, Brazil again). The statistical studies also confirm the lack of such a connection.[13] Two conclusions can tentatively be drawn from this result.

The first is that, whatever the socioeconomic tension caused by rapid economic growth, it does not necessarily lead to a deterioration in income distribution. When such deterioration does occur (as, for instance, in the case of Brazil or Mexico), we should therefore incriminate not the *rapidity* of growth but the *form* this growth has taken. Inverting the causal relationship (or, rather, the nonrelationship), we can propose, as a second conclusion, that egalitarian income distribution (or improvement therein) is a priori neutral vis-à-vis economic growth. If then a change in the pace of growth occurs following a modification in income distribution, we cannot hold responsible this modification as such but rather the form it has assumed (land reform, income transfers, taxation, etc.).

Neither does the volume or growth of industrial exports appear to be significantly linked to income distribution, though we might have expected the contrary. The developing countries' export industries are generally labor-intensive (see Chapter 12); they thus create many jobs for the unskilled and should increase the incomes of the poorest classes. We might therefore expect that a policy change in favor of export industries would be accompanied by an improvement in income distribution. Unfortunately, the facts do not seem to confirm these expectations. If the egalitarian income structure of South Korea and Taiwan apparently supports this theoretical assumption, Brazil and Mexico provide weighty counterexamples. Ever since Brazil and Mexico turned toward export-oriented industrialization, they have experienced, like South Korea and Taiwan, rapid growth in their GNPs as well as in their exports. But their income structures, which were already notably inegalitarian, do not seem to have improved.[14] It is likely that in this case the favorable effects of export industries on income distribution have been unable to compensate for the effects of other factors acting in a contrary direction.

What factors, then, do influence income distribution? First of all, high population growth apparently has harmful effects on this distribution. For an identical level of GNP per capita, those countries with rapid population growth appear to have more inegalitarian income distributions.[15] The causal relationship is presumably reciprocal. On the one hand, inegalitarian distribution contributes to high birthrates and consequently to population growth (see Chapter 5). On the other hand, a high population growth rate will have negative effects on the wages of unskilled laborers (because of the increase in labor supply) as well as on land distribution (since, among the poorest farmers, land will have to be divided among a greater number of children[16]).

Education (secondary and especially primary) and literacy have a favorable impact on income distribution at a given level of GNP per capita.[17] Schooling presumably improves the productivity of unskilled workers, whatever their sector, and thereby permits a rise in the lowest incomes.

Since the great majority of the poorest rely on agriculture as their main source of income and since food represents the largest share of the neediest categories' consumption budget, we could a priori expect that an increase in agricultural or food production per capita would have beneficial effects on the elimination of poverty. In fact, however, statistical surveys show that the relationship is not so simple and that such an increase can easily be accompanied by stagnation or deterioration in the situation of the poorest. In the Philippines and Malaysia, for instance, growth of per capita food production between 1956–1957 and 1970 has apparently been accompanied by an increase in the proportion of the rural population living below the poverty line.[18] A survey of several Indian states shows that, while in several instances there is a positive correlation in the rural sector between the level of per capita agricultural production and the reduction of poverty, in other instances there does not appear to be any significant link between these two variables. Even in the case of certain states that have experienced marked progress in per capita agricultural production (Punjab, Haryana, and Orissa, for instance), such a relationship cannot be established, and the proportion of the poor in the rural population does not seem to have decreased over time.[19]

When we consider the matter, it is not really surprising that growth of agricultural or food production per capita is not always accompanied by positive effects on the poorest categories. In the frequent cases where land and social structures are extremely inegalitarian, small farmers will generally be the last to benefit from technical advances enabling them to increase their production. The mechanization which at times accompanies these technological improvements can in certain cases occur to the detriment of landless workers. Moreover, population growth, resulting, as we have seen, in a reduction in the average farm size and perhaps in a fall in agricultural wages, implies an exogenous tendency to impoverishment which agricultural production growth is not always sufficient to offset.

A developing country's land ownership structure seems to be another determining factor in income distribution. In this respect the contrast is striking between certain countries of East Asia and the majority of the Latin American countries. In South Korea, Taiwan, and China, land reforms carried out during or just after World War II have resulted in an egalitarian land distribution, and the economic development that followed these reforms was marked by an income structure much less unequal than that of most other developing countries. By contrast, most Latin American countries are characterized by extremely inegalitarian land as well as income distribution.

Such a relationship between land concentration and income distribution is not surprising in the case of countries at an early stage of industrialization, where agriculture contributes a substantial part of the gross domestic product and provides most of the population with a means of existence. But it may be more unexpected in the case of countries where, as in Latin America, industrialization is more advanced. In the latter countries it is as though concentration of productive capital — essentially land — at the outset of their development had imposed a structurally inegalitarian pattern of income distribution which subsequent economic evolution has been unable to correct. Although one cannot offer proof of such a causal relationship, it would appear that the initial land ownership structure (and the sociopolitical system underlying it) largely determines the way in which the profits of growth will be divided in subsequent stages of development.

Other lessons may be learned from the experience of countries that have been able to obtain both high and relatively egalitarian economic growth. Shortly after World War II South Korea and Taiwan recognized the importance of the agricultural sector and implemented policies aimed at completing and supplementing land reforms. These countries also set up price and incentive systems to encourage labor-intensive activities in agriculture as well as in industry. After more than a decade of import-substitution policies, Taiwan (around 1960) and Korea (around 1964–1965) modified their strategies to encourage export industries. Their governments also succeeded in preventing the differences between rural and urban wages from worsening, and they strove to develop rural industries. Finally, both countries implemented effective birth control programs.

The experience of China is poorly known; yet we can recognize there again the priority given to agriculture and to small rural industries as well as to the implementation of an effective family planning program. But perhaps China's most original experience has been the implementation of vast rural works programs which appear to have contributed a great deal to the improvement of the employment situation and the elimination of poverty (see Chapter 11).

In closing this rapid survey, we can thus conclude that the link between economic growth, on the one hand, and income distribution and the elimination of poverty, on the other, is far from being automatic, and that governments' economic policies have a decisive influence on the results obtained in the fight against poverty. Thus the sectoral policies implemented in agriculture and industry, the price and incentive systems adopted, public investments, and education policies will all bear upon the evolution of the living conditions of the poorest.[20]

There is still a further question, however, and that is the relative importance of these different factors and their potential effectiveness in the absence of radical initial changes. The contrasting experiences of Latin America and the Asian countries mentioned above lead us to believe that the original distribution of capital and the social and political structure underlying it are decisive in the subsequent evolution of income distribution. If this assumption — for it can only be an assumption — is correct, it follows that if the initial inequalities in land ownership and the political system are not corrected beforehand, subsequent efforts by reformist governments will hardly succeed in improving income distribution. It is interesting to see that many economists — and not only those suspected of political extremism — have come to share this opinion.[21]

The conclusions set forth by P. Bardhan, at the end of his study of

India's experience in the fight against poverty, could presumably apply to most developing countries.

> In sum, the problems of poverty in India remain intractable, not because redistributive objectives were inadequately considered in the planning models, nor because general policies of the kind prescribed in this volume were not attempted. Of course, on the micro level there were specific programs that were ill-conceived and uncoordinated and there were familiar problems of administrative rigidities on the part of an ex-colonial bureaucracy largely oriented to maintaining law and order and collecting revenue. But the major constraint is rooted in the power realities of a political system dominated by a complex constellation of forces representing rich farmers, big business, and the so-called petite bourgeoisie, including the unionized workers of the organized sector. In such a context it is touchingly naive not to anticipate the failures of asset distribution policies or the appropriation by the rich of a disproportionate share of the benefits of public investment.[22]

In the rural sector of many Asian and Latin American countries, the "power realities of [the] political system" are mainly revealed in an extremely inegalitarian land structure. In the absence of real agrarian reform, this system will not be modified, and it would be vain to hope for any notable improvement in present or future income distribution. Of course, such reform is difficult to implement, and the dominant social classes have so far succeeded, in India as in other countries, in checking all velleities of change. It may be safer not to expect that the situation will be different in the coming years. Presumably, most of these countries will keep on fighting the most shocking poverty by measures of a "reformist" type, without touching the existing land system or political structure. In this case, unfortunately, I am convinced that their efforts will not succeed.

In these circumstances, what are the prospects for eliminating poverty in the coming years? From what we have just seen, it is clear that the pattern of growth pursued will largely determine the results obtained. In any case, the disappointing results of the previous decades indicate that it would be unrealistic to hope for a rapid victory in this area.

As noted above, the World Bank estimates that there are now 800 million people living in a state of absolute poverty in the Third World. By projecting these countries' GNP to the year 2000 and assuming that income distribution will evolve according to Kuznets' law, the Bank concludes that there will still be some 600 million poor at the end of the century. If, by contrast, more egalitarian patterns of growth were adopted, the number could fall to 260 million by that time.[23]

Of course, such a projection can easily be criticized. As we have seen, from a conceptual standpoint the definition of the "absolute" poor is not perfectly clear, and in any case, the existing data are too unreliable to enable us today to determine the exact number of these destitute. Furthermore, Kuznets' "law" does not express a rigid determinism but rather a tendency. In these circumstances, then, to what extent can we rely on such a twenty-year forecast?

Yet, if we do not confine ourselves to the actual figures but simply consider the orders of magnitude, such an estimate can prove quite useful. First of all, it confirms the illusory nature of any hope to conquer poverty in the immediate future or even before the end of the century. However great our efforts, in twenty years' time several million people will still be living in a state of utter destitution. But this estimate also reveals the significant impact that the implementation of development strategies purposely aiming to improve the structure of income distribution would have on poverty. Such deliberate policies would involve a change that should not be underestimated, since it would in fact imply that all countries would obtain results that only a few have attained so far.[24] But the very fact that these few countries *have* been able to achieve these results is clear evidence that, while the necessary changes are considerable, they are nevertheless feasible.

The conclusion that emerges from the above analysis is at once disappointing and encouraging. It is disappointing because we have seen that the rapid economic growth of recent years has not been accompanied by equally spectacular results in the fight against poverty and that experiences of the past and forecasts for the future do not permit us to hope for much more rapid advances in this area during the coming years. But it is encouraging because we also know that stagnation in the conditions of life of the poorest is not inevitable. Several countries have demonstrated that certain policies can be extremely effective in the fight against poverty. While we can no longer take for granted that growth, whatever its form, will improve the living conditions of the poorest, we do know that certain types of growth and certain policies have enabled several countries to eliminate the most extreme forms of destitution. It will obviously require more than two or three decades to free the world from absolute poverty, but it is also equally evident that, for the long battle ahead, effective weapons exist that have already been successfully tested.

This chapter and the previous ones have reviewed some of the problems confronting the Third World on the threshold of the Third Development Decade. It is probably not being unwarrantedly pessimistic to state that these problems appear at once more alarming and more complex than they did, for instance, at the beginning of the last decade. Ten years ago, commercial energies did not present any immediate problem, and the crisis in traditional energies, although already brewing, was not yet clearly perceived. The international environment looked favorable, and the developed countries' growth prospects, which are of vital importance for the Third World, seemed free of any serious problem. The heyday of the Green Revolution was not yet over, and many people still believed it to be the coming solution to the food problems of the developing countries. For the Third World as a whole, continuation of the rapid economic growth of the previous decades seemed certain, and few people doubted that, sooner or later, this growth would lead to the elimination of poverty.

All that has now considerably changed. In all these areas, the situation is more alarming today; only the demographic evolution seems to be somewhat less threatening. For those who may be inclined to accuse me of undue pessimism, it may be worth quoting here the two introductory paragraphs of the latest and most comprehensive study of the world's future:

> If the present trends continue, the world in 2000 will be more crowded, more polluted, less stable ecologically, and more vulnerable to disruption than the world we live in now. Serious stresses involving population, resources, and environment are clearly visible ahead. Despite greater material output, the world's people will be poorer in many ways than they are today.
>
> For hundreds of millions of the desperately poor, the outlook for food and other necessities of life will be no better. For many it will be worse. Barring revolutionary advances in technology, life for most people on earth will be more precarious in 2000 than it is now — unless the nations of the world act decisively to alter current trends.[25]

All is not negative, however. Since we understand more clearly today the complexity of the problems we face, it is presumably easier to recognize the main elements of their solution. Common to all these elements is the necessity to challenge a certain mechanistic and authoritarian conception of development. The problems assailing the Third World today will not be solved by the old recipe of waiting for undifferentiated economic growth to trickle down to the poorest. Only through direct actions in favor of the most destitute groups will it be eventually possible to conquer poverty and malnutrition. In addition, solving these problems will require the participation and active cooperation of all the population and particularly of the poorest strata. Thus, policies as different as those aiming to reduce birthrates or combat soil degradation will fully succeed only if the people who benefit from them understand their usefulness, cooperate in their execution, and more generally, share equitably the profits of growth. These few principles could probably guide the ongoing search for new development strategies.

3
OUTLINE OF A STRATEGY

9
FOR OR AGAINST BASIC NEEDS?

Nowadays it has become banal to state that development theories and policies have largely failed in the Third World and that new strategies must be defined and implemented. Whatever the successes — sometimes underestimated — of three decades of economic growth, the development models that have been pursued have unquestionably failed to abolish hunger, poverty, or ignorance. Moreover, as we have seen, the coming decades should present the developing countries with still further difficulties and dangers.

This widely felt need for new directions has resulted in numerous suggestions. Yet these too often tend to be mere slogans, rather than detailed and operational proposals. Basic needs, self-sufficiency, collective self-reliance, new international economic order — so many formulas with, so far, more emotional appeal than concrete substance.

Such an abundance of proposals undoubtedly makes it easier for me to present my own contribution. But the few proposals that I shall make in the following chapters do not constitute an alternative strategy, and for several reasons it is not possible to construe them as one. First of all, I shall not deal here with any of the problems generally covered by the term "North-South dialogue" — not that I underestimate the importance of these problems but, on the contrary, because I do believe that a few pages would not suffice to cover the subject. Secondly, my suggestions, while they are sometimes at variance with certain fashionable ideas, do not themselves claim to be new or original. Finally, these few proposals do not concern all Third World countries: while certain aspects may be applicable to middle-income countries, they mostly concern the poorest nations of sub-Saharan Africa and South Asia.

In my opinion, five specific priorities are essential for a reorientation of development strategies: (1) an intensification of ongoing population policies to accelerate the decline in fertility and birth rates; (2) the long-overdue implementation of policies to develop local energy resources, both commercial and traditional; (3) a greater emphasis on agriculture and food production; (4) direct actions to improve the productive capacity of the poorest; and (5) the rejection of the isolationist temptation and the utilization of the possibilities of foreign trade. The necessity for greater efforts in the areas of birth control and development of energy resources has been sufficiently shown, I hope, in the preceding chapters on these subjects, and I shall not refer again to these topics in the rest of the book. On the other hand, the suggestions of giving greater importance to agriculture, to the poorest strata, and to export possibilities require explanations: the fact that some of these ideas are fashionable today does not constitute a sufficient justification.

Before I attempt to support my proposals, however, it may be worthwhile in this chapter to analyze the idea, recently much debated, of a strategy aiming to satisfy people's basic needs. The controversy this proposal has triggered would in itself justify an attempt to examine the pros and cons of such an approach; in addition this analysis should enable us to reflect further on the characteristics required of a viable development strategy.

A BASIC NEEDS STRATEGY

The failure of the economic growth of recent decades to improve the lot of the poorest has led many economists and government leaders to believe that direct action is necessary to meet these people's fundamental needs. In this regard several proposals have been formulated, and although there is no single canonical text of *a* basic needs strategy, the various existing versions do share a certain number of characteristics.

The first objective of such a strategy would be to guarantee a given underprivileged category with a minimum level of satisfaction of certain needs considered to be especially important. In this, it would differ from a strategy of general growth (which would not specifically identify a target population) or even from a strategy aiming to raise the incomes of a particular group without taking into account the use of these incomes. The strategy being so defined by its *end,* expressed in concrete and at times quantitative terms (for instance assuring a given minimum of calories to a particular social group), the *means* to attain this end would in principle be derived from it. Such a strategy could aim, for instance, at assuring a supply of drinking water to all the members of a destitute category. The means to achieve this end would then be selected, depending on practicality and cost, from among different possibilities: transfer of funds to cover the cost of the construction of a well; direct construction of the well, which would then be handed over to the beneficiaries; supply of loans for the purchase of the materials; provision of technical advice to the beneficiaries, who would then take care of the construction themselves; and so on.

One aspect of a basic needs policy upon which defenders of this strategy place particular importance is that the fundamental needs thus selected include not only material requirements but also others of a psychological, even an emotional nature. Thus the needs for independence, for political freedom, for security, and for participation in decision-making are seen to be just as fundamental as the needs for health, food, and shelter. In practice, however, discussions about basic needs have mostly focused on material needs and the possible ways of satisfying them. Although no firm consensus exists among the partisans of this strategy, many agree in recognizing, as the core of these basic needs, food, shelter, drinking water, health, and education.

The few preceding ideas constitute, for the time being, the essential elements of the basic needs doctrine. A great number of questions remain unanswered, such as those concerning the selection of the needs to be satisfied, the financing and the implementation of this strategy, and its relationship with growth-oriented policies. Many partisans of this strategy openly admit that there is still much to be done, and that their approach cannot yet offer any miraculous solution. In the absence of a clearly defined and thoroughly presented doctrine, it is of course difficult to analyze, much less criticize, its content. Yet it is important to emphasize that for its supporters, the basic needs approach embraces more than mere governmental concern for the poorest: it advocates direct intervention by public authorities to assure that certain predetermined objectives be attained for the benefit of specified social categories.

HOW TO SELECT THE BASIC NEEDS?

The foremost criticism aimed at a basic needs strategy is that the definition of these needs is subjective and thus can be made only by the individuals concerned. Some critics even protest that governments, let alone planners or aid organizations, cannot set themselves up as sovereign judges and decide for the population concerned what that population's most important needs are. According to these critics, governmental intervention would only hinder the free action of the market, which is still the best revelation of the people's preferences as well as the most suitable instrument for eventually satisfying their requirements.

This dispute about principles seems to me out of place and out of date. Ours is not a time when partisans and adversaries of governmental intervention in economic life are pitted against each other, each side upholding equally dogmatic positions. With the almost general acceptance of the welfare state in the developed capitalist countries, these arguments have given place to a more pragmatic attitude; few people today would disagree that government has a role to play not only in a nation's economic life but also in the satisfaction of certain social needs. The idea that a country's governmental authorities decide that certain needs are essential and, consequently, set about satisfying them as far as possible is no more shocking to me than the fact that certain governments establish free and mandatory schooling or set up a social security system. Faced with a certain number of needs — and nobody would deny that these needs are dramatic in the Third World — the most important question is to determine what agents (government, local communities, private sector, etc.) are best able to satisfy them. The answer to this question can only be pragmatic and must be specific to each of these needs.

If the idea, then, of governmental intervention is not a priori anathema to me, the scope of this intervention does pose several problems. First, there is the selection of the needs to be satisfied. The more numerous the governmental interventions — and there would be many in a basic needs strategy — the more frequent and important the choices to be made between competing demands. If the people's preferences and the market "signals" are no longer the guides used for resource allocation, or at least if they are not the only guides, how will the government decide whether, "at the margin," it should spend $100 on health, water supply, or housing? The problem is not merely an academic one, since no specified minimum level of expenditure exists for each type of need. Even if we all agree that health is a fundamental need, this does not tell us what minimum we should devote to this sector: should we plan on having one nurse for 1,000 inhabitants or 5,000? one hospital for 50,000 people or 100,000?

This problem of choice is, of course, not confined to a basic needs strategy; it is also encountered in the management of every public budget, irrespective of the political or economic orientations of the country. The important difference is that, in general, public authorities confine themselves to the financing of a limited number of welfare programs or "public goods," those that cannot be efficiently satisfied by the market. The higher the level of public expenditures, the greater the potential for an error of choice or a deficiency in management. And, by its very nature, a basic needs strategy implies a high level of budgetary expenditures.

To illustrate this kind of difficulty, we can refer to a World Bank estimate of the cost of a basic needs program.[1] For the whole Third World such an investment program, covering food, drinking water, housing, health, and education, would cost approximately $380 billion (1975 value). Housing alone would account for more than half this amount. (These estimates are in fact based on a unit cost of housing of $1,000, a very high expenditure for a family living on the verge of survival!) Considering the urgent needs that exist in other, more vital areas, there is every reason to believe that the beneficiaries would prefer a little less housing and, for instance, a little more food or medical care. And it is difficult to see what criteria would permit governments (or the World Bank) to dispute such a choice. Generally speaking, it is not clear why governmental intervention in the housing sector is an absolute necessity: the people's level of satisfaction would probably be higher if, instead of procuring them a certain standard of accommodation, the government transferred them an equivalent sum of money and let them decide how to use it.

It must be admitted that, at times, certain goods or services cannot be effectively provided by the market; in such cases it may be desirable that governmental or local authorities be responsible for them. In other cases, however, it is usually the market which is best able to satisfy needs. Generally, the reason certain people lack housing or adequate food is not that the market is unable to supply these necessities but that the poor do not have sufficient incomes to obtain them. In these circumstances it would be simpler to try to raise the incomes of the social categories concerned (preferably by increasing their productive capacity or, if this is not possible, by money transfers) and to let them decide how to spend it. It is only in cases when supply in kind offers clearly established advantages that this solution should be envisaged.

FINANCING AND IMPLEMENTATION

To the $380 billion cost of an investment program aimed at meeting the Third World's basic needs should be added the recurrent costs, another $28 billion to $40 billion every year. Approximately two-thirds of these costs would be required in the low-income developing countries alone, the countries where the problem of financing would be particularly acute.

At first sight, and in spite of the magnitude of the amounts indicated, the financing of these needs does not seem impossible. If such a program were realized over twenty years, the annual investment cost would be under 0.3 percent of the annual world income (or 5 percent of annual world expenditures for defense and armament). Yet the required amounts must be set within the context of the developing countries' economic and financial capacity, particularly when the poorest of these countries are concerned.

For the low-income developing countries the investment required over a period of twenty years would reach 12 to 16 percent of these countries' average GNP during the next twenty years, 80 to 105 percent of their gross annual investment, and 85 to 110 percent of their annual budget revenues. In these circumstances it is clear that these countries could not implement such a program without substantial external aid. Yet the simple financing of the investment required every year would correspond to more than half the public aid currently received by *all* developing countries. Even if such external financing could be found, the recurrent costs would far exceed the financial capacity of the receiving countries. Although the financing of such a program over a twenty-year period may thus not be absolutely impossible, it would nevertheless present a formidable challenge to the savings capacity of the poor countries and to the generosity of the rich ones.

Furthermore, whatever aid they receive during the coming years, the developing nations must ultimately ensure the financing of the recurrent costs of such a program themselves if they are not to remain forever dependent on the assistance of the outside world. This will be possible only if their economic capacity grows, which in turn will require that a sufficient proportion of their investments be directed towards increasing production. This problem raises the question of compatibility between basic needs strategy and rapid economic growth, a question to which we shall return later.

But the main weakness of all the basic needs literature is in regard to the means of implementing such a strategy. The idea of producing and supplying directly to the destitute all the goods and services required to ensure these poor a decent standard of living is certainly an appealing one. But the immense problems — economic, administrative, logistic, and, above all, political — of the implementation of such a program has scarcely been touched upon. References to the experiences of certain countries, from Cuba to the Indian state of Kerala, are not sufficient, however interesting they may be; concrete studies leading to specific proposals are unfortunately lacking.

The first problem raised by the implementation of such a strategy concerns the production of the goods required for the consumption of the poorest. To put it in simple terms, how is an economy which so far has manufactured cars and air conditioners for a small minority to produce bicycles and wood stoves for the majority of the people? The first condition appears to be a redistribution of income to modify the demand structure. But a radical modification of the productive system will also be necessary, and this in turn will require the utilization of certain instruments (fiscal, administrative, legal, etc.) to encourage the production of the necessary goods and discourage the production of the luxury ones.

What is the degree of socialization and authoritarianism required to assure that production does indeed correspond to the desired consumption model? To avoid any misunderstanding, I should immediately explain that I am not a priori adverse to such governmental intervention; I would only like to indicate that the previous question points to a host of problems which the literature on basic needs has thus far largely ignored.[2]

Another problem would be the delivery of the desired goods and services to the target population. To a certain extent this problem is linked to the previous one: a water supply company accustomed to installing pipes in cities will not take to drilling wells in villages overnight. But other and no less difficult problems arise. How are we going to assure the delivery of food (or of construction material or of hand pumps) to the thousands of isolated villages in these countries? Where are we going to find and train the necessary nurses and teachers? And, above all, how can we organize the beneficiaries themselves so that they fully participate in these programs? It is clear that the population's participation is the sine qua non for the success of such a strategy. Without this participation, the hand pumps will stop working, the schools will not be maintained, and the dispensaries will remain deserted. As we know, this problem — perhaps the most difficult of them all — has already caused the failure of many governmental programs in the Third World.

To this latter problem is linked the question of the beneficiaries' contribution to the financing of these programs. It is presumably undesirable that the supply of goods and services to the poor be entirely free. First of all, experience has often shown that if the beneficiaries do not participate in the implementation of a program (with their money, their work, or their contribution in kind), they rapidly lose interest and the program founders. Furthermore, in view of the immensity of the needs to satisfy and of the limitations of government budgets, it will always be necessary to marshal to the maximum the population's resources in order to limit as far as possible the government's financial contribution. In this area, the solutions will probably be specific to each country and perhaps even to each program. Studies of other countries' problems and experiences would nevertheless be desirable to clarify some of the possible options; in this instance too, however, the literature remains far too sketchy.

BASIC NEEDS AND GROWTH

In spite of their limited reliability, the estimates of the World Bank enable us to see that a basic needs program would have a fairly high cost and that arbitration among competing needs would be necessary. In addition, at the outset of the implementation of such a program at least, the limited managerial and technical capacity of the administration in charge would entail the necessity of choosing among different priorities. As I indicated above, choices would be difficult and criteria for selection uncertain. Yet two types of criteria do appear important: the intensity or importance of the needs and the impact on productivity of the measures envisaged. Undoubtedly, both are difficult to handle.

The criterion of the intensity of the needs implies selection among priorities to which I have already referred (will one dollar spent on education bring more "satisfaction" than one dollar invested in housing?) [3] and also among target groups (is this social group in greater need than that one?). In both cases, the literature on basic needs has not so far thrown much light on these problems.

While I do not intend to get into the question of target groups here, it may nevertheless be worth making a comment at this stage. Since the justification of a basic needs strategy is the elimination of the most extreme forms of poverty, this strategy should have a pro-rural and pro-agricultural slant, an orientation which still all too rarely appears in the literature on this subject. Clearly, if 85 percent of the poor live in rural areas, the fight against poverty must begin in the countryside, and agriculture must be at the center of this battle. The fact that the prime importance of these sectors is not sufficiently emphasized in much of the basic needs literature is yet another indication of its lack of concreteness. In fact, writers on this subject frequently limit themselves to presenting, side by side, an enumeration of very general basic needs and an exhaustive list of "deprived social categories" without properly emphasizing and analyzing the extent of rural poverty.

The criterion of the impact on productivity is equally difficult to use. The economic theory of development has too long been confined in a mechanistic conception of productivity. Everything that was investment — in the conventional, national-accounting sense — was (with the exclusion of housing) considered productive, while consumption expenditures and housing were, also by definition, unproductive. Gradually, however, economists have come to realize that certain consumption expenditures have an impact on productivity. Statistical studies have shown that not only education but also improvement in nutrition and health have a significant impact on the productivity of the poorest workers.[4]

In these circumstances the distinction between productive and unproductive expenditures grew less clear. It became possible to declare — as many partisans of a basic needs strategy have done — that "investing in man" would increase productivity and consequently accelerate economic growth. Reality, however, is a little more complex. It would be tempting but mistaken to believe that every consumption expenditure per se is productive. Learning to read and write or enjoying better health will not make a worker more productive if, for instance, he is without a job. Moreover, even if all consumption expenditures were productive to a certain extent, it would still be necessary to know which ones have the greatest impact on production.

The question of the contradiction (or, on the contrary, of the convergence) of a basic needs strategy with growth-oriented policies cannot therefore be settled so rapidly. We saw above (Chapter 8) that there is apparently no correlation between income distribution and growth rates. More than income distribution per se, it is the manner in which this distribution is brought about that will influence the pace of growth. Similarly, the impact of a basic needs strategy on economic growth will undoubtedly depend on the content of this strategy and on the specific measures implemented. In this respect the experiences of several countries indicate that, for governments striving to meet their population's basic needs, disregarding the imperative of productivity implies very serious dangers.

SOME COUNTRIES' EXPERIENCES

More than any theoretical speculation, the experiences of countries that have consciously attempted to improve the lot of the poorest could enlighten us as to the feasibility of this approach and its compatibility with a growth-oriented strategy. Of all these experiences, China undoubtedly presents the most interesting. In the space of some thirty years, this country has virtually eliminated famine and malnutrition, raised its population's life expectancy from 33 to 66 years, increased its literacy rate to 66 percent, reached full employment in the towns and the countryside, and brought its population growth rate down to 1.3 percent per year. All this has been achieved with a GNP per capita lower than Uganda's. At the same time its economic growth rate has been relatively rapid: GNP per capita increased at nearly 3 percent per year from 1957 to 1979, almost twice as fast as the average of the low-income developing countries.

As we know, the Chinese government gave priority to the development of the rural sector, where 85 percent of the population live. The collectivization of agriculture during the "great leap forward" made the production team, comprising some thirty families, the basic productive and accounting unit. The establishment of a direct link, within these teams, between each worker's effort and his production share certainly contributed to improving the agricultural sector's productivity; the same applies to the price system, which was systematically slanted in favor of agriculture and the rural sector.[5] Moreover, rural works programs carried out on a massive scale were instrumental in reducing unemployment, and the investments in infrastructure they created were another factor in the improvement of agricultural productivity. Finally, the establishment of basic services in the education and health sectors (the famed "barefoot doctors") has enabled China to attain levels of literacy and life expectancy which many countries with higher per capita incomes have not yet obtained.

By contrast, the experiences of Sri Lanka and Tanzania may be instances where too much attention has been given to the satisfaction of welfare requirements and not enough to productivity. The achievements of Sri Lanka in the social sector are particularly impressive. Between 1946 and 1979, life expectancy rose from 43 to 66 years, while infant mortality fell from 141 to 49 per 1,000 and the crude death rate, from 20.2 to 7.0 per 1,000. At the same time, the literacy rate rose from 58 percent to 85 percent, and the school attendance rate, from 41 percent to 94 percent. The population growth rate, which was as high as 2.8 percent around 1953, fell to 1.7 percent in the seventies. If we compare Sri Lanka with countries having a similar per capita income, its life expectancy is one and a half times, its literacy rate nearly three times, its infant mortality rate one-quarter, and its birthrate one-half of what such a comparison would lead one to expect. Of all countries having a per capita income below $300, Sri Lanka has the highest number of hospital beds per person, and the problems of malnutrition are much less acute there than in any of these countries.

Yet these results have been obtained at a high cost. In the sixties, approximately half the government's recurrent expenditures went to social programs, mainly to the education and health sectors, and to subsidies for food and transportation; food subsidies alone amounted to 5 to 6 percent of the gross domestic product.[6] In the seventies, the contradiction between the high level of social expenditures and the pursuit of sustained economic growth came to the fore. The annual growth rate, which had averaged 4.6 percent in the sixties, fell to 3.1 percent between 1970 and 1977; the rate of gross fixed capital formation, which had risen until 1970, subsequently fell. Public savings gave way to growing dissavings, to such an extent that only government borrowing could permit the financing of a minimum level of public investment. In 1976, food subsidies amounted to half the expenditure on public investment. Unemployment, which had already been the cause of violent incidents in 1971, grew even worse, reaching 20 percent in 1977 and affecting particularly primary and high-school graduates. Faced with this deterioration, the government which came to power in June 1977 had to conclude that a modification of the ongoing policies was necessary to correct these growing imbalances. The first measures taken included various programs aiming to accelerate economic growth as well as to reduce food subsidies.

During the six years which followed their country's accession to independence in 1961, the leaders of Tanzania pursued a policy not very different from the one adopted by most other developing countries. In 1967, however, the declaration of Arusha defined new priorities: socialism, rural development, autonomy at the national and local levels, education, and economic growth were the main axes of a program which has been consistently followed since then. Fifteen years later, improvements in the social sectors are unquestionable. At 52 years, life expectancy is higher than the African average, two-thirds of the population are literate, and 40 percent of the people have access to drinking water. While the level of GNP per capita still remains low, the GNP growth rate is quite respectable for a country embarked on a program of major structural change.[7] At first sight, Tanzania thus seems to have succeeded in carrying out simultaneously a growth-oriented policy and radical programs aimed at improving the population's living conditions.

Yet the situation appears somewhat less simple when we look at it more closely. Although the development of the rural sector (where 90 percent of the population live) has been one of the first priorities since 1967, agricultural production has increased at a rate barely higher than the population growth rate.[8] For the poorest farmers, in fact, the seventies presumably witnessed a fall in their real income. There are many reasons for these disappointing results from agriculture; among the most often mentioned are the ineffectiveness of the system of production incentives, the insufficiency of agricultural research and extension efforts, and the inadequacy of the infrastructure and the marketing systems. Perhaps the most important of these different factors was the counterproductive effect of a structure of agricultural prices which, until recently, were kept deliberately low lest it should advantage the big farmers and raise food prices in the cities.

As in Sri Lanka, the seventies witnessed a degradation in the level of investment and public saving (the latter, in fact, became negative towards the middle of the decade).[9] In this case also, excessively rapid growth in recurrent government expenditures was responsible for this deterioration in the level of public saving. An additional factor was that, while priority had effectively been given to rural development, the main efforts had been made in social sectors such as education, health, and drinking water supply, rather than in programs that directly increase agricultural production and incomes.

A comparison of the experiences of these three countries thus apparently confirms that, while programs to eliminate poverty can be reconciled with high economic growth, a strategy exclusively oriented towards the satisfaction of the population's welfare requirements might be carried out to the detriment of growth and could to this extent be called into question because of the imbalance it entails. More than an academic question, balancing social and productive policies is a vital necessity, and the risks taken by ignoring it are quite real.

In all likelihood, the implementation of a basic needs strategy can be reconciled with the productivity imperative only if priority is really given to increasing the productive capacity of the poorest. To the extent that it will assure the growth of their income and their consumption, this strategy will enable them to meet their most immediate needs. And to the extent that it will permit increases in their production and savings, it will also lead to sustained and balanced economic growth. Since the vast majority of the poor rely on agriculture for their subsistence, increasing their productive potential will require that the importance of this sector be fully recognized. A basic needs strategy can be effective and viable over the long term only if it gives first priority to increasing the productive capacity of the poor in the rural sector.

It would be difficult to deny that there are good reasons behind the concern that led to the idea of a basic needs strategy. Clearly, the development strategies of recent decades have not succeeded in improving the lot of the poorest, and it is no longer possible today to recommend waiting patiently for the "trickle-down" effects of economic growth. Other, more direct strategies are necessary: only if we undertake to improve directly the living conditions of the destitute will poverty eventually be eradicated.

In this regard, the reorientation of government policies toward the underprivileged should be a priority. In many countries, government budget expenditures on infrastructure and social sectors should thus be redirected, within these sectors, toward these destitute categories. Less should be spent on university education and more on primary schooling, less on urban hospitals and more on rural health clinics, less on the embellishment of residential suburbs and more on the improvement of the shantytowns.

But, as the Brandt Commission reminds us, "domestic efforts to achieve development cannot be restricted exclusively to direct anti-poverty policies and programs; they must be seen within the broader framework of policies for promoting rapid growth and structural transformation of the economy." [10] Reconciling the two imperatives of high growth and equitable distribution constitutes a real problem which cannot be evaded. Part of its solution presumably lies in giving priority, among the measures in favor of the poorest, to those programs which increase these people's productivity. Such a productivity increase seems, indeed, to be a necessity, both for the viability and for the effectiveness of a basic needs strategy.

10
AGRICULTURE AND DEVELOPMENT

The argument for giving greater priority to agriculture in development strategies cannot be based simply on the facts that this sector has largely been neglected so far, that it employs two-thirds of the labor force, or that it provides three-quarters of the Third World's poorest with a source of income. After all, one could reply — and the reply has often been made — that this sector has been rightly neglected because its productivity is low, that the very essence of development requires a transfer of the active population from agriculture to the sectors of industry and services, and that, however deplorable the situation of the poor in the rural areas, they can expect more from rapid development of the "modern" — meaning industrial — sector than from agricultural development, whose potential will always remain limited. And very often historical examples of certain industrialized or industrializing countries are given in support of these arguments.

These replies are not wholly convincing, however. In fact, a more thorough study of the industrial revolution in the developed countries as well as of the development of the Third World countries since World War II shows that the importance of agriculture in the industrialization process has been underestimated. Furthermore, particular conditions specific to the developing countries will, in the coming decades even more than in the past, justify giving priority to the agricultural sector. But such a change in orientation would no doubt involve challenging a certain number of prejudices concerning agriculture — from the low productivity of this sector to the conservatism of the farmers — prejudices which are deeply ingrained in the very heart of economic science itself.

139

THE EXPERIENCE OF THE DEVELOPED COUNTRIES

The causes and mechanisms of the industrial revolution are still debated among historians today. Why did it start in England? What are the particular conditions which set off this cumulative process in this country, first of all? What were the mechanisms which sparked development in the other now-developed countries? Whatever the answers to these questions, it is probable that there is no single factor at the origin of this process: a whole series of factors certainly played a role. And rather than centering on the search of a unique cause, discussions have usually been directed toward the relative importance of the various explanatory factors.

The research carried out during the last twenty years has nevertheless led to the recognition of the importance of agriculture in this process. Thus Paul Bairoch, after having dismissed various traditional explanations — technical progress, population growth, price increases, accumulation of capital — concludes that the growth of agriculture was a decisive factor in starting development in the now-industrialized countries.[1]

In all the countries for which the necessary information is available, the take-off of industrial production was in fact preceded by a significant increase in agricultural production. In England in the second half of the seventeenth century wheat yields had already increased at a rate nearly three times higher than in previous centuries. This progress accelerated at the beginning of the eighteenth century and by 1750, the grain trade surplus had grown to 15 percent of the country's requirements. Thus it was well before the middle of the eighteenth century — which is traditionally considered to mark the beginning of the industrialization process — that English agriculture had started a phase of rapid growth.[2]

Similarly, in France, agricultural progress preceded the beginning of industrialization. Agricultural production, which had grown at an average annual rate of 0.3 percent during the first half of the eighteenth century, increased at a pace nearly five times more rapid in the third quarter of this century. On the other hand, it was only around 1770, with the increase in the demand for iron and the growth of the cotton industry, that the first signs of the industrial revolution appeared in this country.

In the same manner, agricultural production increased rapidly in Germany during the first half of the nineteenth century, while the industrial sector was growing slowly during this period and did not really begin to expand until after the middle of the century. The fact that Belgium had already attained a high level of agricultural production in the eighteenth century is presumably one of the reasons why it apparently began its industrialization as early as the end of that century. In the United States, agricultural production per capita increased rapidly between the beginning of the nineteenth century and the Civil War (between 1800 and 1840, for instance, the number of man-hours required to produce a bushel of grain decreased by 20 percent for corn and 38 percent for wheat), but it was only at the end of this war that the industrial transformation of the country really began. Finally, in Japan, an exceptional increase in the agricultural production per worker at the beginning of the Meiji era (more than 50 percent in the last two decades of the nineteenth century) preceded a period of rapid industrialization which in fact only began during the first decade of the twentieth century.

In all these countries the increase in agricultural productivity stimulated the demand for industrial goods. It is in these terms that Bairoch explains, for instance, the rapid development of the iron, steel, and textile industries which, in most countries, was one of the particularly striking characteristics of the industrial revolution. The modernization of technology, which was at the origin of the "agricultural revolution," was in fact partly due to the growing use of equipment made of iron, cast iron, or even steel. Indeed, the increase in the agricultural sector's demand for iron during the fifty to seventy years which followed the transformation of this sector is apparently sufficient to account for virtually all the demand for iron during this period.

Subsequently, of course, the mechanization of the textile industry substantially contributed to the demand for iron and steel products. The take-off of the textile industry itself was caused by a growth in demand resulting from an increase in agricultural productivity and incomes. Thus productivity per agricultural worker doubled in England during the eighteenth century, while in France it increased by 70 percent between 1760 and 1860. Finally, the increase in agricultural incomes permitted an accumulation of savings which financed investment in this sector and also, presumably, in industrial enterprises: a transfer across sectors which was greatly facilitated by the social links existing between industrialists and landowners.[3]

We see, then, that in all the now-developed countries, the prior development of the agricultural sector was a decisive factor in the start of the industrialization process. However different the circumstances in which the Third World countries are trying to develop their economies today, we can recognize in their experiences, be they successful or not, the same crucial role of agriculture.

SUCCESSES AND FAILURES IN DEVELOPING COUNTRIES

For most developing countries, productivity in the agricultural sector is lower, even today, than it was in the now-developed countries at the outset of their industrial revolution. Productivity per male agricultural worker, expressed in millions of calories of annual production, was approximately 7 in each of the European countries when they started their industrialization process.[4] Around 1960–1964 this index was approximately 12.9 for

Latin America (9.2 if we exclude Argentina) and 8.4 for the Middle East; by contrast, it was only 4.7 for Africa and 4.3 for Asia (China excluded). Indeed, productivity in Africa and Asia was presumably even lower than the level reached by the European countries at the outset of their agricultural revolution.[5] Even if we take into account the increase in agricultural productivity that has occurred over the last two decades, productivity in most African and Asian countries remains lower than the level it had reached in the now-developed countries when they started their industrialization process; in this respect, the situations of the two groups are quite dissimilar.

In spite of this difference in situations, most developing countries have tried during recent decades to promote industrialization, with disappointing results in many cases. The same relationships that explain how a previous increase in agricultural productivity enabled the now-developed countries to start their industrialization presumably also explain, in a reverse manner, how low agricultural productivity has held back or even arrested the industrialization efforts of many developing countries. In these countries the growth of the industrial sector has been hampered by insufficient demand from the rural sector. This insufficiency is, in turn, explained by the low technological level of traditional agriculture (which requires few products from the industrial sector) and by its limited productivity (which condemns agricultural workers to low incomes that must be spent almost entirely on food).

Fortunately, during recent years a few developing countries have experienced rapid industrialization. A study of their economic development only confirms the importance of the agricultural sector in the industrialization process. In this regard it seems appropriate to analyze the experience of those countries whose industrialization efforts have been the most successful. Especially noteworthy among them are certain countries in East Asia, particularly the "gang of four" (Hong Kong, Singapore, South Korea, and Taiwan), and in Latin America, notably Brazil and Mexico.

Hong Kong and Singapore, archetypes of export-oriented industrialization, appear to be perfect examples of successful industrial development without prior increases in the productivity of the agricultural sector — in fact, even without an agricultural sector! Their experience clearly shows that the situation has changed since the eighteenth century and that an agricultural revolution is no longer always necessary to prime the pump of the industrialization process. This change is due to the rapid decline in transport costs since the nineteenth century: today entrepreneurs can find in distant markets the initial demand that is necessary to trigger industrialization. This does not prove, however, that agriculture no longer has a role to play in the developing countries' industrial revolution. The cases of these two city-states are obviously special, and there is no reason to believe that export-primed industrialization would necessarily lead to overall development in the case of a much larger country with an important agricultural sector.

Whatever our first impression, the examples of South Korea and Taiwan do not contradict the preceding statement. Export markets have been unquestionably important in the industrialization of these two countries, but it would be a mistake to conclude that the development accompanying this industrialization process was merely automatic. In fact this development owes as much, if not more, to a number of sectoral policies which have greatly encouraged the growth of the agricultural sector; quite often, actually, these policies even preceded the reorientation of industry toward the export markets at the beginning of the sixties.

In South Korea, the war of 1950–1953 had devastated the economy, and the ten following years were devoted to reconstruction, defense, and augmentation of private incomes and demand. The agrarian reforms of 1947 and 1950 had paved the way for balanced agricultural growth. Thanks to an active education policy, the literacy rate rose from 30 percent in 1953 to more than 80 percent in 1963. While agriculture was relatively neglected (its growth rate from 1953 to 1963 was only about 2.5 percent per year), improvement in land distribution and investment in "human capital" were to permit rapid growth of agricultural production after 1963. The same year, 1963, also saw a revision in the industrial policy which gave priority to export industries, but this change did not imply a lessening of governmental involvement in the agricultural sector. Growth of agriculture after 1963 was fast and lasting; from 1960 to 1979, agricultural value added increased at an annual rate of 4.6 percent, one of the highest among the developing countries during this period. The increase in agricultural incomes led to the development, in the rural sector, of small industries supplying consumer products to households and intermediate goods to agriculture. This exceptionally rapid development made an important contribution to industrialization and creation of employment: in the sixties, employment in these rural industries increased by about 6 percent annually.

Taiwan's experience is similar to Korea's. During their long occupation (from 1895 to 1945) the Japanese had developed a very productive agriculture, and after World War II, land reform led to a better use of the land's potential. The early postwar years were devoted to agricultural development and import-substitution industrialization. In the agricultural sector, the well-developed infrastructure the Japanese had left behind was to permit particularly high production growth rates: 5.5 percent per year from 1952 to 1960 and 7 percent from 1960 to 1969. In this instance, too, the increase in agricultural incomes led to the development of many small labor-intensive industries. This development, encouraged by the government's active policy of decentralization, had a much wider scope than in all but a few other developing countries. Employment in these industries increased at an annual rate of 7.4 percent from 1956 to 1966, and by 1970 about 70 percent of the families working in the agricultural sector derived part of their incomes from nonagricultural activities.[6]

We see then that it would be too simple and partly erroneous to regard the achievements of Korea and Taiwan as essentially examples of an export-oriented industrialization that would automatically have affected and carried along the rest of the economy, the agricultural sector in particular. In both cases export-oriented industrialization was preceded by an import-substitution phase, when bolstered domestic demand, agrarian reform, and the development of physical and human capital were paving the way for an exceptionally rapid growth of the agricultural sector. During the following phase, it was this high growth of agriculture which permitted the overall extension of the industrialization process and the general economic development.

In their economic experiences, Brazil and Mexico appear to be the antipodes of Korea and Taiwan. While Korea and Taiwan are generally considered examples of export-oriented industrialization, Brazil and Mexico probably constitute the best examples of industrialization based on import substitution. We should note, however, that these import-substitution strategies experienced serious problems and that, after the second half of the sixties, these two countries, especially Brazil, reoriented their policies towards export promotion.

Value added in the manufacturing sector represented about 21 percent of Brazil's gross domestic product in 1947 (a percentage similar to the proportion in Senegal today). The system of protection which encouraged import-substituting industrialization was established at this time, primarily as a reaction to a crisis in the balance of payments. During the fifties and early sixties, the nominal rate of protection on all traded goods reached 50 to 100 percent; this rate was particularly high for industrial products, thus biasing the terms of trade against the agricultural sector. Yet other policies (low interest rates, price subsidies for fertilizer and tractors) probably offset the handicap created for agriculture by this differentiated protectionist structure. In any event, total agricultural production grew at the rapid rate of 4.2 percent per year from 1947 to 1964, while production per agricultural worker increased by about 2.7 percent annually. Subsequently, these rates were to increase further, reaching, respectively, 5.2 percent and 3.7 percent from 1967 to 1976.

Of course, the increase in agricultural incomes was very unequally shared, mainly because of inegalitarian land distribution. Nevertheless, the significant rise in average agricultural incomes during the two decades which followed World War II did permit substantial growth of *average* consumption per head in the rural sector. Stimulated by this demand and protected by high tariff barriers, manufactured production also increased rapidly (10 percent annually from 1947 to 1962). From 1968 onward, following a change in the government incentive system, the expansion of industrial exports replaced import substitution as an engine of growth, thereby permitting an even higher growth rate of industrial output;[7] today the manufacturing sector accounts for nearly one-third of the gross domestic product.

The industrialization of Mexico has been in many ways similar to that of Brazil; but industry has always remained less protected in Mexico, and import substitution has been less significant. In the fifties and sixties, the development of irrigation and the new varieties of wheat and corn led to a particularly rapid increase in food production (see Chapter 7). Agricultural production increased at an annual rate of 3.6 percent from the end of World War II to the beginning of the seventies. While this rate was only marginally higher than the population growth rate (3.3 percent), it was nevertheless more than the rate of increase in the agricultural labor force (0.8 percent). As a result, average production per agricultural worker increased rapidly, and as in the case of Brazil, this increase in the average rural income permitted a rapid augmentation of manufactured production (7.3 percent annually during the same period). The fact that — as in Brazil, once again — the profits of economic growth have been most unequally distributed in no way diminishes the importance of the role played by the development of agriculture in this industrialization process.

The Brazilian and Mexican experiences thus reveal the importance of agricultural development for an industrialization policy oriented toward the satisfaction of domestic demand. We find the same to be true at a local level, in the economic evolution of the states of Punjab and Haryana in India. In this region, the "bread basket" of the Indian Union, the spectacular growth of the agricultural sector during the years following the beginning of the Green Revolution was accompanied by equally rapid expansion of industrial production. This industrialization process is somewhat reminiscent of the industrial revolution in Europe to the extent that textiles, agricultural inputs, and capital goods for local consumption have similarly played a major role.

The importance of the agricultural sector in the development process can also be illustrated by the counterexamples of countries that have pursued an objective of rapid industrialization without placing enough emphasis on agriculture. These counterexamples are numerous, but we shall limit ourselves here to India, Algeria, and China, all of which, at different times and for various durations, have followed policies of forced industrialization while neglecting their agricultural sectors.

The second Indian Five-Year Plan (1955–1960) can be regarded as an archetype of an "industrialization first" strategy; it gave priority to the production of capital goods and to the use of capital-intensive technologies, while light industries and especially the agricultural sector were largely neglected. The negative implications of this model from the standpoint of private consumption and alleviation of poverty were acknowledged, but the advocates of this strategy argued that the emphasis on capital goods industries would permit high savings and, consequently, substantial reinvestment and rapid growth.

Actual growth was, however, much lower than projected. From 1955 to 1960 the industrial growth rate was a respectable 7.2 percent per year, but because of slow agricultural growth, per capita income increased by only 1.1 percent a year on average. Nor can it be claimed that the second plan built the heavy infrastructures which subsequently permitted more rapid growth: from 1960 to 1979 industrial production increased at 5.0 percent annually and income per capita at 1.4 percent. On the other hand, during this period, the neglected rural sector was increasingly falling behind, with consequences that are still plaguing the Indian economy today; food imports, which in 1955–1956 represented about $110 million, quadrupled during the second plan period. During the sixties, the setbacks of agriculture finally led the government to reconsider its priorities and to give more importance to this sector.

The strategy followed by Algeria since its independence (or more exactly, since the Seven-Year Development Forecast for 1967–1973 was prepared in 1966) is somewhat reminiscent of the options which Mahalanobis had chosen for the second Indian plan: accelerated industrialization, priority to capital goods industries, and deliberate neglect of the agricultural sector. In the pursuit of these objectives, however, Algeria has shown a constancy and a determination which far exceed India's performance. Algeria's gross investment had already reached 28 percent of GDP in 1969 and exceeded 50 percent in 1978; the proportion of industrial investment in intermediate and capital goods industries alone averaged 87 percent from 1967 to 1977.

Yet the results obtained after such an extraordinary effort appear somewhat disappointing. Of course, industrial production increased rapidly from 1960 to 1970 (12.9 percent annually), but its growth subsequently slowed down (6.5 percent from 1970 to 1979). As for agricultural production, it almost stagnated: the annual growth rate from 1960 to 1980 was about 0.5 percent. While the demand for employment was growing rapidly (it now increases by some 140,000 people every year), industry was offering only limited opportunities (25,000 additional jobs per year from 1969 to 1977), and agricultural employment was stagnating or declining. Food production, which accounted for 73 percent of consumption in 1969, corresponded to only 41 percent in 1977. It is clear today that, for want of modernization, agriculture and the rural sector have not been able to provide industry with the expected markets. Toward the end of the seventies it had become evident that the priorities of the Algerian strategy would have to be revised and that, in this reorientation, the importance of agriculture would have to be clearly recognized.

The success of China's strategy is generally — and rightly — attributed to the importance given to agriculture and the rural sector. We must remember, nevertheless, that in the years immediately following the Communists' arrival to power, the Chinese government, under the influence of Soviet advisers, paid more attention to industry. In retrospect, such an orientation appears even more questionable in the case of China than in that of the Soviet Union: in 1952, on the eve of its first Five-Year Plan (1953–1957), per capita grain production in China was one-half what it was in Russia in 1928 when Russia embarked upon its series of Five-Year Plans. In spite of this, China actually tried to surpass the industrial effort made during the Soviet Union's first Five-Year Plan: nearly half the investment of the first Chinese plan was thus allotted to the industrial sector. Moreover, most of the industries so established were highly capital-intensive, in the image again of the Soviet model.

In spite of the priority it had received, Chinese industry contributed little to the creation of employment during the first plan. While industrial employment increased by nearly 50 percent in five years, it still had reached only 8 million in 1957, that is to say, 2 to 3 percent of the total labor force. Agriculture was not completely neglected, since it was during this period that the collectivization of the land was carried out. But the deficiencies in this sector were clearly revealed at the end of the fifties, when three years of bad weather led to a fall in agricultural production and to food scarcity. Other factors, such as the excesses of the Great Leap Forward and the departure of the Soviet advisers, contributed to the deterioration of the economic situation, with the result that, in 1960–1961, domestic production fell 20 to 25 percent. Faced with these problems, the Chinese government reversed the orientation of the first Five-Year Plan and put at the head of its new priorities (which have been maintained since then) agriculture, light industry, and heavy industry, in that order.[8]

What lessons can we draw from these different experiences? In a strategy of import-substituting industrialization, agriculture plays a fundamental role, since productivity increases in the agricultural sector are necessary to stimulate the demand for industrial products. In the case of export-oriented industrialization, while agriculture may not play a vital role at the beginning, its modernization soon becomes necessary to prevent the development process from remaining confined to an enclave. In all cases, therefore, the development of the agricultural sector largely determines the eventual success of the industrialization process. The counterexamples of certain countries whose development has been arrested because they had given exclusive priority to industrialization again confirm the importance of the agricultural sector in the initial phase of development.

SPECIFIC CONDITIONS OF THE THIRD WORLD

Both the history of the now-developed countries at the beginning of their industrialization phase and the experience of the developing countries during the last thirty years argue in favor of paying greater attention to the agricultural sector in Third World development strategies. In addition, in the coming decades, certain conditions specific to developing countries will reinforce the argument in favor of such priority.

The severe food problems forecast for the coming decades certainly justify heightened attention to agriculture, particularly to food production. Furthermore, as we have seen, only direct intervention, through measures aiming to increase incomes, will improve the situation of the poorest. This implies that the first priority should be given to the agricultural sector, the main source of income for most of these poor. Finally, in order to check the ongoing soil degradation and deforestation, specific programs should be implemented in the agricultural and, more generally, in the rural sector.

As we saw in Chapter 1, the present population growth in the developing countries is much higher than it was in the now-developed countries at the beginning of their industrialization phase. From this standpoint, the parallel between the development of the latter countries in the eighteenth and nineteenth centuries and the development of the Third World today should not lead us astray; it will be necessary to take these particular circumstances into account when considering the developing countries' economic strategies.

For several reasons the problems raised by the Third World's population growth further reinforce the argument in favor of giving greater priority to agriculture and the rural sector. First of all, the still excessive rapidity of this growth demands that current efforts to reduce it be pursued. This will of course require strengthening birth control programs, but, as we have seen, the effectiveness of these programs will undoubtedly remain limited in the absence of policies to improve the incomes and well-being of the people concerned. Since most of the Third World population live in rural areas and depend on agriculture for their living, improvement in their well-being will be contingent on the development of the agricultural sector. From this standpoint, a particular effort in favor of the rural population would seem all the more justified, since fertility rates are generally higher among the rural than among the urban population.[9] The serious danger that population growth represents for the future of the Third World would in itself justify greater priority being given to the improvement of living conditions in the rural areas.

The employment problem is another aspect of the relationship between population growth and the evolution of the agricultural sector. The population explosion of the postwar years was due mainly to a decrease in infant mortality and to the resulting increase in the number of children per family. With a time lag of fifteen to twenty years, this decrease has led to a rapid increase in the number of people arriving in the labor market. In this respect, the situation is completely different for the developing countries from what it was for the now-developed countries at the outset of their industrialization. During the nineteenth century, the active population of the industrializing countries increased by about 0.9 percent a year. The corresponding rate for the developing countries today is over 2.0 percent.[10] Because of the time lag between reduction in infant mortality and increase in the labor force, only now are the full consequences of the population explosion on employment beginning to be felt. The active population of the Third World increased by 1.6 percent a year during the fifties and by 1.8 percent during the sixties; during the seventies and eighties it should increase at an annual rate of 2.2 percent, and this increase should slow down only slightly (2.1 percent) during the nineties.

The implications of these high growth rates are even more striking when we measure the absolute increase in this labor force. From 1980 to 2000 the active population of the Third World will increase by about 450 million (from 850 million to over 1,300 million) a number approximately equal to the *total* active population of these countries toward the end of World War II. The active population of sub-Saharan Africa was multiplied by two during the last thirty-five years; it will probably require less than three decades to double again. The active population of Latin America has doubled in only thirty years, and the next doubling should scarcely require more than a quarter of a century.

Because of the rapid growth of the developing countries' active population, industrialization has made only a limited contribution to the solution of the employment problem. Even today, industry employs only 16 percent of the Third World's active population; by way of comparison, in the now-developed countries this percentage was about 30 percent at the beginning of the twentieth century. Yet this relative failure is not explained by the slow development of the industrial sector in the Third World: the annual growth rates of industrial value added and employment in the developing countries over the last few years have been more than twice what they were in the developed countries at the beginning of this century.[11] There are, in fact, two main reasons why this rapid industrial growth has had only a limited impact on employment. First, industry still accounts for only a small part of GNP and total employment, and consequently even very rapid growth of this sector would have only a limited effect, in the first years, on the breakdown of value added and employment among the different sectors. Second, whatever the growth of industrial employment, industry will never be able to absorb anything but a small proportion of the annual increase in the active population. Thus, during recent decades the industrial sector has absorbed less than 35 percent of the additional workers in the middle-income developing countries and less than 20 percent in the poorest ones.[12]

This incapacity of industry to solve the employment problems of the Third World is particularly clear in the case of the low-income countries (those with incomes below $380 per capita in 1979). In these countries the percentage of the industrial labor force in the total active population rose only from 8 percent in 1950 to 11 percent in 1979. In many countries of Africa this proportion has not changed since the Second World War; in India, the breakdown of the active population among the three sectors (agriculture, mining and manufacturing, services and other) has remained practically unchanged since 1921.[13] As Gunnar Myrdal said, for these countries, industrialization is a myth, meaning both that it has represented an actual ideology for their elites and that it has not fulfilled the hopes it aroused.

During the eighties, because of the accelerated growth of the active population in low-income countries, the contribution of industry to the absorption of the additional labor force is bound to remain limited. In its draft Five-Year Plan for 1978–1983, the Indian government noted that the increase in the "share of landless workers in the unorganized work force . . . reflects several tendencies which should cause concern, namely, growing population pressure in the rural areas [and] lack of opportunities for non-agricultural work"; and further that "if growth of industrial production continues to be only 5% per year as at present, the organized sector will absorb only 2.7 million of the 29.5 million new workers . . . and if the growth [rate] increases to 7%, the extra absorption in the whole organized sector will be only 0.26 million."[14] A similar analysis could apply to many countries. In fact, a rough calculation shows that, even if the growth rates of industrial value added and employment in the low-income countries were to increase by half in the coming years, industry would still be able to absorb less than one-quarter of the additional workers arriving on the labor market every year.[15] It is clear that, for these countries, agriculture must continue to supply most of the new jobs in the coming years.

The problem is, in fact, very similar in certain middle-income countries. In Latin America, for instance, the doubling of the labor force over the next quarter of a century will increase the seriousness of the employment problems already existing. Although the share of the agricultural labor force in the total active population is less than it is in Africa or Asia, it was still as high as 41 percent in 1970, higher than the percentages in industry or in the service sector.[16] Whatever the absorptive capacity of the latter two sectors, they will be able to provide employment only to a small share of the incremental labor force; it will therefore be necessary that agriculture contribute significantly to employment creation if the present situation of unemployment and underemployment is not to deteriorate further in this region. In the coming years, other middle-income countries faced with rapid growth of their labor force will also have to look for new employment possibilities in the agricultural sector.

For many countries the problem is likely to be further compounded by the degradation of the world economic situation. Less rapid growth in the developed countries could lead to a slowdown in the developing countries' export growth, while increases in energy prices will contribute to the deterioration of their balance of payments. Several of these countries are thus likely to be led to pay more attention to their agricultural sector, with the double aim of creating the jobs that the export sectors will have more difficulty providing and of finding substitutes for the food imports that will weigh heavily on their trade deficits.

In the coming decades, therefore, the developing countries will be confronted with a host of problems which, in most instances, the now-developed countries did not have to face when they started their industrialization process. On the whole, these particular circumstances will further reinforce the necessity of giving greater priority to the development of the agricultural sector.

ECONOMIC THEORY, MYTHS, AND AGRICULTURE

The exclusive attention given by many Third World countries to industry is mainly a result of the prestige of this sector, which is considered the hallmark of development. In addition, a certain number of myths have prevented the governments of these countries from recognizing the importance of the agricultural sector in development. While government policies have improved somewhat in recent years, these myths nevertheless die hard and continue to discourage the implementation of desirable strategies. Thus, I shall — after many others — devote a few pages to an attempt to expose the hollowness of these so-called truths.

It is not really surprising to find that the origin of these myths can often be traced to the theories of some famous economists or to the occasionally erroneous interpretations which their disciples have made of their work. As Keynes noted, "The ideas of economists and political philosophers, both when they are right and when they are wrong, are more powerful than is commonly understood. Indeed the world is ruled by little else. Practical men, who believe themselves to be quite exempt from any intellectual influences, are usually the slaves of some defunct economist." [17] I shall not venture to endorse the overall implications of this remark, any more than I shall attempt here to make a critical study of the place of agriculture in economic theory and practice. There are, however, three economic questions related to this sector that have had a significant bearing on the orientation of development strategies and that I would like to discuss here: the linkage effects of agriculture on the other economic sectors, the economic behavior of the farmers and their so-called conservatism, and agricultural productivity in general.

The linkage effects of agriculture

The links between agriculture and industry, and the mutual linkage effect of these two sectors, were probably explicitly shown for the first time by Quesnay and the physiocrats.[18] After him, however, the classical economists were more interested in the stimulus industry provided for agriculture than in the reverse process. While Adam Smith recognized that "the cultivation and improvement of the country, . . . which affords subsistence, must, necessarily, be prior to the increase of the town, which furnishes only the means of conveniency and luxury," he subsequently devoted a whole chapter to showing "how the commerce of the towns contributed to the improvement of the country."[19] Among more recent writers, Hirschman could still write scarcely more than twenty years ago: "Agriculture certainly stands convicted on the count of its lack of direct stimulus to the setting up of new activities through linkage effects — the superiority of industry in this respect is crushing."[20]

The best refutation of Hirschman's accusation would probably be an analysis of the developed countries' economic history at the outset of their industrialization or of the developing countries' experiences during recent decades. As I have tried to show in the first two sections of this chapter, in these countries the linkage effects of agriculture on industry have been vital for the development of the latter. Moreover, Hirschman's analysis — which we can presumably consider here as representative of a particular school of thought — prompts me to make three comments.

First of all, linkage effects as Hirschman defines them result either from the demand for other sectors' products as inputs to one sector (backward linkage) or from the supply of one sector's final products as inputs to other productive sectors (forward linkage). While it is true that traditional agriculture uses few industrial products, its modernization will require increased utilization of this type of good. This was already true at the time of the agricultural revolution which preceded the industrial revolution in the developed countries. It is even more true today, when modern agriculture uses fertilizers, insecticides, irrigation facilities, farm equipment, and so on. We saw in the two Punjabs (in India and Pakistan) that the Green Revolution brought about increases in the production of precisely this type of industrial product. Similarly, forward linkages have sometimes been important factors in a country's industrialization. In the Ivory Coast, for instance, agricultural and food industries account for more than half the industrial value added and a still higher proportion of manufactured exports.

Second, Hirschman's definition of linkage effects is probably too restrictive; other interactions should also be taken into account. One of these is the effect that the growth of farmers' consumption (resulting from an increase in agricultural productivity and incomes) can have on industrial production. In the rural areas of Asia, for instance, nonfood products generally represent between one-quarter and one-half of household consumption. Here also the examples of the Punjabs, Taiwan, and Korea show that the effects of such consumption expenditure can be decisive in the creation of rural industries or in the development of urban industries supplying rural markets.

Finally, another form of interaction which should be taken into account is that which financial flows establish among the different sectors. In this respect, agriculture can play a significant role in the financing of industrial development. Because of the importance of agriculture in the economies of the developing countries, especially during the early stages of their development, the resources required for the financing of industrialization must come in part from the agricultural sector. The way in which this transfer is achieved can determine the success, or the failure, of development efforts. The most frequently used method consists in modifying, wittingly or not, the terms of trade to the detriment of the farmers by keeping prices low for agricultural products and high for industrial goods. Unfortunately, the effects of this method have generally been to discourage agricultural production and consequently to hinder industrial development. By contrast, countries that have attempted to use an appropriate system of land taxation or to mobilize rural savings through financial institutions have generally been more successful. In this regard, there is a striking contrast between, on the one hand, South Korea and Taiwan, where high agricultural prices and an effective system for the mobilization of rural savings have led to rapid growth of agriculture and a net transfer of funds out of this sector and, on the other hand, the countries of South Asia, where, partly because of an unadapted price structure, agriculture has progressed only slowly in spite of a net financial transfer from the other sectors to agriculture.

The conservatism of farmers

In the developed as in the developing countries, farmers generally have a bad reputation. Politicians and economists have accused them, on flimsy evidence, of carelessness, wastefulness, and conservatism, and these beliefs have often led governments to prefer development strategies oriented toward industrialization rather than toward modernization of the agricultural sector, which is considered hopelessly backward. Classical and Marxist economists are largely responsible for these prejudices, which have contributed to the distortion of many development policies. To mention but a few, David Hume did not hesitate to accuse farmers of laziness and wastefulness, while Marx and Engels saw the peasant class as a pillar of the established order, unlikely to evolve or accept modernization spontaneously.[21]

The idea that farmers are slow to adopt technical innovations and do not respond to the incentives of the market is directly linked to these prejudices. After the rapid modernization of agriculture in the developed countries had given this idea an unchallengeable refutation, it was asserted, in an attempt to breathe new life into this time-honored prejudice, that while the farmers of the developed countries could show dynamism and rationality, the peasants of the Third World, imprisoned in an ancient and traditional culture, would be unable to display the same aptitude for evolution. One implication of this supposed inertia was that it would be vain to hope that these farmers could respond "rationally" to a rise in the prices of agricultural products by increasing their production. In these circumstances, why should policymakers attempt to raise these prices, since this would only dissatisfy the urban consumers without leading to any increase in the available quantities?

In fact, this idea has been largely refuted by examples coming from every region of the world. In Thailand, for instance, when Japan's purchase of corn caused prices to rise in the sixties, farmers quickly reacted by increasing the planted area as well as the yields, and in five years production was multiplied sevenfold. In the Sudan, bean production increased fivefold from 1948 to 1955 when prices rose; it subsequently fell by almost half in two years following a fall in prices. In India and Pakistan, studies on the elasticity of cultivated areas with respect to crop prices show that the farmers of the Indian subcontinent behave in very much the same way as their American colleagues and respond just as quickly to changes in relative prices.[22]

The link between yields and average producer prices was clearly revealed by a study on rice production in different Asian countries.[23] As can be seen in Table 10.1, there is a direct relationship between the yields achieved and the price structure. The countries where the ratio of the prices to agricultural producers (measured by the price of a kilogram of rice) to the cost of agricultural inputs (estimated by the price of a kilogram of fertilizer) is high are also those where the yields are the highest. It would be difficult to argue that this apparent relationship is merely the outcome of chance. Differences in prices among countries are substantial and result from long-standing government policies; furthermore we may note that the three countries with the highest yields (Japan, South Korea, and

TABLE 10.1   Comparative Price Data for Fertilizer and Rice

Country	Paddy price to producers (in U.S. cents per kg.)	Price of fertilizer nutrients to producers (in U.S. cents per kg.)	Ratio of paddy price to fertilizer price	Paddy yield in 1970 (in million tons per hectare)
Japan	30.7	21.5	1.428	5.64
Korea	18.4	19.1	0.963	4.55
Taiwan	11.7	26.2	0.447	4.16
Malaysia	8.8	20.3	0.433	2.72
Ceylon (Sri Lanka)	11.3	15.8	0.715	2.64
Indonesia	4.5	15.2	0.296	2.14
Thailand	4.5	14.3–50.0	0.315–0.090	1.97
Philippines	7.0	17.3	0.405	1.72
Burma	3.1	25.1	0.124	1.70

SOURCE: C. Peter Timmer and Walter P. Falcon, "The Political Economy of Rice Production and Trade in Asia," in Lloyd G. Reynolds, ed., *Agriculture in Development Theory* (New Haven: Yale University Press, 1975).

Taiwan) have soils which are among the poorest of the nine countries surveyed.

The use of the price system to encourage agricultural production is not merely a bourgeois stratagem of the capitalist countries. In a deliberate and, apparently, continuous manner, the government of Communist China has modified the terms of trade between agricultural and industrial products in favor of the farmers. Thus, toward the end of the fifties, a given quantity of agricultural products bought 35 percent more industrial goods than at the beginning of the decade, and at the end of the sixties this percentage had risen to 67 percent.

Confronted with new agricultural technologies, the farmers of all countries are not long in adopting them, provided they perceive their advantages vis-à-vis traditional techniques. The rapidity with which the high-yield cereals have been adopted by Third World farmers (see Chapter 7) should be sufficient to disprove all statements about the conservatism of farmers and the traditionalism of rural classes. When a so-called improved technology is not adopted by farmers in spite of the efforts of extension services, we can without much risk reverse the usual presumption: instead of accusing the farmers of inertia and stupidity, we should try to find out what drawbacks of this new technology more than offset its apparent advantages in the eyes of its users. Then we may discover that this high-yielding variety of corn has a different taste and does not sell as well, that that variety of wheat can be cultivated only by farmers who have at their disposal a reliable water supply, and that a particular variety of rice, while it yields more grain, produces less straw for animal fodder. When farmers do not progress and agriculture stagnates, the fault does not lie with laziness or economic irrationality on the part of the farmers but with the inability of researchers, extension agents, and governments to provide the technical and economic conditions required for this progress.

Agriculture and productivity

The low productivity of the agricultural sector is presumably as old a theme in economic literature as the question of the "innate conservatism" of farmers. The fact that this theme has also been refuted by more than two centuries of economic history has not succeeded in dispelling this notion: for many Third World governments, industry still remains the productive sector par excellence.[24]

Although it directly contradicts certain writings by Adam Smith, the idea that agriculture is condemned to have a lower productivity than the other sectors can be traced to this founding father of modern economic theory. He was in fact one of the first to recognize that, in contrast to industry, economies of scale do not exist in agriculture; after him, classical, Marxist, and neoclassical economists all accepted the idea that agriculture suffered from decreasing marginal returns, while industry benefited from economies of scale, that is, from increasing marginal returns. This idea — which is at any rate difficult to challenge — does not automatically entail that the productivity of agriculture today is necessarily inferior to the productivity of industry (at most it could be concluded that at *constant technological level,* unlimited increases in productive factors would ultimately bring about this relative inferiority of agricultural productivity). Yet many nineteenth- and twentieth-century economists have believed that agriculture is bound always to have lower productivity than industry — this, despite the fact that agricultural productivity was making unprecedented progress at the very time when they were writing!

To the argument based on the idea of decreasing marginal returns can be added another one, a less theoretical argument, since it is based on statistical observations. The inequality in per capita incomes between the rural and the urban sector, or between agriculture and other economic activities, can be interpreted as the result of the differences in productivity per worker in these different sectors. Even if we modify the usual estimates to take into account the fact that the relative prices of agricultural products are often artificially depressed, the *average* productivity per worker is still generally lower in agriculture (and in all likelihood the same applies to the *marginal* productivity per worker).

Nevertheless, it would be a mistake to conclude from these limited results that agriculture should receive a smaller share of *all* productive factors and that the share of the other sectors should be increased. If the marginal productivity of labor is indeed inferior in agriculture, it would

TABLE 10.2   Capital/Output Ratios, Value Added, and Investment in Agriculture: Annual Averages, 1960-1965

Country	Gross marginal capital/output ratio		Value added in agriculture as a percentage of GDP	Agricultural investment as a percentage of total investment
	Agriculture	Overall		
Bolivia	0.7	2.9	26.0	3.2
Taiwan	2.8	1.8	27.7	18.3
Cyprus	1.0	4.1	19.0	12.0
Ethiopia	0.3	3.0	66.1	4.0
Jamaica	6.8	3.4	12.3	10.9
South Korea	0.7	2.1	40.7	10.5
Malawi	1.3	10.7	54.2	12.0
Philippines	0.7	2.2	34.0	5.7
Senegal	0.2	. . .	33.3	3.9
Sudan	1.3	2.5	54.0	23.3
Syria	0.6	2.0	32.8	19.1
Tanzania	1.9	3.3	59.0	18.2
Thailand	2.1	2.5	36.0	17.4
Trinidad and Tobago	3.3	8.9	10.6	2.1
Tunisia	4.7	3.6	23.7	19.9
United Arab Republic	3.4	2.6	30.6	16.2
Uruguay	5.1	11.6	16.7	11.9
Venezuela	5.9	3.7	7.5	12.8
Weighted average	1.73	3.2	29.5	12.3

SOURCE: E. Szczepanik, "The Size and Efficiency of Agricultural Investment in Selected Developing Countries," FAO, *Monthly Bulletin of Agricultural Economics and Statistics,* December 1969, p. 2.

certainly be in keeping with sound marginalist logic to encourage the transfer of labor to other, more productive sectors.[25] But such a transfer should not be envisaged for the other productive factors unless it can be ascertained that their marginal productivity is higher in the other sectors than in agriculture.

Yet this is precisely where there is a flaw. The rare indications available tend to show that the productivity of these other factors — capital in particular — is higher in agriculture than elsewhere. Thus, as can be seen in Table 10.2, in most of the countries for which data exist, the gross marginal capital/output ratio is lower — thereby indicating higher productivity — in agriculture than in the other sectors.[26]

Table 10.2 also enables us to see that while investment in agriculture has, on average, a higher productivity than in the other sectors, its share in total investment nevertheless remains relatively low. Thus this share is lower than the share of agricultural value added in GDP for all countries except Venezuela. This paradoxical situation can be explained in part by the insufficiency of government efforts and by the difficulties that small farmers encounter in trying to obtain, on reasonable conditions, the inputs, equipment, and credit required for their investments (see Chapter 11).

The accusation of low productivity that has been leveled against agriculture must therefore be specified and qualified. While such an assertion can be justified with regard to the productivity of labor, it is presumably erroneous with regard to the productivity of capital. Statistical data are too sketchy to permit any judgment on the productivity of all productive factors. Yet, in the United States, the only country for which we have a sufficiently long statistical series, the total productivity of all factors has increased faster in agriculture than in the other sectors.[27]

Microeconomic studies confirm this overall impression (one can scarcely speak of "results" because of the imprecision of the data). While the economic rates of return of traditional agricultural activities are generally low, modern technologies permit the obtainment of rates which, for many activities, equal or exceed the rates of the other sectors. The idea of an agricultural sector suffering from low productivity was probably justified in the context of traditional technology. In all likelihood, however, it was already no longer accurate in the countries where the nineteenth-century economists were writing. And it is even less so today in many developing countries where modern technology permits, or could permit, high yields and economic rates of return equal or superior to those obtained in other sectors.

ELEMENTS OF A STRATEGY

Before I attempt a rapid sketch of some elements of an agricultural strategy, it may be useful to explain how I see the role of this sector. In my opinion, agriculture has not received the priority it deserves in the government policies of most developing countries. But I would like to avoid any misunderstanding with regard to the origin of this opinion. My position is not the result of any dislike of urban life, or reluctance with regard to industrial civilization, or ecological preference for a rural society. I do not believe that industrialization is an unattainable objective, and I certainly consider it to be a desirable goal.

But the experiences of many countries have shown that giving an exclusive priority to industrial growth has often led the development process to a dead end. The growth of the agricultural sector is necessary for the balance and the viability of the development model, and its stagnation will generally doom industrialization efforts in the long term. Instead of being considered an end in itself, agricultural development should be thought of as a means toward balanced growth in all economic sectors — including the industrial sector.

It is not possible to detail agricultural policies here, since their specifics will vary from country to country. Yet the main lines of these policies are generally alike in the developing nations, and in this respect, it is surprising to note how similar the deficiencies or weaknesses of the policies are. Two frequent errors seem particularly important. First, price structures are often artificially modified to the detriment of agriculture; second, public financing of investments and recurrent expenditures in this sector are far below the levels that economic efficiency or social justice would require.

The modification of the price structure to the detriment of agriculture is the outcome of a variety of measures, usually implemented in different sectors in a more ad hoc than systematic manner. In many countries the prices of agricultural products are thus authoritatively set by the government or influenced by a system of compulsory procurement; in both cases the prices so determined are usually set in the consumers', rather than the producers', interest. By contrast, the prices of industrial goods are generally artificially raised because of protectionist measures adopted to discourage imports and encourage substitution industries; when similar protection exists for the agricultural sector, its relative level is generally much lower, so that this sector is here again at a disadvantage.[28] As a result, the prices of inputs for the agricultural sector and of industrial goods consumed by the farmers are artificially raised, while the prices of agricultural products are lowered, and consequently, agriculture's profits decline. Even the enforcement of low interest rates for the loans made by credit institutions works to the detriment of agriculture, and of small farmers in particular: the agricultural sector receives only a small proportion of these loans, and within this sector, almost all the institutional loans go to large farmers.

Aware of the disadvantages that these artificial price modifications entail for farmers, governments sometimes try to compensate for them by subsidizing certain agricultural inputs, such as fertilizers, water, and seeds. But these measures often lead to a considerable drain on the government budget at the expense of other, more productive investments. Moreover, the advantages thus given are generally monopolized by the big landowners and seldom reach the other farmers.

The first and perhaps most effective measure that should be taken by governments wishing to encourage agriculture would therefore be to review and modify the complex system of economic policies determining prices — and thus economic incentives — in the various economic sectors. Policies aiming to keep prices low in the food production sector are often defended as necessary to maintain an adequate consumption level for the poorest; it is sometimes added that high prices would only benefit the large farmers and worsen the situation of the landless workers.[29] These arguments are certainly serious and cannot be swept aside offhandedly.[30] Yet objective, case-by-case surveys often show that this type of problem is of a more limited nature than is often believed.[31] Moreover, the food ration programs which already exist in many developing countries could be markedly improved in many instances without increasing their cost so as to reach the poor more effectively and thereby reduce the impact that an increase in food prices would have on these classes.[32]

In most Third World countries, the share of public investment and recurrent expenditures going to agriculture is considerably less than the proportion of the active population depending on this sector. Generally, this share is even lower than the percentage of total production coming from this economic sector. In the Asian countries, for instance, agriculture receives on average about 20 percent of public investment, yet about 60 percent of the active population depend upon agriculture, and the share of this sector in total production is around 40 percent. The share of public investment going to the agricultural sector appears equally inadequate if we use as a criterion the productivity of the invested capital.[33] In fact, the low level of public investment in agriculture is probably the most telling indicator of the prourban and proindustrial bias of most Third World governments.

In most developing countries, because of budgetary limitations and administrative restrictions, the salaries and conditions offered to civil servants in the agricultural services are inadequate to attract and keep the quality personnel required. These civil servants are in fact generally less well paid than those in the general administrative service or even in the other technical departments. Moreover, hardship allowances for out-of-town assignments are low or nonexistent, while equipment and transport are also inadequate. As a result, the best agricultural civil servants try to join other services or the private sector; those who remain try to obtain an assignment in a large town, and those who have been unable to avoid an assignment to a rural post use their lack of equipment and transport as a pretext for limiting their work load. The modification of this state of affairs should be a priority for governments; in particular, a revision of the salary scale in the public services should aim at making agricultural services more rewarding and prestigious, in keeping with the importance of this sector for the development of these countries.

Within the agricultural sector, the distribution of public expenditures has generally tended to favor investments which are immediately profitable and politically appealing, to the detriment of long-term programs, whose financial and political gains appear doubtful to the governments. Thus, generally speaking, irrigation has been preferred to research, extension, reforestation, or soil conservation programs. In the early seventies, for instance, irrigation received 80 percent of the public investment financing in the agricultural sector in Thailand; in India and Pakistan the proportion was as high as 95 percent.

Agricultural research, a long-term investment par excellence, has been systematically neglected. Yet the history of the Green Revolution has shown that this activity could lead to spectacular – and profitable – results. The surveys that have been carried out also confirm that the economic profitability of agricultural research can be very high. In Mexico, the agricultural research carried out from 1943 to 1963 resulted in an annual rate of return of 290 percent; for the research in wheat alone this rate even reached 750 percent.[34] In spite of this, as we have seen, research efforts remain restricted to a small number of plants and crop types. Furthermore, while international organizations and aid donors have considerably increased their efforts in this area, most developing countries still do not give sufficient priority to this activity. In 1975, for instance, these countries devoted to research only 0.3 percent of the income they had drawn from agriculture (in the developed countries the corresponding percentage was 1 percent). For the whole world, only 3 percent of research expenditure goes to agriculture, and 90 percent of this amount is spent on the agricultural problems of temperate regions. The inadequacy of these efforts is probably the most serious threat to the long-term prospects for agricultural growth – and, consequently, for economic development – in the Third World.

Agricultural extension is another area which has been too often neglected. Lacking personnel, transport, and equipment, the departments in charge generally content themselves with routine visits to a restricted number of farmers. The absence of any link between agricultural extension and research and the inadequate training of the extension agents rapidly result in these agents' advice losing all novelty and interest for the farmers. Yet in all countries there is a significant gap between the results obtained by the research stations – and even by the best farmers – and the achievements of the average farmers; here there is a reservoir of agricultural technologies not yet used by most farmers that the extension services could disseminate. The creation of such an effective link between farmers and research workers would have the additional advantage of enabling researchers to understand better the problems encountered by the farmers and, consequently, to orient their research programs in an appropriate manner. Several developing countries have shown that extension services can function effectively and serve as a link between research and farmers. In fact, in many instances, a simple restructuring accompanied by a minimum of additional expenditures has led to spectacular results in the farmers' fields.[35]

Finally, forest departments and soil conservation services are tragically inadequate in the vast majority of the developing countries. Very few countries are free from the ills of deforestation and soil deterioration, but governments are rarely aware of the full extent of these problems. The will to act is even rarer. After all, afforestation or soil conservation programs would not yield any immediately visible benefit, and there is therefore nothing in them to attract a government, even if it is not subject to the periodic pressure of genuine elections. We saw in Chapters 6 and 7 that in any event such programs are difficult to implement and that it is not always easy to enlist the cooperation of the beneficiaries. In these circumstances it is not surprising that, in the absence of governmental determination, the implementation of these programs has encountered so many problems. Yet in the vast majority of Third World countries there are forests and soils which are already reaching a point of no return, if they have not already passed it. Haiti and Nepal are not the only countries threatened by ecological disaster; a delay of a few decades, even of a few years, could be fatal. It is now that the governments of these countries should launch their counteroffensives.

The above few points do not cover, of course, all the orientations of an agricultural policy. There would be much to say with regard to credit, marketing, equipment, and input supply and the administration and planning of this sector. I shall return to some of these topics in the following chapter when I discuss programs specifically oriented toward the small farmers.

In the first half of the seventies a series of poor harvests in South Asia, the Sahel, and the U.S.S.R. brought about a worldwide food crisis. This led several developing countries to conclude that the Green Revolution and the American grain surpluses might not always be at hand to save them in case of difficulty and that it was time to give more emphasis to their food production. Agricultural and rural development was consequently promoted to the rank of development "priorities," and international organizations hastened to propagate the new orthodoxy.

If the alarm sounded in 1973-1974 remains the only basis for these new priorities, however, it is to be feared that they will not last for long. Governments have short memories, in the South as in the North. The food crisis no longer makes headlines, and worries about the slowdown in growth may well renew the popularity of the "fast-growing" sectors — such as industry. As for the economists and development specialists, they could not, without ennui, repeat the same themes for long: a minimum of two to three fashions per decade is apparently necessary to keep the profession awake. In turn, basic needs have now presumably dethroned rural development, and at times, one feels that even this new theme is beginning to wear thin.

Yet there are other, more fundamental reasons for giving greater priority to the development of the agricultural sector. The economic history of the now-developed countries and of the most advanced developing countries enables us to see that agriculture has played a prime role in the success of the industrialization process; by contrast, many other examples show that neglect of the agricultural sector has compromised the development programs of a great number of countries.

But history does not repeat itself, and the Third World pursues its development efforts today in circumstances very different from those which confronted the now-developed countries when they began their industrialization. Perhaps the main difference is the rapid population growth in the developing countries, which is without parallel in the past experience of the developed countries. In the coming years, the most dramatic manifestations of this population explosion will be an unprecedented increase in food deficits, as well as a rapid surge in the labor force, at a rate which industry will never be able to absorb. These two factors only reinforce the argument for giving greater priority to the agricultural sector. More than a passing fad or an obedient — and self-serving — response to the whims of aid donors, this new orientation must signify a profound change in the development strategies of the Third World. Only when this priority is translated into action — through revisions in budget expenditures and price structures, for instance — will it become a concrete reality rather than a mere intention.

11
DEVELOPING THE PRODUCTIVE CAPACITY OF THE POOREST

The experience of three decades has shown that economic growth did not always suffice to ease the burden of poverty. Statistical evidence has challenged the idea of an automatic diffusion of the profits of growth toward the poorest strata. Because most of the poor live in the rural areas and earn their living from agriculture, a reorientation of development strategies in favor of this sector could lead to an improvement in their living conditions. Yet in this instance, too, there is nothing automatic about such an improvement. Examples as different as those of the Philippines and El Salvador show that rapid agricultural growth may very well be accompanied by impoverishment of the rural poor.[1] Beyond a modification in sectoral priorities, what is actually required is a change in the pattern of growth and the distribution of its benefits.

There is a risk that strategies of the basic needs type, however well-intentioned they may be, could lead to contradictions in policies or stoppages of development if the objective of economic growth is forgotten. The only way to reconcile the imperative of growth with the necessity of improving the living conditions of the poorest is to use and develop the productive capacity of these destitute people. Moreover, since the vast majority of the poor live in the rural areas, this effort should begin in the countryside.

In many countries of Asia and Latin America, land reform is the prerequisite of an improvement in the incomes and living conditions of the poorest. This reform should be accompanied by policies to organize small farmers and support their productive efforts. In addition, implementation of rural works on a wide scale could supply employment and income to the unemployed in the countryside. Finally, industrialization strategies should be revised to promote more effectively the creation of employment and the development of small firms.

LAND REFORM

The history of the last thirty years has shown that in countries where land resources are limited, improvement in the rural poor's living conditions will not be possible unless the land is distributed in a relatively egalitarian manner. In China, Taiwan, and South Korea, for instance, an initial land reform subsequently permitted an exceptional improvement in the economic situation of the poorest, while in Brazil, India, and the Philippines, where land structures are quite inegalitarian, small farmers and landless workers have experienced stagnation or even deterioration in their situation.

The advocates of land reform have generally defended their cause on grounds of equity and social justice. However fundamental this aspect of the problem, it tends to conceal other equally important considerations. As a survey by the Asian Development Bank notes:

> Some of these problems [encountered during the implementation of land reforms] exist because, even among those policy makers who are sympathetic to the idea of land reform, it tends to be regarded mainly as a means of securing social justice. With increased production being given first priority in development plans, a "social justice program" does not receive adequate attention and less care is given to implementing and monitoring it. In contrast with the attention given to recent developments in technology, the potential gains from land reform in terms of augmenting production are not well appreciated. This is partly because the economic research attendant on various land reform measures has only recently attained a depth and rigor comparable to, for example, that accompanying the release of new high-yielding crop varieties. While the potential dislocations due to land reform are readily apparent, the fact that it can simultaneously promote the productivity and employment goals of the development is not so widely recognized.[2]

Until recently, in fact, the traditional view of economists was that, on the whole, the consequences of land reform on economic development were negative. Their opinion was very often based on the idea that large farms generally obtained better results than small ones in the areas of production, savings, or the production of a marketable surplus — an idea which is, however, theoretical and rarely justified by facts.[3] To the extent that this opinion is still widely held and frequently underlies the arguments against land reform, it deserves to be examined more closely. If we attempt to compare small and large farms from the standpoint of economic development, four aspects are particularly important: production per acre,

TABLE 11.1   Agricultural Output by Farm Size in Latin America

Country	Year	(1) Smallest subfamily farms	(2) Largest multifamily farms	(3) Ratio of col. 1 to col. 2
		National monetary unit per agricultural hectare		
Argentina	1960	2,492	304	8.20
Brazil	1950	1,498	170	8.80
Chile	1955	334	41	8.20
Colombia	1960	1,198	84	14.30
Ecuador	1954	1,862	660	2.80
Guatemala	1950	63	16	3.90
		National monetary unit per worker		
Argentina	1960	40	192	0.21
Brazil	1950	1,197	8,237	0.14
Chile	1955	268	1,171	0.23
Colombia	1960	972	9,673	0.10
Guatemala	1950	74	523	0.14

SOURCE: Barraclough and Collarte, *Agrarian Structure in Latin America,* a resume of the CIDA Land Tenure Studies of Argentina, Brazil, Chile, Colombia, Ecuador, Guatemala, Peru, Studies in the Economic and Social Development of Latin America (Lexington, Mass.: Lexington Books, 1973).

employment, savings and investment, and the volume of marketed surplus.

Numerous surveys tend to prove that, contrary to preconceived ideas, productivity per acre is often higher on small than on big farms. Comparisons of various countries by the Food and Agriculture Organization (FAO) of the United Nations and the World Bank have shown that a smaller average size of landholdings and a lesser concentration of land ownership are generally accompanied by higher production per acre. This indication is confirmed by comparisons, within particular countries, of the production by farms of different sizes. In central Thailand, paddy yields decrease from 765 kilograms per acre for farms having between 2 and 6 acres, to 485 kilograms per acre for farms of 140 acres and more. In the Philippines, yields vary from 2.9 tons of paddy per hectare for holdings of less than 2 hectares, to 2.2 tons for farms of more than 4 hectares. A systematic analysis of the differences between small and large farms in six Latin American countries shows that, on average, the value of production per hectare is from three to fourteen times higher on the small than on the large farms (see Table 11.1). In these circumstances, it can be expected that, all else being equal, land redistribution would lead to an increase in agricultural production.[4]

Likewise, statistical data consistently show that employment per unit of area is higher on the small than on the large farms. Thus a survey of a district in the Indian state of Punjab shows that in 1968 employment per acre ranged from 33 to 39 man-days on the farms of fewer than 30 acres, and from 20 to 23 on the bigger farms. The number of workers per hectare is thirty to sixty times higher on the small farms than on the big ones in Argentina, Brazil, Chile, and Guatemala. In Colombia in 1960 this number declined steadily from 2.7 man-years on holdings of less than 0.5 hectares, to 0.17 man-years on farms of 500 to 1,000 hectares. It is in fact because they use more labor (essentially family labor) per acre that the small farms produce more per unit of land.

It is often argued that since small farmers have a savings rate inferior to that of larger farmers, land redistribution in favor of the former would have negative consequences on the total volume of savings and therefore on investment. In fact, both the premise and the conclusion of this argument are questionable. In the first place, while the *average* savings rate is indeed lower among the small farmers, the variable which we must consider here is not the average but the *marginal* savings rate, and there does not appear to be a marked difference in this rate according to farm size.[5] Furthermore, as we saw in Chapter 9, for people living on the edge of survival, the distinction between consumption and investment is not very clear; "consumption" expenditure can, for instance, improve the health, and therefore the productivity, of small farmers and agricultural workers. Finally, even if it were true that small farmers have a lower marginal savings rate, it is still possible that this would be compensated for by the fact that their production — and therefore their income — per acre is higher. Land transfer from the large to the small farmers will bring about an increase in the latter's income which will be higher than the fall in the former's income. In these circumstances, the increase in savings of the small farmers may also be higher than the decrease in savings of the big ones (even though the small farmers' marginal savings rate is lower than the large farmers'): if this is the case, it would imply an increase in the total savings of all farmers.[6] In this respect, it is interesting to note that, in China, land reform was accompanied by a rapid increase in the consumption of most farmers as well as in their savings and investments.[7]

An argument similar to the one above concerning savings could be developed with regard to the impact that land reform would have on farmers' marketed surplus. Traditionally it has been said that since the large farmers sell a larger proportion of their crops, a redistribution of land in favor of the small farmers would lead to a decline in the marketed surplus. This argument, however, implies that land reform would not affect the volume of total production; yet we have seen that we could expect a marked production increase from such a reform. Under such circumstances, the impact on the marketed surplus would not necessarily be negative; it would in fact depend on the extent to which this reform would actually increase total production.

It can be seen then that, from an economic standpoint, it is far from certain that the consequences of land reform will be harmful. The impact of such a reform on savings, investment, or the marketed surplus need not be negative and could even be positive; moreover, it is likely that this reform would increase production and employment.

There is, however, another aspect of land reform — perhaps the most important one — which cannot be couched simply in economic terms. This is the question of its consequences on the sociopolitical system in the villages and rural areas. This system is still of a feudal type in several areas in Asia and Latin America, where the condition of the farm laborers is very similar to serfdom. Over the past centuries, colonization and the multiplication of the links connecting these countries to the world economy has brought about the progressive integration of many of these landholdings into the market economy. This has, in turn, caused a transformation of the socioeconomic structure, with large commercial estates gradually replacing feudal farms as the dominant landholdings. Yet this change has brought little improvement in the workers' situation; they remain as dependent today on the estate management as they were yesterday on their feudal landlord. In either case, they are at the total mercy of their "masters" for their jobs, incomes, food supplies, or credit; even sending their children to school or marrying their daughters may depend on the financial goodwill of these all-powerful beings. This static system, where social or economic mobility remains virtually impossible, has the same stifling effect on economic development that a similar system had in Europe during the Middle Ages. By eliminating a system of profoundly conservative political and social constraints, land reform will thus permit the liberation of potentially productive forces, a prerequisite of any economic development.

We may conclude from the above that the effects of land reform on economic growth can, on the whole, be positive. A great deal will depend on the social and political circumstances in which this reform is carried out and on the accompanying programs to organize and support the beneficiaries. The experiences of various countries confirm that, if such programs are carried out effectively, land reform can have a beneficial effect on long-term economic development. This is in fact the conclusion reached, in numerous studies, for several Asian countries where such reforms have been implemented: Japan, South Korea, mainland China, Taiwan. To a lesser extent, it also seems to be true in Latin America for Bolivia, Chile, Mexico, and Venezuela.[8] In all cases the result has also been an improvement in income distribution and a lessening of the differences among social categories. A sufficient number of examples therefore exist today to show that the objective of production and economic growth is not necessarily incompatible with the goal of social justice and that well-managed land reform can lead to the attainment of both.

ORGANIZING THE SMALL FARMERS

As we have seen, in the countries where land distribution is extremely inegalitarian, it would be vain to hope for a real reduction in rural poverty in the absence of land reform; yet land reform will be insufficient if it is not accompanied by measures to organize and assist the beneficiaries.

In the vast majority of countries, a host of social, administrative, and especially political reasons have prevented the smallest farmers from benefiting as much as others from agricultural extension and credit programs; these farmers have also encountered greater difficulties in obtaining the inputs (including water) required for their crops and in marketing their products. Indeed, the government programs set up to help them have very often been appropriated by the large farmers.

In most developing countries, extension agents are too few to be able to look after all the farmers in their area. In the developed countries the number of farmers per extension agent averages about 400; in the developing countries this number is about twenty times higher. In these circumstances it is not surprising that agents confine their activities to a restricted number of farmers; neither is it surprising that the privileged ones are invariably large landowners. Larger farmers are generally easier to reach; they also have the influence and the financial means required to secure the services of an adviser;[9] moreover, the results of the advice given will be more visible on the large than on the small farms. Furthermore, the advice of the research and extension services is often based on optimal conditions (implying, for instance, good water control as well as access to the necessary inputs and credit): these conditions are closer to the actual situation of the big farmers than to that of the small ones.

Small farmers have only very limited access to institutional credit. In the first place, most of this credit goes to the urban areas: in India, for instance, less than 25 percent of the institutional credit is distributed in the rural areas; in Thailand, the Philippines, and Mexico the corresponding percentage is below 15 percent; and it is less than 10 percent for Iran and Bangladesh. And then of course only a very small share of the institutional credit given in the rural areas is used by small farmers. Banks and credit cooperatives have only limited confidence in them: their holdings are too small to offer sufficient collateral, and they always function on the border of survival. Moreover, the costs of administration and supervision are higher for small loans than for big ones; for a banker it is more profitable to concentrate his operations on a small number of large clients. The credit cooperatives are generally under the sway of big landowners, who make certain that they will be the first to benefit from loans, while forgetting, at times, to repay them later. Although small farmers are generally considered credit risks, it has often been noted that their recovery rate is higher than that of the big landowners. The latter know, in fact, that, because of their social importance and political influence, they are very unlikely to be harassed in case of default.

Even the programs of credit on concessional terms specifically intended for the small farmers are often appropriated by the richer ones. In these circumstances, small farmers often have no recourse except to family loans (if they are available) and credit from a usurer (who is often a rich landowner himself). In this regard, government policies of subsidizing credit to the small farmers do not seem to be the best way of helping them. Very often, in fact, the profitability of agricultural operations would enable these farmers to reimburse their loans at unsubsidized rates. Instead of subsidy programs — which are unnecessary for the small holders and will in fact mostly benefit the big landowners — it would be preferable to increase the amount of institutional credit put at the disposal of these small producers.

Because they cannot get the credit they need, small farmers find it difficult to obtain the inputs and agricultural equipment they require: fertilizer, insecticide, seeds, irrigation pumps. On the whole, these farmers spend less than 20 percent of the amount necessary on these inputs, simply because they lack the financial resources. In Asia, for instance, the cost of the fertilizers and insecticides required for the utilization of high-yield varieties of wheat and rice amounts to some $20 to $80 per hectare; as an average, small farmers spend only $6. And most of the latter sum does not come from institutional loans, but from some local usurer.

Furthermore, when these inputs and farm machinery are supplied at prices set by government organizations, the influence of the large farmers enables them to be served first in case of scarcity. As in the case of credit, these farmers often misappropriate government supplies of subsidized seeds and fertilizers, even though these supplies are generally intended for the small holders.

The small farms are less likely to have irrigation facilities. One reason is that small farmers do not generally have the political weight that big landowners can wield to obtain the desired site for dams or irrigation channels. In addition, the irrigation of many small farms from the same source raises organizational problems which are more complicated than in the case of a single big farm. Laying out the channels, distributing the water, or dividing the operating costs will always create friction when some twenty farms share the water from the same deep tube well; when only one large holding is concerned, all these questions are settled more easily.

Finally, small farmers face serious handicaps with regard to the marketing of their products. Because of their limited financial resources, they cannot afford to hold onto their crops to take advantage of a favorable evolution in prices, and they are obliged to sell them soon after harvest, at the time when prices are at their lowest. Also, because of lack of transport, they cannot sell their products directly to the nearby town (where prices are generally higher); instead, they have to use the costly services of an intermediary.

Only too often, government efforts to increase the production of small farmers have met with little success. The usual programs of support to agriculture have primarily benefited the large landholdings; even the specific programs for small farmers have been misappropriated to the advantage of the richer cultivators. Experience has shown that whatever the initial success of cooperatives — a success often due to the dedication and dynamism of a few pioneers — it is difficult to avoid such distortion in the end. In Bangladesh, for instance (or rather in East Pakistan, as it was called at the time), the efforts of the Rural Development Academy led to an improvement in the sixties in the incomes and living conditions of the small farmers in the Comilla region. When this program was taken up again at the national level in the seventies, it nevertheless met with numerous difficulties, and its benefits were often misappropriated by the big farmers. As we have seen, the extremely skewed land distribution which exists in many developing countries is in fact nothing but the most visible sign of a profoundly inegalitarian sociopolitical system. In these circumstances it is presumably naive to hope that rural development programs and government efforts to improve the living conditions of the poorest farmers will have much effect on their situation.

Where these structures are relatively egalitarian, however, the organization of farmers into cooperatives or associations can be an effective tool for economic and social improvement. China probably presents the most impressive achievement in this area. The organization of the farmers was carried out in stages: cooperatives, "advanced" cooperatives or collectives, then, during the "Great Leap Forward," transformation of the latter into communes. Today there are some 50,000 communes, which are organized on three levels: the production team (about thirty-three families), the brigade (comprising six to seven teams), and the commune (made up of about fifteen brigades). The brigades play an essential role in this organization because they supply the work teams with a great number of services: credit, delivery of agricultural inputs, marketing of the products, and primary education and health, for instance.[10] In South Korea, agricultural cooperatives, to which 90 percent of the farmers belong, play a fundamental role in extension and credit. The success of Taiwan in the agricultural sector is due largely to its farmers' associations, which provide their members with many services. From 1950 to 1970, the 900,000

Taiwanese farms of less than one hectare increased their production more rapidly than the whole agricultural sector (though the latter grew at the high rate of 5 percent per year on average).

These various experiences in very different political contexts show that the organization of small farmers can be an effective tool for rural development when the agrarian, political, and social structures are relatively egalitarian. The best-adapted forms of organization (communes, cooperatives, associations) will no doubt vary from country to country, and we cannot define a universal model. But these examples show that solutions are possible and have already been implemented.

RURAL WORKS

The organization of small farmers to develop their productive capacity will not be sufficient to improve notably the lot of landless agricultural workers or the poorest of these small cultivators (those whose holding is in any case too small to assure them a living). Of course, overall growth of agriculture should create additional employment within and without the agricultural sector, but generally these new jobs will not be sufficient to absorb the growing number of landless workers and marginal farmers.

The problem of landless rural workers is found in all the regions of the Third World. In fact, a growing body of evidence indicates that, in many countries, their number — and even their proportion in the rural population — has probably increased during recent decades. Thus, in Latin America, the number of agricultural workers apparently increased during the sixties (in Brazil, Panama, Costa Rica, and Haiti, among others), while the average size of small farms decreased in several countries (see Table 8.4). Similarly, the proportion of wage earners in the agricultural labor force (which is itself growing) increased over the last few years in Morocco and Egypt. The less ambiguous data, however, concern Asia, where various studies agree in concluding that the proportion of landless workers in the active rural population has increased in several countries, such as Bangladesh, India, and Indonesia (see Chaper 2).[11]

This situation can only worsen during the coming years because of the foreseeable increase in the rural labor force (see Chapter 10). In these circumstances, growth in the agricultural sector will not in itself be sufficient to improve the employment situation and the incomes of these landless workers — no more than economic growth alone sufficed to improve the lot of the poorest in the fifties and sixties. In both cases, direct action will in fact be necessary.

The first measure, of course, should be a land reform to give these landless workers and marginal farmers a plot big enough for them to earn a minimum income. In certain countries, however, this measure would not be sufficient, since, even if all the cultivable land were redistributed equally among the active rural population, the size of the holdings would be too small to yield the minimum required for a family to survive. Thus, the average arable area per rural dweller is 0.22 hectare in Nepal, 0.16 in Bangladesh, 0.10 in Haiti — less than in a country like Japan (0.26 hectare), which is considered a country of small farms.[12] And, of course, population growth is not going to improve matters. In these countries, it is clear that agriculture alone will be unable to provide full employment and adequate incomes to the whole population; to this end other activities will be necessary. Similarly, in many other countries, nonagricultural activities will be required to improve the incomes of the poorest and diversify the economy of the rural areas. The main occupations that can be envisaged are the development of small industries (which I shall discuss in the last section of this chapter) and the implementation of rural works programs.

In the vast majority of the developing countries, past experiences with rural works have not been very encouraging, and their contribution to employment creation and economic development has remained very limited. Yet these mediocre results are primarily the consequence of the improvised manner in which rural works have been planned and implemented. As the World Bank stated in a study of these activities, "The most frequent use of public works programs is as a response to crises, economic fluctuations, seasonal unemployment or sustained open unemployment. They have generally been planned and implemented in isolation, not as a part of a broader strategy to attack fundamental problems." [13] This is particularly true in South Asia, where rural works programs are frequently launched without preparation when inadequate harvests make it necessary to distribute food and create additional jobs to assist the famine-stricken rural population.

Under such rural works programs, the implementation of projects has rarely been accompanied by complementary development actions to bring about the full use of the investments put in place. For instance, roads have been built to supply rural markets, but no simultaneous program to help the farmers increase their production has been launched; schools have been built which do not get any teachers; health care centers have been set up and left without medicine. Furthermore, these projects are in general insufficiently prepared. In the hurry to create jobs in response to a crisis, officials implement projects that fail to meet desirable standards of technical quality and economic profitability. Finally, the vast majority of the programs have been concerned exclusively with immediate execution of the project and have totally neglected its maintenance in the course of the following years. The benefits of several months or years of work can thus be rapidly lost when the irrigation channels become obstructed, the soil conservation structures collapse, and the dead trees are not replaced in the reforested areas.

Such negligence is all the more regrettable because maintenance could be a significant source of employment. In the definition and implementation of rural works programs, unfortunately, only the jobs created during the construction period are generally taken into account; no thought is given to the employment that could be supplied later by the maintenance and operation of the investments. Yet maintenance activities generally have a higher labor intensity than those related to construction. In addition, they require a smaller number of skilled personnel (technicians or foremen) and, consequently, are easier to carry out. Similarly, the directly productive projects (irrigation, drainage, fishing) can have a substantial impact on employment during the operational phase. In Indonesia and Bangladesh, for instance, the reconstruction of irrigation and drainage structures has led to the creation, every year during the operational phase, of twice as many jobs as were created altogether during the whole investment period. Moreover, the types of projects, designs, and technologies selected for these works are not always the most appropriate — contrary to what is usually believed — for programs whose main objectives include the creation of jobs. A survey of the programs carried out in different countries shows that the share of the wage bill in total expenditures varies a great deal (from 16 percent in Bangladesh to 70 to 75 percent in South Korea), indicating that, with adequate preparation, there is substantial opportunity to select programs permitting the creation of a greater number of jobs.

Finally, the benefits of these rural works have been distributed very unequally. In fact, certain surveys have shown that landowners benefited from these programs at least three times more than workers.[14] Furthermore, among these landowners themselves, it is often the richest who have obtained the greatest advantages. Because the big farmers have a larger share of cultivable land at their disposal, they would benefit more than the small landowners even if the selection of the areas to be developed were made in a "neutral" manner. In fact, by using their political influence, large farmers make sure that this selection is anything but neutral and that the choice of beneficiaries is not left to chance.

The very fact that these benefits are so unequally distributed harms the productivity of rural works. It is difficult to win the enthusiastic cooperation of workers when they are well aware that the big landowners will be the first to profit from their efforts. In this respect an incident which occurred several years ago in Ethiopia is particularly instructive. A reforestation program had been launched to control soil erosion and to meet local wood requirements; the plantation work had been entrusted to some destitute groups (mostly landless workers), to whom seedlings had been distributed. The program apparently started without any major problem, but when supervisors later visited the project area, they discovered that in many places the trees had been planted upside down! The workers, of course, knew the roots from the branches, but they knew equally well that the big landowners were going to be the main beneficiaries of their work. In their own way, these poor laborers were showing their lack of enthusiasm at the idea of working for the betterment of these wealthy farmers.[15]

This anecdote also demonstrates the importance of enlisting the active cooperation of the local people. Too often well-meaning programs have not yielded the expected results because the administration responsible for carrying them out had been unable to obtain the participation and support of the beneficiaries. An effective decentralization of the programs will be necessary, so that the people concerned can participate in the projects, not only at the implementation stage but also at the time of selection and definition of the investments. Such participation will also make maintenance easier after the completion of the investments.

In spite of past failures, the experiences of several countries show that rural works programs can be instrumental in creating new employment and productive investments, and in improving the incomes of the poorest. But governments cannot use these programs as an easy alternative to land reform. We have seen how, in the absence of a relatively egalitarian land structure, large farmers will always be the first to benefit from rural works; to this extent these programs will in fact reinforce the inequality of the socioeconomic system. Furthermore, in such a situation, even the productivity of these works could be reduced for lack of cooperation on the part of most people. Genuine land reform is in fact a prerequisite of rural campaigns, since it will largely determine the effectiveness of these rural works programs with regard to productivity as well as social justice.

In addition, as we have seen, governments need to change their conceptions radically and consider these rural works campaigns as one element of an overall rural development strategy. This will require that these programs be prepared in conjunction with the other components of this strategy: assistance to production, supply of agricultural inputs, marketing support, deployment of the needed personnel in the health and education services, and so on. The projects to be undertaken in the context of these programs should be carefully studied and prepared. This would imply in particular that the studies required are carried out sufficiently in advance. In the case of the South Asian countries, which are periodically confronted with famine, it should be possible to start preparing immediately the studies and designs for projects to be carried out during the next crisis — a crisis whose eventual occurrence is only too certain.

A serious effort with regard to rural works programs would also require a marked increased in their financing. In most countries, average annual expenditures for these programs do not reach 1 percent of GNP; in South Asia, where these rural works are particularly necessary, this percentage is generally below 0.5 percent.[16] In fact, the Asian Development Bank estimates that during the next decade, the countries of this region should devote 1 to 2 percent of their national income to rural works.

China probably supplies us with the best evidence that rural works programs can lead simultaneously to a substantial increase in employment, the development of infrastructure, and the creation of productive investments. Since the beginning of the sixties, large-scale public works campaigns have become a characteristic of rural life in the winter. While the construction of big dams has particularly caught the attention of foreign observers, a wide range of activities are in fact covered: afforestation, irrigation, flood control, construction of hydroelectric stations, well drilling, land leveling, construction of earthwork terraces, restoration of arable land. The number of jobs created has been exceptionally large: in recent years, about 100 million people, one-quarter of the agricultural labor force, have participated each winter in these rural works campaigns. If we rate rural works programs by the number of working days created per person in the labor force, these programs can be said to have been three times more effective in China than in South Korea or Morocco, and ten times more so than in India or Bangladesh.[17] Their total contribution to employment was comparable or superior to that of the industries located in the rural areas, a result which is all the more remarkable since rural industrialization has been more successful in China than in most developing countries.[18] Moreover, the investments thereby created are, on the whole, carefully selected and contribute effectively to the economic and social development of the country.

A MORE APPROPRIATE PATTERN OF INDUSTRIALIZATION

We have so far mostly considered the problems of agriculture and the rural sector, mainly because these sectors constitute the economic bases of the poorest developing countries and because their importance for the development of these countries has often been underestimated. This does not mean of course that the Third World countries should neglect the other economic sectors; in this regard, the role of industry will always be vital in the development process.

The industrialization policies implemented in most countries have had only a limited impact on the employment and living conditions of the population. As we saw in the previous chapter, this is due to the rapid growth of the total labor force and to the fact that the industrial base was initially too small. A further reason is the fact that generally the patterns of industrial development followed have not been those most adapted to the conditions of the developing countries. Three frequent orientations have been counterproductive. First, the policies of these countries have usually been biased in favor of capital-intensive, labor-saving technologies. Second, industrial policies have favored large firms to the detriment of small enterprises and artisans. Finally, the potential of industrialization in rural areas has been largely neglected.

One does not have to be an economist to understand that in a developing country — characterized by abundance of labor and scarcity of capital — the most appropriate technologies will use many workers and little equipment. Yet it is only recently that economists have become interested in this problem. In fact, until a few years ago, many specialists still believed that the possibilities of alternative technologies were very limited and that, consequently, the selection of different techniques better adapted to the specific conditions of these countries was hardly possible. [19]

This view is widely rejected today, however; there is a considerable amount of evidence to show that, for many production processes, such alternatives do indeed exist. [20] For instance, the World Bank notes that "engineering and process analysis studies of a limited number of industries show that factor substitutability does seem to be quite possible, and the differences in factor ratios can be quite substantial." [21] A recent publication of the United Nations Industrial Development Organization (UNIDO) lists more than one hundred technologies developed by research institutes in developing countries; [22] even for the production of urea and ammonia — the very archetype of a capital-intensive industry — certain possibilities for substitution seem to exist. Econometric studies measuring the elasticity of substitution between labor and capital confirm this view; this elasticity is in general relatively high, indicating a significant potential for substitution. [23]

In view of the above, one might expect that in countries with a large labor force, labor-intensive techniques would be automatically preferred. In fact, however, capital-intensive technologies are usually adopted. In practice a host of factors conspire to discourage the selection of more appropriate technologies. Among the most important of these factors are the following facts:

— The cost of capital is often lower than its "opportunity cost." For instance, imports of capital goods generally benefit from preferential exchange rates, tariffs, and tax regulations; moreover, the interest rates of the banking institutions are frequently subsidized, thereby encouraging the use of these capital goods.
— In contrast, the cost of labor in the modern sector is generally higher than its opportunity cost (as can be measured by the cost of labor in the traditional sector) because of government or trade union regulations, in particular.
— Entrepreneurs, civil servants, and banks succumb to the prestige of Western technology and are reluctant to try alternatives which are considered inferior.

TABLE 11.2   Production Structure in Japan by Scale of
Manufacturing Enterprise, 1957

Number of employees	Y/L		K/L	
	(¥000)	Index	(¥000)	Index
1–9	192	38	79	31
10–19	272	53	76	30
20–29	315	62	81	32
30–49	347	68	90	35
50–99	420	82	120	47
100–199	489	96	166	65
200–299	566	111	209	81
300–499	695	136	309	120
500–999	784	153	407	158
1,000 +	921	180	624	242
Average	*512*	*100*	*275*	*100*

SOURCE: Katushi Ohkawa and Mutsuo Tajima, *Small to Medium Scale Manufacturing Industry: A Comparative Study of Japan and Developing Nations,* Working Paper series no. A-02 (Tokyo: International Development Center of Japan, March 1976).

— The possible alternatives are not well known by the potential users.
— Suppliers of technology and equipment as well as expatriate consultants propose only the techniques with which they are familiar.
— The assistance of the developed countries is often tied to purchases made in these countries.

In these circumstances, it will no doubt be difficult for a government to implement policies that effectively encourage the use of the most appropriate technologies. Yet various Asian countries – Japan, China, South Korea, Taiwan – have succeeded in promoting the utilization of technologies that are better adapted to these countries' conditions, and the lessons of their experiences should enable other countries to implement similar policies.

The first measure needed would probably be to correct the system of price incentives by modifying, in particular, government policies which artificially lower the price of capital. A significant effort in technological research and, above all, in the education of the potential users will also be required, but it would be a mistake to expect very much from these policies as long as the existing price system makes the choice of the most appropriate technologies financially unprofitable.

The same factors that discourage the selection of capital-saving techniques work against the small firms. These firms are generally less capital-intensive than the big ones, or, to put it differently, the capital per job created is less for the small than for the large firms. Although the studies on this subject are few and relatively recent, they tend to show that the small firms also have a lower value added per worker, a lower wage rate,

Y/K		W/L(= w)		Lw/Y	(Y-Lw)/K(P)	
Ratio	Index	(¥000)	Index	Percent	Ratio	Index
2.43	122	118	61	34.6	1.59	123
3.59	180	132	69	44.9	1.98	153
3.90	196	144	75	43.8	2.19	170
3.85	193	144	75	42.1	2.23	173
3.45	173	156	81	38.1	2.16	167
2.95	148	168	88	35.7	1.90	147
2.70	136	192	100	33.6	1.80	140
2.25	113	204	106	29.9	1.58	122
1.92	96	228	119	29.6	1.35	105
1.48	74	300	156	33.1	0.99	77
1.99	100	192	100	35.1	1.29	100

NOTE: Y = value added; L = employment; K = value of tangible fixed assets (excluding land); W = amount of wages; P = rate of return on capital.

and a higher value added per unit of capital. This can be seen, for instance, in Table 11.2, which presents the results of a survey of Japanese firms. In capital-scarce countries, small firms therefore appear more efficient, to the extent that for the same amount of capital they would produce higher value added and create a larger number of direct jobs. (Even though the lack of reliable statistics precludes any definite statement, it seems that the same holds true of the *total* number of jobs, that is to say, direct plus indirect jobs created by backward and forward linkages.) If we add to this the other advantages of these firms (creation of incomes among under-privileged social categories, formation of a class of small entrepreneurs, possibility of creating new activities in the rural areas), it can be seen that the particular attributes of these enterprises would justify an active government policy in their favor.

Finally, a policy in favor of small firms would complement a development policy aimed at eliminating poverty and increasing the incomes and consumption of the poorest. As can be seen in Table 11.3, the small firms' share in production is particularly high for basic consumption goods (industry groups I and II), and the growth in demand for these goods which would result from an increase in the incomes of the destitute strata would therefore particularly encourage the development of small firms.

Small firms therefore possess many characteristics which should have attracted the planners and industrial policymakers in the developing countries. In fact, however, this subsector has been neglected in the vast major-ity of these countries — in some cases, despite official declarations explic-itly stating its priority. For instance, the Indian government declared in 1956 in an industrial policy resolution: "Then, as now, the government

TABLE 11.3   Share of Small-Scale Production Units in Manufacturing Value Added
of Developing Countries
(percentages)

Industry group[a]	Small units			All units	Group share in total manufacturing value added
	Less than 5 employees	Less than 10 employees	Less than 50 employees		
Industry group I	10.9	16.2	37.2	100.0	43.0
Industry group II	14.8	19.7	38.0	100.0	19.0
Industry group III	6.0	8.7	22.0	100.0	38.0
All groups	7.9	11.2	23.6	100.0	100.0

SOURCE: Based on Ranadev Banerji, "Small-Scale Production Units in Manufacturing: An
International Cross-Section Overview," *Weltwirtschaftliches Archiv* 114, no. 1 (1978).
  [a] Industry group I includes food and beverages, wood, furniture, printing and publishing,
nonmetallic mineral products and diverse industries. Industry group II includes textiles,
clothing, and leather. Industry group III includes paper, rubber, chemicals, petroleum, basic
metals, fabricated metals, nonelectrical machinery, electrical machinery, and transport equipment.

pursued the development of [the small industries] subsector on the basis of
its capacity for creating considerable employment per unit of capital
investment, its potential for reducing inequalities in existing personal and
regional income distribution patterns, and its ability to mobilize otherwise
underutilized scarce resources." [24] Yet in 1970 a special commission called
attention to the objectives that had not been attained and stated that this
subsector "has not been given the position of high priority which should be
its due." [25]

In most countries small establishments are handicapped vis-à-vis big
ones. They often lack access to credit institutions and have to resort to
usurers. They have more difficulty obtaining the permits and licenses
required for their activities, and they are frequently less protected from
foreign competition than large enterprises, which benefit from governmental solicitude. Finally, they lack access to the improved technologies that
would enable them to diversify their production and enlarge their markets.

The implementation of government policies to help small firms would
therefore seem to be doubly justified, by the advantages that these enterprises offer from an economic standpoint and because of the handicaps
they meet in the course of their activities. These policies would require,
first of all, the adaptation of existing institutions so as to improve their
capacity to respond to the needs of these small firms; in certain cases, the
creation of specialized new institutions for this specific purpose should be
considered. An industrial extension service adapted to the particular conditions of small establishments would lead to improvement in their
technical, marketing, and accounting know-how. Other possible measures

include modifying the regulations and practices of government procurement procedures to enable these firms to participate in a market now
generally reserved for large enterprises, and adapting the industrial zones
so they can also be used by small firms.

We should not have any illusions, however, about the facility of such
changes. As a study by the Asian Development Bank concludes:

> In short, the industrial policies, the pattern of development, and administrative
> considerations all combine to favor large industrial firms which thrive in many
> developing countries because of their "economies of scale." But the existence of
> economies of firm size cannot be meaningfully considered in isolation. As
> discussed above, a variety of appropriate technologies already exist in manufac-
> turing activities: thus, the very existence of size economies may depend on
> policy-induced distortions in factor price ratios, the operation of non-price
> rationing systems, the pattern of income distribution, the nature of the industrial
> administrative structure and a host of other considerations. And, of course, the
> momentum of such a complex, interlocking system makes it difficult to effectu-
> ate a major shift toward labor-intensive production.[26]

Thus it will not be easy to correct the existing bias in favor of large firms
and capital-intensive technologies. And it will be even more difficult to
implement policies effectively promoting rural industrialization. Yet this
type of industry presents many advantages. Rural industries are mostly
small; in addition, because of their location in the countryside, they can
supply additional incomes to the rural population, which is, as we know,
particularly destitute. In spite of this, few countries have implemented
rural industry programs, and among these few, those that have met with
some success are even fewer. Yet the examples of China, Japan, South
Korea, and Taiwan show that such policies can be effective, provided they
are well defined and implemented.[27]

In this area, the success of China is undoubtedly the most remarkable.
Industrial employment in the rural areas of this country accounts for 10 to
17 million workers, half the total employment in the manufacturing and
mining industries. The example of this country — and of others that have
succeeded in implementing an effective strategy for industrial development
in rural areas — indicates both the importance and the feasibility of select-
ing technologies suited to local conditions. It also shows that rural industrialization programs must be conceived as elements of an overall development strategy for these areas.

In this context it is worth quoting a passage from a study devoted to this
subject:

> The success of rural industrialization efforts in China has been owing to a
> number of reasons. The encouragement and establishment of rural industries
> have been closely integrated with agricultural improvement and other rural

activities (including the development of infrastructure, training, science and technology development etc.) within a sectoral strategy that entails conscious choices of technology (by scaling down large-scale technology) and of appropriate products, quality and designs to suit local markets. At the same time, the technology of traditional village crafts has been scaled up. The sectoral strategy includes both the development of backward-linkage industries to meet the demand for consumer goods and agricultural inputs, and forward-linkage industries based on local resources. The promotion of small-scale industries in rural areas has not been at the expense of or in competition with the development of medium or large-scale enterprises at appropriate locations. The aim has been to facilitate the eventual development of a balanced industrial structure with the scales of enterprises varying widely.[28]

It would be difficult to overemphasize the necessity of closely integrating the rural industrialization programs with the development strategy of these areas. The failure of these programs has often been due to the neglect of the necessary accompanying measures in the other sectors. In this respect the development of the agricultural sector is essential. As we have seen, this development is important for the success of industrialization programs; it will be even more so for the success of rural industrialization efforts. Thus the size of the local market, which is the main outlet for rural industries, will depend on agricultural production, whose growth will induce backward and forward linkage effects on rural industry. First, the growth of agricultural incomes will bring about an increase in the demand for industrial goods. On average, rural families in poor regions spend 40 to 50 percent of their incomes on the purchase of processed food products, nonfood products, or services; moreover the elasticity of this demand with respect to income seems to be quite high. As a significant proportion of these goods and services is produced in rural areas, the increase in demand will lead to backward linkage effects on the industries in these areas. Second, the growth of agriculture will increase the demand of this sector for inputs from the industrial sector. Apart from fertilizers and heavy agricultural equipment like tractors, these inputs used by the agricultural sector are generally processed locally; this increase in demand will therefore stimulate the production of the rural industries.[29]

Finally, we should note that the extent to which the development of the agricultural sector will stimulate rural industrialization will itself depend on the structure of income distribution. It seems, in fact, that small farmers and landless workers consume more of the relatively unsophisticated products of rural industries than do large farmers, who tend to use more "modern" goods produced by urban or foreign firms instead. To this extent, an agricultural and rural development strategy giving special importance to poor farmers and landless workers would complement and support a policy of rural industrialization.

If one accepts the premise of this book — the necessity of modifying development strategies in order to increase the productive capacity of the poorest — it is fairly easy to deduce the policies required. Land reform to give a plot to each agricultural worker, development efforts specifically oriented toward small farmers, rural works programs, and promotion of labor-intensive industries and of small firms in rural areas would undoubtedly be the main components of such a strategy. The logical coherence of such a proposal may be convincing — or so I hope — yet one important question still remains: does it *really* work?

The fact that several countries have successfully implemented such a strategy is certainly more convincing than any theoretical demonstration. Countries as ideologically different as China and South Korea have recognized the importance of the agricultural sector in the development process, carried out agrarian reforms, actively supported the efforts of their small farmers, increased nonagricultural employment in rural areas, and promoted the use of appropriate industrial technologies. The results have been impressive in both cases, and rapid economic growth has been accompanied by an overall improvement in living conditions.

Strategies similar to those presented here have been successfully carried out by various countries for several decades, and in this sense there is nothing "revolutionary" about the present proposals. Using a different meaning of the word "revolutionary," however, we may wonder whether such a collection of radical measures could in fact be effectively implemented in the absence of violent political change. Programs supporting marginal farmers and small industries would certainly be unpopular with the rich farmers and the industrial bourgeoisie. As for land reform . . .

Indeed, in all the nations which have pursued a strategy similar to the one proposed here (China, South Korea, Taiwan, Japan) the violent chaos of revolution or war preceded the implementation of land reform. Can we hope that a country may one day effectively implement such reform without destruction or violence? The example of most countries in South Asia or Latin America, where the stubborn resistance of the property-owning classes has succeeded in thwarting all government efforts in this direction, makes it look doubtful. Yet the experiences of a few countries — such as Chile in the sixties or Sri Lanka in the seventies — show that agrarian reform can be carried out in a relatively peaceful manner, even if the extent and the results of such reform have not always been at the level of initial hopes.

Of all the policies presented here, land reform would undoubtedly be the most fiercely resisted by a gathering of forces regrouping large farmers, industrialists, and government bureaucrats. In this respect the example of India is presumably representative — and certainly discouraging. In this country, thirty years of — admittedly not very wholehearted —

effort have not succeeded in giving concrete expression to the proclamations of all the successive governments regarding the urgent need for such reform. In these circumstances it might seem preferable to give up these vain efforts and attempt to improve the lot of the poorest by other measures: improvement in contracts between landowners and tenants, rural industrialization, special programs for marginal farmers and landless workers.[30]

Yet I believe that it would be an illusion to hope that the necessity of land reform would be thereby avoided. In the absence of such fundamental restructuring, any alternative policies that are implemented will always be misappropriated to the benefit of the richest groups and will thus prove ineffective. Agricultural development, rural works, and small industries will scarcely improve the lot of the poorest as long as the sociopolitical structure remains inegalitarian. After all (and without being cynical) such policies differ little from those that India has pursued over the last two decades — with results, in the field of social justice and elimination of poverty, that are anything but convincing. Without previous land reform, the benefits of these various programs will continue to end up where they usually have in the past: in the pockets of the rich.

12
TAPPING THE POTENTIAL OF INTERNATIONAL TRADE

International trade is not particularly popular among left-wing economists, especially among those who are interested in the development of the Third World. Thus, some of them believe that exchange between developed and developing countries is bound to be unequal and that trade is one of the main instruments by which "the center" dominates "the periphery." From these premises, they conclude that "the break with the world market is the first condition for development"[1] and that only a "self-reliant" development strategy, on the scale of either a country or an entire region, will be able to satisfy the needs of the vast majority of the people. Frequently, the visions they outline (but rarely describe in detail) of this new development model evoke agrarian reform, rural development, and small industries, and refer profusely to the experience of China.

Whatever my sympathy for a development strategy that would start from the bottom up and give priority to the rural sector, and in spite of my admiration for China's economic development, I do not share the above views concerning the role of international trade in development policies. Foreign trade has already played an important part in the development of many Third World countries, and I believe that it can continue to do so in the coming years. Before I develop this argument, however, I believe it might prove helpful if we step back a little and return to the evolution of trade in the developing countries since World War II.

EXTERNAL TRADE OF THE THIRD WORLD SINCE WORLD WAR II

In the aftermath of World War II, the most eminent economists were extremely skeptical about the possibility of developing countries' using

TABLE 12.1   Composition and Growth Rate of Manufactured Exports
in Developing Countries
(percentages)

	Composition of total exports		Annual growth rate (in volume)
	1960	1975	1970–75
Machinery and transport equipment	7.5	21.9	20.3
Clothing	1.8	17.1	20.3
Textiles	27.8	15.1	17.8
Chemicals	11.9	10.5	16.5
Iron and steel	3.6	4.0	10.7
Other products	47.4	31.4	10.2
All manufactures	100.0	100.0	14.9

SOURCE: Based on World Bank, *World Development Report,* 1978, and idem, "World Trade and Output of Manufactures," Staff Working Paper, January 1979.

profitably the potential of international trade. Back in the fifties, Gunnar Myrdal and Raùl Prebisch were particularly pessimistic in this respect.[2] Even in 1961 Nurkse wrote that "the world's industrial centers in the mid-twentieth century are not 'exporting' their own rate of growth to the primary-producing countries through a corresponding expansion of demand for primary products." He added that for developing countries "industrialization for export markets may encounter . . . difficulties on the supply side" and considered equally serious the obstacles that this type of industrialization would meet on the demand side because of the protectionism of the industrialized countries.[3] Perhaps the manner in which these specialists, twenty years ago, underestimated the potential of international trade should keep us today from being overpessimistic with regard to its future possibilities.

In any event, the developing countries' exports had already started growing rapidly in the fifties, and they further accelerated in the following decade. As we saw in Chapter 1, these exports did not consist exclusively of primary products; they also included manufactured goods, whose progression has been quite remarkable. In 1960, the export value of nonfuel primary products represented almost five times the amount of industrial exports; in 1980 the proportion was approximately one to one, and industrial goods should soon exceed nonfuel primary products. While the Third World is an important exporter of raw materials, it is clear today that it is also more than that.

The rapid growth of manufactured exports has been accompanied by a process of diversification and structural change. The exports of finished products or technically more elaborate goods have experienced higher growth; this is all the more remarkable, since the obstacles due to the lack

TABLE 12.2 Growth Rate and Share of Product Class in Manufactured Exports of Selected Developing Countries
(percentages)

Product class	Annual growth rate 1968-74	Class share in total	
		1968	1974
Intensive in R & D and wages	50.3	0.9	2.1
Intensive in R & D, human and physical capital	34.9	8.2	10.3
Intensive in human and physical capital	36.9	9.4	13.7
Intensive in physical capital	41.4	3.7	5.7
Intensive in unskilled labor	28.0	77.8	68.2

SOURCE: UNIDO, *World Industry since 1960: Progress and Prospects* (New York, 1979).

NOTE: The 17 developing countries and areas are Argentina, Brazil, Egypt, Guadeloupe, Hong Kong, Iran, Libyan Arab Jamahiriya, Pakistan, Philippines, Republic of Korea, Singapore, Sudan, Thailand, Trinidad and Tobago, Tunisia, Turkey, and Venezuela.

of knowledge of markets and marketing structures are particularly formidable for this type of product. As can be seen in Table 12.1, machinery, transport equipment, and clothing, which represented less than 10 percent of the developing countries' manufactured exports in 1960, amounted to almost 40 percent in 1975. Furthermore, within each of the groups of products presented in this table, considerable diversification has taken place, particularly for the product groups which experienced the fastest growth. As a consequence, the number of manufactured products exported by developing countries is much higher today than it was twenty years ago.[4]

This diversification into a gamut of more elaborate products has been accompanied by the development of capital-intensive exports. Contrary to what might have been expected, the fastest-growing exports have not been within the categories of labor-intensive products but within those of capital-intensive goods, whether physical or human capital, or even the capital embodied in research and development (R&D). As can be seen in Table 12.2, labor-intensive products, which made up 78 percent of manufactured exports in 1968, represented only 68 percent of these in 1974.[5]

Linked to this growth of capital-intensive exports was a marked increase in the exports of capital goods. In fact, a study of manufactured exports by final use shows that the exports of this kind of product have increased in recent years about twice as fast as the exports of intermediate or consumer goods. Of course, this phenomenon should be seen in its appropriate context. This rapid growth was made possible only because capital goods still represented a small percentage of the developing countries' exports: 5 percent in 1979, as against 38 percent in the OECD countries. Also, this type of export is presently limited to a small number of countries: in 1979 five countries were responsible for about four-fifths of the developing countries' exports.[6] Nevertheless, the accelerated growth of this category of exports does reflect the general tendency toward a diversification of the exported products into new products which are technologically more sophisticated.

The analysis of the evolution of developing countries' exports in recent decades thus shows the rapidity and dynamism of their growth — rapidity, because these countries' exports have increased at a rate unprecedented in their history; dynamism, because the gamut of exported products has been widely diversified, from primary products toward industrial goods whose demand is growing faster, from labor-intensive products manufactured with a relatively simple technology toward more elaborate, capital-intensive goods. Of course, as we saw in Chapter 1, we should not exaggerate the importance of a phenomenon in which the various developing countries have participated very unequally. But today we must recognize that, far from being the expression of static determinism, the international division of labor corresponds to a dynamic concept and evolves rapidly in the course of time.

The impression of vigor conveyed by the developing countries' trade is further confirmed if we consider the evolution of their manufactured exports during the seventies. Thus in 1975, for instance, while the world recession caused a fall of about 5 percent in the volume of the developed countries' industrial exports, the developing countries' exports experienced a positive — albeit small — change. Between 1970 and 1980, industrial exports of the non-oil developing countries increased in volume almost three times faster than those of the developed countries. In fact, despite significantly slower growth and new protectionist barriers in the industrialized world, the developing countries expanded their manufactured exports more rapidly in the seventies than in the sixties. During the last decade, the volume of this type of export from the middle-income oil importers almost quadrupled; even the low-income oil-importing countries did not fare too badly, since the volume of their manufactured exports increased by 90 percent (Table 12.3).

This rapid growth in the developing countries' industrial exports is all the more surprising considering that, during recent years, many protectionist measures in the developed countries have slowed down imports, especially those from the Third World. This dynamism is only partly explained by the significant increase in the exports of products like electrical and nonelectrical machinery, which are less affected by quantitative restrictions. In fact, even for textiles and clothes, the principal targets of the newly erected protectionist barriers, the volume of exports to the industrialized countries continued to increase rapidly during the last

TABLE 12.3   Manufactured Exports of Oil-Importing Developing Countries, 1970-1980

(in billions of 1970 dollars)

Country group	1970	1980	Percentage change
Low-income countries			
In Africa	0.2	0.2	− 2
In Asia	2.8	5.6	+ 104
Total	3.0	5.8	+ 90
Middle-income countries	11.4	43.1	+ 278
All oil-importing developing countries	14.4	48.9	+ 240
Developed market economies	161.4	303.4	+ 88

SOURCE: Based on World Bank, *World Development Report* (Washington, D.C., 1981).

decade. To quote a World Bank report: "Developing country exports to industrial countries expanded fastest [during the seventies] in those labor-intensive products most subject to trade restrictions. This reflects the large cost differences between industrial and developing countries, which trade barriers were not able to offset. It is also a tribute to the ingenuity of developing country exporters who found ways to meet these administrative requirements and to vary products and markets so as to minimize their impact." [7]

There has also been a significant growth of trade among the developing countries themselves. While the exports of developing countries to other Third World nations still represent only about one-quarter of their total exports, this proportion has tended to increase in recent years. [8] Today, for instance, Brazil trades more with other developing countries than with the United States. The developing countries (South Korea and Taiwan in particular) have been able to obtain a share of the new markets in the oil-exporting countries: from 1973 to 1980 their exports to these markets were multiplied by more than eight (in value). Since 1973, trade in manufactured goods among developing countries has progressed twice as fast as exports from these countries to the developed countries. Between 1973 and 1977 trade among developing countries represented almost 50 percent of the increase in their manufactured exports, as against slightly more than 25 percent in the 1963-1973 period. The development of this "South-South" trade seems to owe more to the commercial dynamism of certain Third World countries and to the new vigor of their industries than to the establishment of preferential regional agreements. [9]

The new dynamism in developing countries' exports, particularly in manufactured exports, is only the expression, at the level of international trade, of the growing industrialization of several Third World countries; far from being a passing phenomenon it is therefore clearly the result of the structural evolution of these countries' economies. The fact that, in recent years, the depressed condition of the world economy and the erection of protectionist barriers have not succeeded in limiting the growth of these exports is yet another indication of Third World industrial vigor. For this reason we can expect that, in the coming years, the industries of the Third World will continue to assert themselves on international markets.

Finally it is worth recalling that Third World industrialization does not represent a threat for the industrialized countries. The rapidly expanding markets of the newly industrializing countries have supplied and will continue to supply new sales opportunities to the industries of the rich countries. The trade balance of industrial products between developed and developing countries shows a growing surplus to the benefit of the former (of $169 billion in 1980). In addition, numerous studies have shown that the trade in manufactured goods between these two groups of countries has had a negligible and sometimes positive effect on employment in the rich countries. Thus, the OECD estimates that the trade in manufactured goods between the "newly industrializing countries" of the Third World and the developed countries from 1973 to 1977 created a net average of 200,000 to 500,000 jobs per year in the developed countries; for France alone, the trade in manufactured goods with all developing countries probably created some 100,000 jobs on balance between 1970 and 1976.[10]

EXPORTS AND ECONOMIC DEVELOPMENT

On the whole, the arguments for increased participation of the developing countries in international trade follow the lines of Ricardo's theory. To the extent that these countries possess a comparative advantage in certain areas (abundant raw materials, cheap labor, etc.), it is in their interest to export to other, differently endowed countries the products obtained from these resources and to import from these countries the goods for which the latter have a similar advantage. The result will be a more efficient allocation of the resources used and a net gain for all partners; in particular, this more efficient resource utilization should lead to accelerated economic growth in the exporting developing countries.

However criticized – or refined – the Ricardian theory might have been, it still remains apparently true that participation in international trade does indeed accelerate economic growth. We saw it happen in the developed countries when the tariffs were lowered within the frame of the European Economic Community or the GATT-sponsored trade negotiations. Similarly, for the developing countries a significant statistical relationship exists between the growth rate of GNP and that of exports. For instance, the correlation coefficient between changes in export growth (in volume) and changes in GNP growth was $+0.62$ for a sample of twenty-eight countries.[11] Individual studies for various countries that have achieved rapid export growth (the "newly industrializing countries," for instance) also confirm what appears to be commonsense evidence.

Exports will stimulate economic growth in several ways. To the extent that production is increased by export, the existing capital will be better used, new jobs will be created, and incomes distributed.[12] This in turn will induce forward and backward linkage effects on other productive activities; moreover, the incomes distributed will stimulate demand through a Keynesian multiplier process. Finally, the foreign exchange obtained through exports will permit the import of consumer products and, most important, of the capital goods required for future investment.

The attention of economists has been more particularly drawn to two specific aspects of this rather theoretical argument: the creation of direct and indirect jobs through production for export, and the foreign exchange earnings resulting from the sale of the exported products. The first aspect is important, although it has often given rise to exaggerated hopes. The second one still supplies, in my opinion, the most solid argument in favor of export-oriented development strategies.

During the seventies, when economists more accurately measured the Third World's employment problems as well as the prospects for the following decades, their attention was drawn to labor-intensive activities. The spectacular success met by some semi-industrial countries in their conquest of foreign markets had frequently been accompanied (in South Korea and Taiwan, for instance) by no-less-exceptional performances in the reduction of unemployment; as a result, certain economists were able to see in the development of export industries the panacea that would enable the developing countries to solve their employment problems. If we are to judge the realism of these hopes, however, we must compare the effects of these industries on employment with the present situation and the future prospects of the labor market.

On careful examination, the contribution of export industries to employment seems relatively small. Thus, the World Bank estimates that the total number of *direct* jobs created by export industries in the Third World does not exceed 2 to 3 million, about 10 percent of total industrial employment in these countries. Considering the multiplier effect, the total number of *direct* and *indirect* jobs created would come to 5 to 10 million, perhaps 1 percent of these countries' total labor force.[13] As this labor force is growing today at an annual rate of 2.2 percent, the number of workers added *every year* to the active population of the Third World is about twice as large as the *total* labor force of these countries employed in activities generated by manufactured exports. At the global level, clearly, export industries cannot succeed in absorbing the additional labor force arriving on the labor market — not to mention the resorption of current unemployment. Even if we consider the countries that have succeeded in rapidly developing their manufactured exports, the impact of this growth on employment remains, on average, limited. A study of the results obtained by eight of these countries (Brazil, Egypt, India, Mexico, the Philippines,

South Korea, Taiwan, and Yugoslavia) during the sixties concludes that direct plus indirect jobs created by the exports of manufactured goods represented, as a weighted average, only 3 percent of total employment.[14]

For small countries with a high level of industrial exports, the contribution of these exports to employment can nevertheless be significant. Thus in Taiwan in 1969, one job out of six was created by manufactured exports, while in South Korea in 1970, one job out of ten was created by exports of all kinds.[15] In all likelihood, these proportions are even higher today because of the surge in these two countries' exports which took place during the seventies. Moreover, for city-states like Hong Kong or Singapore, the figures would also certainly be superior. For small countries, then, it seems that foreign trade can make a significant contribution to employment.

The above conclusion will be especially true for export industries, since these activities are generally labor-intensive. Textiles, clothing, and electrical and mechanical assemblage use a great deal of labor per unit of production, and this labor is relatively unskilled. The rare existing data clearly confirm that the labor coefficient of the manufactured goods exported by developing countries is generally higher than that of the industrial products they import or manufacture for their domestic markets. Thus in South Korea in 1968 the average labor to capital ratio (measured in number of persons for labor and in millions of won for capital) was 3.55 for industrial exports, while it was 2.64 for the products made for the domestic market and 2.33 for manufactured imports. Incidentally, this also seems to indicate that this country has skillfully exploited its comparative advantage by exporting labor-intensive products while importing capital-intensive industrial goods. Similar results concerning the labor coefficient of export activities have been obtained for countries as different as Brazil, Colombia, Indonesia, and Thailand.[16]

In addition, the fact that export industries have a high coefficient of unskilled labor implies that relatively more of the incomes distributed by these industries will go to the poorest categories and less to the social classes rich in technical skills or capital. For this reason, these industries generally have a favorable impact on income distribution: this is probably one of the reasons why exporting countries like Taiwan or South Korea have income structures that are among the least inegalitarian in the Third World. In large countries, of course, this positive impact will be less visible, especially if in these countries land and wealth are divided very unequally, as in Brazil and Mexico. But in the latter cases it would be a mistake to blame export industries for the inequity of the income structure, since the origin of these distortions is to be found elsewhere.

To conclude, it seems that export industries can make and have already made an important contribution to the creation of employment and to the improvement of income distribution in certain small countries. Yet it would be a mistake to believe that these industries can make any but a marginal contribution to the employment situation in the Third World as a whole. To quote the conclusion of a study on this subject: "Those who hold out export-oriented industrialization as a panacea seem to be deluding themselves and those who listen to them, as well as providing a rationale for not undertaking more radical measures to resolve the problems of labor underutilization and marginalization." [17]

While the potential of export activities for creating employment may have been overestimated, it is difficult to deny their importance as a source of foreign exchange. As we saw in Chapter 1, the developing countries' imports have increased rapidly in recent decades, and the financing of these imports depends, for the most part, on these countries' export earnings. Thus, during the 1973–1978 period, the exports of the non-oil developing countries financed more than four-fifths of their imports, the remainder being financed mainly by official development assistance for the poorest countries and by official assistance and private capital for the others. [18] A rapid increase in official assistance appears unlikely for the coming years. As for private capital, it will continue to neglect the poorest countries, and even the middle-income countries will only be able to attract it if their reimbursement potential — that is to say, their export prospects — look satisfactory. In the final analysis, then, the only possible alternative to an increase in exports is a reduction in imports.

Yet such a reduction would have disastrous consequences for these countries' growth and would, in certain cases, entail a high human cost. There are, in fact, scarcely any frills which could be easily sacrificed in the developing countries' imports. In 1979, for instance, nonfood consumer goods amounted to less than 10 percent of the imports of non-OPEC developing countries. By contrast, food products — an important part of which are the cereals required to meet growing food deficits — represented 12 percent of this total, and electric and mechanical products contributed more than 30 percent. Fuel (mainly oil) accounted for about 21 percent of these imports in 1979, but it had already increased to 26 percent by 1980.

In the coming decades, it is likely that the cost of numerous items on this import list will become much heavier. Food deficits should bring about an increase in the imports of cereals and other foods. The volume of energy consumption will increase if the growth of these countries is to continue, and the unit cost of a barrel of oil itself is also likely to keep on increasing. [19] Finally, the developing countries will continue to import the capital goods required for their growth, since a large number of them will not be in a position to produce these goods themselves.

From this standpoint, a development strategy based on regional self-reliance will not provide an immediate solution to these problems. Commercial and financial relations among developing countries can undoubtedly be developed; they have, in fact, intensified during recent years, and it is desirable that this trend continue. For instance, certain regional groups could presumably aim at a higher degree of self-sufficiency. Yet the history of these regional associations during the last thirty years, marked as it has been by frequent problems and rare successes, shows that we should not underestimate the difficulties of this undertaking.

Furthermore, balance of payments and foreign exchange reserves will pose the same difficult problems for the member countries within each of these self-reliant groups. Whatever the regional association to which it belongs, Brazil will have to find the resources required for the payment of its energy imports, whether they come from Venezuela or the Middle East. Similarly, unless the miraculous virtues of collective self-reliance enable the Sahel countries to reach food self-sufficiency, they will continue to need foreign exchange to pay for their food imports, whether they are purchased in Argentina or in the United States.

Monetary unions linking several developing countries would not supply a viable long-term solution either, unless each country in the union succeeds, over the years, in approximately balancing its foreign exchange revenues and expenditures. Whatever the reality of regional solidarities, we may still wonder whether the countries with a balance of payments surplus would agree to finance, on a permanent basis, the foreign exchange requirements of the structurally deficit countries within such associations. Neither regional associations nor monetary unions will obviate the necessity for each developing country to develop its exports in order to finance the growth of its imports.

The strategy pursued by China, which is often mentioned in this context, could not be transposed directly to the majority of the developing countries, if only because this huge country is fortunate enough to have at its disposal natural resources that are lacking in most other Third World nations. Furthermore, we should recall that China's international trade is far from insignificant; as a percentage of GNP it is probably not much lower than that of India, another developing country of comparable size.[20] For the smaller and less well-endowed countries, the problem of financing essential imports would be even more serious. To think that formulas of individual or collective self-reliance will miraculously solve this problem risks, in fact, making these countries more dependent, to the extent that it could cause them to remain unable to finance their most vital import requirements themselves.

For the non-oil developing countries it appears that the financing of the foreseeable deficits in their balance of payments will be one of the major problems of the 1980s. No matter how we approach the question, there are only two solutions which appear feasible over the middle term. Either these countries will succeed in increasing their exports to finance the imports they need, or they will fail to do so and will then be obliged to reduce their imports and, consequently, their economic growth and the well-being of their population.

The foregoing analysis would certainly not be accepted by all economists or politicians; presumably it would encounter two main lines of criticism. The first would question the possibility of authentic development for a Third World country as long as it remains involved in the international system of trade and finance. The second would argue that an export-oriented development strategy, whatever its intrinsic advantages and disadvantages, cannot succeed in the present situations of most Third World countries and of the international economy. I must now address these two types of criticism.

INTERNATIONAL TRADE AND DEPENDENCE

The idea that international economic relations work to the benefit of the rich countries and to the detriment of the poor ones is an old theme in economic literature. Even the most adamant supporters of free trade have not always been free of doubts, and the father of laissez-faire, Adam Smith himself, occasionally had some unorthodox comments: "The discovery of America, and that of a passage to the East Indies by the Cape of Good Hope, are the two greatest and most important events recorded in the history of mankind. Their consequences have already been very great; but, in the short period of between two and three centuries which has elapsed since these discoveries were made, it is impossible that the whole extent of their consequences can have been seen. . . . To the natives, however, both of the East and West Indies, all the commercial benefits which can have resulted from those events have been sunk and lost in the dreadful misfortunes which they have occasioned." [21] Certainly this assertion would meet with the approval of the most ardent partisan of self-reliant development.

There has been a revival of interest in this theme during the last decade, and today it is frequently argued that the development of Third World countries (the periphery) will not be possible unless they break off all relations with the industrialized ones (the center) and pursue an autonomous, self-reliant development model. Of course, the implications of such a rupture go far beyond commercial aspects alone; they also concern, for instance, financial or cultural relations, since these also enable the center to dominate and exploit the periphery.

Let us examine the main elements of this thesis. The economic relations between the center and the periphery, which were often established through violence at the beginning of the colonial era, still remain essentially unbalanced today. At the time of the "colonial pact" the poor countries were supplying the mother countries with the raw materials necessary for their development and serving as markets for their industries. While the political context has apparently changed with the accession to independence of the former colonies, the international division of labor which the center today proposes to the periphery remains just as inequitable. Apart from its traditional role as a supplier of raw materials, the Third World would in fact be responsible for the production, for export to the developed countries, of labor-intensive manufactured goods — the countries of the center keeping the "noble" capital- or technology-intensive products for themselves. This division would work for the greater benefit of the multinational corporations, which would thus be able to compensate for the low rates of profit they realize in the rich countries by more substantial rates in the poor ones.

In the countries of the periphery, economic and political relations with the center are in the hands of a bourgeois "comprador" class whose interests are the same as those of the center countries and which thereby profits from the relationship established with the latter countries. This bourgeois leadership imposes a development model that serves its own interests and those of the center, to the detriment of the Third World population. This is the case for development strategies based on import substitution, since the industries thus created — sometimes with the assistance of multinational corporations — cater to the needs of the well-off classes at the expense of the poorest majority and of subsistence agriculture. But it is also true of export-oriented strategies, since they aim at satisfying the needs of the center countries and not those of the people in the periphery countries; in particular, the rural sector and agriculture would remain just as neglected in the case of export orientation. In these circumstances, the only solution is to break off with the center and to follow a self-reliant development strategy, where "industrialization must first of all be placed at the service of rural productivity." [22] Self-reliant development does not necessarily signify autarky at the country level, however, and this autonomy should instead be envisaged at the level of a region or of a group of neighboring countries.

This critique of the center-periphery relationship thus goes beyond simply calling into question the role of export activities in the Third World's development strategies. The noncommercial aspects (financial, political, even emotional) are probably the most important, even if they lend themselves less easily to rational discussion. [23] Thus, in confining my comments mostly to the commercial aspects of this thesis, I am aware of not doing justice to a theory which intends to be global. Its supporters could no doubt reproach me for separating various aspects which are in fact not separable and for distorting their thought as a consequence. My own argument, however, would be that these aspects are indeed separable to a certain extent and that a prudent and reasonable exploitation of the potential of foreign trade can in fact make the Third World less dependent politically and financially.[24] In this respect I would like to discuss in more detail here three specific aspects of the developing countries' international trade: the role of the multinational corporations, the international division of labor, and the implications of this trade with regard to the satisfaction of the population's needs.

The subject of the Third World's trade relations at once evokes the question of the multinational corporations, a controversial subject if there ever was one. A vast — and frequently contradictory — literature has been devoted to these firms in recent years. In spite of its interest, I do not intend to enter this debate here, nor shall I attempt to prove that these firms are "good" or "bad" for the development of the host country. The idea that I would like to defend is that a country that wants to develop its exports need not necessarily surrender its independence to the almighty authority of these firms.

It is important to recall, first of all, that the development of the Third World's exports during the last few years is not uniquely — and, in all likelihood, not even essentially — due to the activities of the multinational corporations. These countries' domestic firms have played an important role in this recent development: this is particularly true of the "traditional" export sectors, such as textiles, clothing, and shoes, where local firms have always been preeminently involved. I should also emphasize that while the multinational firms have played a particularly noticeable role in South and Central America, they have been less heavily present in the rest of the Third World, even in the exporting countries of these other regions. Moreover, North American multinationals first moved into Latin America to exploit the natural resources or to set up import-substituting industries; it was only later, during the sixties, that their role in the development of export industries became more important.[25]

In the case of the Asian countries the responsibility of multinational firms for export development has been less significant than is often believed. For the whole continent, in fact, the share of manufactured exports attributable to them is in the range of only 5 to 15 percent.[26] This percentage may reach 30 percent in the case of Singapore, but it is below 15 percent for exporters as important as Taiwan or South Korea. A study on South Korea concludes that its success with regard to exports must be attributed more "to the efforts of its entrepreneurs or the incentive policies under which they operate" than to this country's ties with multinationals; the same conclusion would probably apply to most countries of the region.[27] A comparison of the experiences of several countries and of different continents thus leads one to conclude that the expansion of the multinationals and the growth of Third World exports are two phenomena which, while they frequently overlap, are not as closely linked as is sometimes believed.

Furthermore, the developing countries' governments are better able today than they were twenty or thirty years ago to control the activities of the multinationals. First of all, information on this subject circulates more effectively nowadays, and the Third World nations are in a better position to take advantage of the experience of other countries. Thus, several of the laws concerning foreign investments, repatriation of profits, participation in key industries, and transfer of technology enacted by the countries of the Andean Market have been rapidly adopted by Argentina and Peru, and are now being considered by the Caribbean Free Trade Association.[28] Similarly, the contracts signed by several multinationals with Eastern socialist countries and providing for these countries' majority participation in the capital of the subsidiary created are now used as an argument by the Third World countries for demanding similar contracts to their benefit, instead of the usual agreement giving the majority of the capital to the multinational corporation.

Moreover, the range of the multinationals is no longer limited to American firms, as it mainly was in the fifties; firms from other countries (such as Germany and Japan) have now appeared on the international scene. To a certain extent, this has increased the bargaining leeway of Third World governments by enabling them to play these corporations off one against another. The developing countries are also better armed and more sophisticated in their negotiations with these firms. For instance, they have learned how to avoid falling under the dominance of one single firm, either by dividing their procurements among several firms or by "unpackaging" the "investment-technology package" so as to separate its different elements (investment, technology, finance, marketing, management). Finally – and without indulging in any illusion – we may hope that the Code of Conduct on Transnational Corporations or the International Code of Conduct on the Transfer of Technology, both being negotiated in the United Nations, will succeed in lifting the moral standards of an international activity which has not always been above suspicion in the past.

This does not mean, of course, that the multinationals have been tamed by the attacks they have been subjected to in recent years, and it would be absurd to believe that the development of their host countries has now become their first priority. But it remains true that the developing countries are better able today to control the operations of these corporations; also, and more importantly, these countries are not always compelled to resort to these firms to develop their own exports.

It would equally be a mistake to say that the new international division of labor will necessarily confine the developing countries to the role of suppliers of labor-intensive manufactured goods. We saw that the situation has already evolved and that the proportion of capital goods and capital-intensive products in these countries' manufactured exports is growing. Various studies confirm that in the course of economic development, the export structure of Third World countries changes to adapt itself to the evolution of their comparative advantage: while the least developed economies export mainly labor-intensive products, the most advanced countries export more goods with a high coefficient of capital (physical or human).[29] Such an evolution (similar to that of Japan) is clearly visible today in countries like Singapore, Taiwan, and South Korea.[30] In fact, more than any "natural" adaptation to the changes in comparative advantage, this evolution is frequently the result of a deliberate effort on the part of these countries to diversify their exports toward more sophisticated and capital-intensive products. For instance, Singapore has recently significantly increased its industrial wages to discourage labor-intensive industries, and the Taiwanese government has now adopted systematic measures to send students abroad for training in the most modern industrial technologies. Incidentally, it is interesting to note that, while certain economists accuse the multinationals of confining the Third World to labor-intensive industries, the U.N. Industrial Development Organization (UNIDO) attributes the growth of capital-intensive manufactured exports from these countries in part to the transfer of activities to developing countries which some of these corporations have carried out.[31]

It is a truism to say that export activities satisfy the needs of foreign consumers and not those of the local population. It would be a mistake, however, to conclude from this that the domestic population does not benefit from the activities thereby established. In fact, these activities create new jobs and incomes in the exporting countries; in turn, these incomes have a multiplier effect, which will be all the more significant to the extent that they are widely shared. In this respect, labor-intensive export industries have a favorable impact on both growth and employment. The demand for industrial products due to the resultant additional incomes in turn encourages the development of industries supplying the local market. As a result, even in export-oriented countries, industries catering to domestic demand frequently remain preponderant. As can be seen in Table 12.4, in the main exporters of manufactured goods, these exports represent only 12 percent of the gross production value; to put it differently, even in these countries, close to nine-tenths of the manufactured output is produced for domestic consumption.

A related question concerns the relationship (and alleged contradiction) between export development and satisfaction of basic needs. The immediate consequences of export activities are likely to be, on balance, a positive (albeit limited) impact on the reduction of poverty. By increasing the employment of unskilled workers (directly or indirectly through the multi-

TABLE 12.4   Ratios of Manufactured Exports to Gross Value of Manufacturing, and of Manufacturing Value Added (MVA) to GDP, 1970
(percentages)

Country group[a]	Ratio of manufactured exports to gross value of manufacturing	Ratio of MVA to GDP
Largest exporters	12.4	19.5
Primary-oriented exporters	10.2	10.9
Others	12.0	14.2
All three groups	11.5	14.9

SOURCE: See Table 12.2.

[a] The largest exporters are Brazil, India, South Korea, Singapore, and Thailand. Primary-oriented exporters (countries whose exports of manufactures were less than 10% of their total exports) include Chile, Ethiopia, Honduras, Indonesia, Iran, Kuwait, Libya, Nigeria, Panama, Sudan, United Republic of Tanzania, and Zambia. Other countries are Barbados, Colombia, Congo, Egypt, Fiji, Ghana, Guatemala, Kenya, Madagascar, Malawi, Mauritius, Peru, Philippines, Somalia, Sri Lanka, Tunisia, and Turkey.

plier effect) they will provide the poorest strata of the urban population with some additional income. Also, protrade policies are more likely to be based on a realistic price structure (for labor and capital) that will, in all economic activities, encourage the use of labor-intensive technologies. In contrast, import-substitution policies have usually biased this price structure in favor of capital-intensive technologies, by maintaining an overvalued exchange rate and then allowing duty-free import of capital equipment for "priority" industries. As I noted before, however, the employment effect of export activities, while positive, is unlikely to solve the developing countries' unemployment problem; to this extent these activities are unlikely to make more than a dent in the overall poverty of the population.

Attacking the problem of mass poverty is therefore going to require additional, direct policies. In this connection it is sometimes asserted that protrade orientation is incompatible with domestic antipoverty strategies and that the political regimes favorable to export promotion are unlikely to support social and economic justice as a priority objective. Possibly the best refutation of this accusation is given by the experience of several East Asian countries that have pursued export-oriented strategies while implementing policies to improve the lot of the poorest (often, admittedly, for opportunistic, political reasons). Whatever can be said of Taiwan's or South Korea's political regimes, one has to recognize that these countries have pursued, and achieved, simultaneously the objectives of export development and income redistribution. It could in fact be argued that, in the past, lack of concern about the plight of the poor has, by and large, more often been associated with antitrade than with protrade policies and regimes. On the whole, however, there does not appear to be any direct relationship between a government's external economic policy and its interest and effectiveness in combatting poverty. To quote the conclusion of a study on this subject, "In summary, it is not clear that adoption of pro-trade policies will be inimical to social reforms in the direction of redistribution or that anti-trade policies will lead in any dependable way toward redistributive policies, much less redistribution with growth. Rather, there seems to be no reliable political mechanism under either type of trade policies, to trigger early redistribution efforts." [32]

Similarly, there is no reason that export growth should necessarily work to the detriment of agricultural development. It seems, on the contrary, that a system of economic incentives which encourages export industries — and therefore does not unduly protect import-substituting industries — will not modify the terms of trade at the expense of the farmers and consequently will be more favorable to agricultural activities than the system of industrial protection required by import-substitution strategies. In any event, the development of agriculture will depend mainly on the economic policies implemented by the government, and it is not clear why an isolationist government would necessarily be more interested in this sector or more effective in its policies. After all, agricultural development has not been particularly successful in Burma and Guinea, while South Korea and the Ivory Coast have obtained quite remarkable results in this sector.

Yet I do not wish to give the impression that I am in favor of unbridled free trade and complete laissez-faire in the areas of trade, finance, or technological transfer. A measure of selectivity is certainly desirable, particularly in the latter two fields. But prudence and selectivity do not imply autarky, and in the area of trade, the developing countries probably have more to gain by taking the developed countries at their word with regard to their free-trade declarations than by retreating into an ivory tower. In addition, whatever proclamations have been made on this subject, self-reliant development and egalitarian development are not necessarily synonymous; in and of itself, the closing of the borders is not enough to give a progressist label to a development strategy. It is certainly desirable that development policies be redefined to take into account, in a more systematic manner, various considerations of social justice and income redistribution; yet trade isolationism is neither a necessary nor even a sufficient condition for such a reorientation.

PROSPECTS FOR EXPORT DEVELOPMENT

Another line of criticism often directed at the idea of orienting development policies toward export does not question so much the intrinsic advantages of such a strategy as its chances of success. Prospects for growth in the developed countries — which are the main markets for Third World exports — do not appear very promising, and there are considerable risks that the economic crisis will worsen the already manifest protectionist tendencies. Is this really the right moment, then, to preach to the developing countries about the miracles of export-oriented strategies? We certainly have a serious argument here, and it would be a mistake to underestimate the real dangers that a deterioration in the industrial world's economic situation could entail for Third World exports. In spite of this, however, several reasons lead me to believe that there is not yet cause for despair.

It is with regard to manufactured exports that the concern about the possibilities of future growth is more acute. Industrial goods have so far constituted the most dynamic element of the developing countries' exports. From 1960 to 1975 the manufactured exports of these countries increased in volume at an annual rate of 12.3 percent, twice as rapidly as their total exports and about four times as fast as their exports of agricultural products. But these industrial exports have also been the main target of the new protectionist measures taken by the developed countries during the last decade. Should we not fear that, in the years to come, the difficult economic situation of the industrial countries will further hinder the development of this type of exports?

The answer to this question will depend in part on the degree to which the industrial products of the Third World have penetrated the developed countries' markets. This penetration is, in fact, quite limited on the whole: thus, in 1978, the products of the developing countries represented only 2.9 percent of the developed countries' consumption of manufactured goods. The penetration of the European markets is a little higher (4.1 percent), but that of the North American, Canadian, and Japanese markets is lower: 2.9 percent, 1.9 percent, and 1.5 percent, respectively. Even for the sectors where imports from the Third World have rapidly grown, the proportion of these imports in the consumption of the industrial countries remains relatively low: in 1975, it was 8.6 percent for clothing, 3.2 percent for textiles, and 1.7 percent for chemical products.[33]

In these circumstances, it would seem that the developing countries have sufficient room to develop their exports; we may also wonder why the Third World ever appeared a threat to the developed countries. The main reason for the attention which this problem has recently received is in fact the difficult economic situation in the latter countries. The high unemployment plaguing all developed nations makes them much more sensitive to the problems of labor transfer and relocation which foreign competition may cause. Another reason is probably the fact that the industries which are the most threatened by Third World competition (textiles, clothing, shoes) were already in difficulty before this competition was even felt; in addition, they are frequently established in economically depressed regions and employ a labor force (women or relatively old people) which cannot easily be relocated. Finally, these industries often specialize in one single product type and consequently cannot without difficulty diversify their production into other lines less threatened by foreign competition.

These factors probably explain why the protectionist measures taken by the developed countries against Third World imports have been essentially confined to these critical products. There are other sectors, however, where the developing countries can use their comparative advantage without competing in the developed countries with industries as sensitive as textiles or shoes. Precision instruments, photographic equipment, even electronic machinery, are but a few examples of such products into which the developing countries can diversify — and are in fact diversifying — their production without exposing themselves to the vigilant protectionism of the developed countries.[34] The newly industrializing countries, which pursue a dynamic and systematic policy of diversification, have already proved that there are important markets for the developing countries outside the traditional sectors of clothing and textiles. This should counteract undue pessimism with regard to the future of the Third World's industrial exports, and in this respect, the vigorous manner in which these exports have overcome the protectionist obstacles erected in recent years is certainly encouraging.

Neither should we exaggerate the difficulties that countries embarking today upon an export-oriented industrialization strategy could meet because other developing countries might have already conquered the markets. As we have seen, these markets are in fact far from having been conquered, and on the whole there is still scope for some increase in the developing countries' industrial exports. Moreover, we also know that the types of exports evolve in the course of economic growth: when the exporting countries reach a more advanced stage, they tend to abandon certain industries, which can then be taken up by newcomers. Thus, we have witnessed since World War II successive transfers of various labor-intensive industries from Japan to Hong Kong and from Hong Kong to South Korea; in turn the Koreans are now trying to shift to other developing countries several activities for which these other countries have a comparative advantage. The evolution of the international division of labor thus goes on, not only between developing and developed countries but also within the Third World itself. Among the developing countries, consequently, the late starters in the industrialization race are not necessarily condemned to see their more rapid neighbors monopolize indefinitely the positions they have been able to win in world markets.

Finally, whatever the importance of the protectionist measures adopted by the developed countries, serious efforts have been made to limit their extension. The conclusion of the Multilateral Trade Negotiations is the most recent manifestation of the rich countries' awareness of the dangers presented by protectionist pressures. While the results of these negotiations have not been as positive for the developing countries as might have been hoped, they have nevertheless expressed the will of the industrial countries to resist the temptation of protectionism. For this reason it would presumably be too hasty to take for granted a marked expansion of trade barriers in the coming years.

I certainly do not want to claim that there are no obstacles to the development of Third World exports; even less do I wish to justify the actions of the developed countries in erecting certain of these obstacles. In the present atmosphere of discouragement, however, it may be worth quoting a World Bank report, which, after a careful review of the situation, concludes that "despite a number of problems, on balance over the 1970s the international trading system did not become less open." [35] And it would be harmful to overestimate the importance of the existing difficulties if this were to discourage the developing countries and lead them to give up the efforts required to develop their exports. It may be useful to recall here that, after the world recession of 1974–1975, the semiindustrialized countries which chose to maintain their policy of export-orientation continued to increase their foreign sales rapidly; for instance, Korea's manufactured exports increased by two-thirds in one year after the second quarter of 1975. By contrast, countries — like Brazil, Colombia, or Mexico — that instead reacted to the difficulties created by the crisis by turning inwards and discriminating against imports, obtained much lower growth of their exports.[36] In any event, the semiindustrialized countries taken as a whole stood up remarkably well to the shocks of the recession and the protectionism of the developed countries: after having marked time around the middle of the decade, their exports resumed vigorous growth. As we saw, this presumably indicates that, for all its seriousness, the deterioration in the economic situation of the developed countries has not destroyed the developing countries' export potential.

In this regard, one may fear that the poorest countries might be the first victims of this loss of confidence regarding export possibilities if these countries turn away from a strategy that has been so successful for the more advanced developing countries. To quote another World Bank report, "The worst result of the increased protectionism may be a greater unwillingness on the part of many developing countries to risk more outward-looking trade policies, even when these are urgently needed. . . . Partly for this reason, . . . the adverse effects of heightened protection may be felt more by the poorer and less successful developing countries than by the most successful and visible targets." [37]

EXPORT POLICIES

The success that several countries have encountered in the development of their foreign trade has not been merely the fortunate outcome of favorable circumstances. In all cases, in fact, these performances have been the result of deliberate government policies aiming to encourage exports.

It is sometimes said that the remarkable achievements of certain newly industrializing countries are due to a number of particular circumstances – one implication of this assertion being that the other, less fortunate developing countries would not be able to duplicate such performances. Thus, because of their small domestic markets, Hong Kong and Singapore would have had no other choice than to aim at the conquest of foreign markets. This is to forget, however, that many countries in Africa, America, or the Caribbean, constrained by equally limited domestic markets, have not felt the same necessity and have, on the contrary, chosen to pursue the development of their import-substituting industries – with little success in most cases.

Similarly, the achievements of South Korea and Taiwan have sometimes been attributed to the privileged economic relations between these countries and the United States and Japan. Without underestimating the importance of these relations (and notably that of American aid in the reconstruction of these two countries), I would nevertheless suggest that their role in the development of these countries' exports has not been primordial. In the case of Korea, for instance, the share of the sales to Japan and the United States in total exports has constantly declined since 1960, the role of these two countries' investments in the first phase of export development has been very limited, and Korean goods have not benefited from preferential import treatment on the part of these two countries.[38] At the end of their study of the "exceptional circumstances" explaining the Korean success, two economists have thus been able to conclude that "while a variety of factors have contributed to Korea's successful development, the key fact nonetheless remains that economic policies have made a large contribution to fostering what appears to be a reasonably efficient and equitable process of industrialization. Thus Korea provides an almost classic example of an economy following its comparative advantage and reaping the gains predicted by conventional economic theory."[39]

Many studies confirm that government economic policies are a decisive factor in the development – or the stagnation – of industrial exports. Governments of the Third World have frequently pursued import-substitution policies combining high levels of protection with an overvalued exchange rate. It is well established today (by statistical studies inter alia) that these policies have in fact discouraged exports by enabling the industries producing for the domestic market to realize monopolistic rents.[40] Other studies have also been able to establish, in an equally conclusive manner, the existence of a link between the adoption of an export incentive scheme and the growth of exports.[41] Thus the exports and GNPs of the newly industrializing countries have generally grown much faster after such a scheme of export incentives had been adopted. This is not to say, of course, that it is sufficient to implement various tested policies, to use certain "recipes," for exports to soar. But today it is recognized that government policies do contribute decisively to the success — or failure — of entrepreneurs' efforts to export.

It is certainly difficult to indicate at what stage of a country's development a strategy of export development should be implemented. Import-substitution strategies have often been justified as a prerequisite phase to create the industrial basis required for later export growth. This argument is not totally convincing, however. Certain exporting countries have had only a very short import-substitution phase (six years in the case of Singapore) or even have not had any (in the case of Hong Kong). Moreover, in countries like South Korea, Taiwan, or Singapore most of the present export industries (including synthetic textiles, electronic machinery, and shipbuilding) have not passed through a previous import-substitution phase. In the case of Latin America the industries that were set up during the import-substitution stage were frequently inefficient and insufficiently integrated; to this extent, they generally constituted more of an obstacle than an aid during the following phase of export development. Finally, overly extended import-substitution phases have frequently created entrenched networks of vested interests and political influences that have subsequently resisted — at times successfully — the necessary policy changes. This does not mean that the preliminary phase of substitution should always be bypassed, but it would nevertheless seem desirable to limit its duration — contrary to what many countries have done.

From the experiences of recent decades it is possible to recognize and outline the main components of an export incentive policy. In many cases, the first element would be a devaluation to bring the exchange rate of the national currency closer to its real value and to improve the competitiveness of exports on the world market. Whatever the advantages of such a policy, however, it is important to recognize that in certain instances other political or economic considerations can make its implementation impossible. In such a case, it may be preferable to maintain the parity of the currency and the existing system of tariff protection while compensating for this tariff protection by establishing export subsidies of an equivalent level. From the standpoint of foreign trade, such a policy amounts to a devaluation that would increase the official exchange rate in equal proportion to the tariff average. In particular, because of the subsidies given to exports, the outward-oriented industries would not be at a disadvantage vis-à-vis those catering to the domestic market.

As compared to a straightforward devaluation there is nevertheless a double disadvantage to the latter approach. First, its implementation is certainly more complicated than a mere modification of the exchange rate. Second, the governments of the importing countries, especially those of the developed ones, are generally very sensitive to the use of export subsidies and are always quick to suspect intentions of "dumping." For that reason, developing countries may often find it in their own interests to confine themselves to types of subsidies that have the blessings of the GATT (such as duty rebates on imported inputs) or that are used by the developed countries themselves (such as preferential export credits, credit insurance schemes, or income tax deferrals).[42]

The purpose of such restructuring of the incentive system should not be to give export activities more support than is given to the industries supplying the domestic market, but simply to establish an approximate equivalence between the incentives granted within these two sectors. It would thus be possible to correct a situation which in fact prevails in most developing countries, since these countries' export activities are generally at a disadvantage vis-à-vis those catering to the local market. Similarly, the level of these incentives should, as far as possible, be the same in the various exporting sectors; it is only when it can be definitely established that an activity brings special benefits (not taken into account by the criterion of financial profitability) to the economy that specific support measures should be implemented. Temporary exceptions could be envisaged for new export industries (following an argument similar to the one justifying provisional protection for infant industries), but in this instance too, their duration should be clearly specified at the outset.

Generally speaking, to avoid any harmful disruption in productive activities, it is desirable that these changes in the incentive system not be sudden. Such modifications should be carried out by stages, according to a preestablished timetable, so as to enable the firms to prepare the necessary evolution of their activities.

As is the case with many other aspects of international relations, the problem of the developing countries' foreign trade would often be more clearly understood if it were approached in a more realistic and pragmatic manner. In particular, an analysis of the facts would often permit calling into question certain preconceived ideas.

It thus seems difficult to maintain today that developing countries have nothing to gain by developing their trade with the rest of the world in general, and with the developed countries in particular. However unequal, the exchange between North and South has enabled many Third World nations to accelerate their development. The experience of various countries has also shown that a development strategy that takes advantage of the potential of foreign trade is not necessarily unbalanced or inequitable. Without claiming that a systematic and indiscriminate opening to international trade is always in the interest of the Third World, we must nevertheless acknowledge that foreign trade does offer real possibilities to the developing countries if they are able to use them.

At the other extreme, it would be just as mistaken to overestimate the capacity of international trade to solve these countries' problems. Thus the development of exports toward the industrial countries will never be able to bring any miraculous solution to the problem of Third World unemployment. The growth of these exports can contribute to reduce unemployment, especially in the small countries; it cannot, however, constitute a viable alternative to the necessary implementation of specific policies to improve the employment situation and the incomes of the poorest strata. It is, in fact, mainly by enabling the developing countries to loosen the constraint of their balance of payments that export development can contribute to the Third World's economic growth. This role should be particularly important in the eighties because of the non-oil developing countries' vast financial requirements foreseen for this decade.

In the same manner, it would be desirable not to let the present economic situation excessively darken our evaluation of the developing countries' trade prospects. A similar pessimism existed twenty-five years ago, but it has been refuted by a quarter of a century of rapid export growth. Today we are told that circumstances have changed and that such growth is no longer possible: in the meantime, however, Third World exports continue to increase at sustained rates.

We also hear that "miracles," whether they are Korean, Brazilian, or "made in Hong Kong," are due to particular circumstances and cannot be replicated. On closer examination, however, the "particular circumstances" turn out to be intelligent economic policies and – to plagiarize Keynes – a few entrepreneurs and their animal spirits. If miracles cannot be replicated, they can be imitated, and this is exactly what many Third World countries, currently busy developing their export industries, are now doing. The same economic policies which yesterday permitted the reorientation toward export and the miracles of certain countries can tomorrow enable newcomers to carve themselves a share of the international market.

This is not to claim that no difficulties exist and that there are no obstacles to the development of Third World exports. But the manner in which these exports have resisted the unfavorable circumstances of the previous decade is certainly heartening. It would indeed be regrettable if an unwarranted pessimism were to discourage the developing countries from pursuing their efforts in this direction at the very time when the world economic situation makes this orientation more necessary than ever.

CONCLUSION

In many respects World War II was a watershed for the Third World countries. On a political level, the immediate postwar period witnessed the birth of independent nations and the establishment of new governments in Africa and Asia. In the demographic sphere, a general improvement in health conditions brought about an unprecedented population explosion. Finally, shortly after the independence of the new countries and for the first time in their history, economic development became one of the main priorities of their governments and ruling classes.

The 1970s may have marked a new turning point in the economic history of these countries. During this period, the exceptionally rapid growth of the two previous decades was called into question. Considerable evidence had been assembled showing that economic development had been accompanied by frequent failures and serious shortcomings. Moreover, the very possibility of continued growth appeared less certain, and various "shocks" — in the areas of energy, food, and raw materials — seemed to confirm the existence of physical limits to growth. At the beginning of a new decade, it has now become clear that growth has to be reformulated to take into account past failures and future obstacles.

It is obvious, however, that the basis for such reflection must be an objective evaluation of the experience of the last decades as well as of the prospects for the coming years. Underestimating the results of past growth or exaggerating the importance of future problems can only lead to discouragement and helplessness. By contrast, ignoring past failures or minimizing future difficulties will only prevent the definition and implementation of appropriate strategies.

During the last three decades, the developing countries have experienced exceptional economic growth. Their growth rate during this period was twice as high as it had been during the first half of the twentieth century. In spite of rapid population growth, income per capita has also increased at an unprecedented pace. For the Third World as a whole, average income had increased by about one-third during the first half of this century; it doubled during the third quarter. Achievements have been just as exceptional with regard to living conditions. In thirty years, life expectancy at birth in the Third World has undergone an increase that had required more than a century in the now-developed countries. In twenty years, from 1950 to 1970, the number of students in primary schools tripled; it increased sixfold in both secondary and higher education.

Because the achievements of recent decades are unquestionable, their failures are even more striking. The rapid economic growth of these countries has brought little or no benefit to the poorest third of their population. In some cases, in fact, the situation of the poorest has probably deteriorated. Moreover, growth has not led to the elimination of hunger, ignorance, or disease; it is even likely that the numbers of malnourished and illiterate have increased during the last few decades. Today it is no longer possible for us to believe — as we still could ten years ago — that these problems which we have been unable to solve will eventually find their solution in the continuation and acceleration of growth. What is in question here, in fact, is not the pace of this growth but its quality and content.

During recent years, we have also reached a clearer understanding of the possibilities and the risks of growth in the next few decades. It now seems that the main problem of the coming years will not be one of physical limits but of implementing appropriate policies to develop the resources required for the continuation of this growth. The difficulties of the coming decades will not be insurmountable if we can, without further delay, define and carry out the necessary strategies. Their implementation has already been much delayed, unfortunately, in spite of the multiplication of warning signals: in the areas of energy and food, for instance, it may now be feared that the required measures will be taken too late to avoid the impending crises.

For the Third World countries, therefore, a modification of development policies seems necessary, both to remedy past failures and to face up to future problems. Several priorities appear to be essential for such a redefinition. The ongoing efforts to reduce demographic growth must be intensified. The development of commercial and traditional energy resources will have to receive priority attention. The growth of agricultural production and particularly of food production must also be considerably accelerated. Finally, because of the foreseeable increase in their import requirements, these countries will have to strive to increase their exports in order to obtain the foreign exchange required for these purchases.

In addition, the orientations of growth must be modified to take into account the needs of the poorest. We can no longer believe that undifferentiated economic growth alone will be sufficient to improve the living conditions of these destitute peoples; the experience of the last decades has shown that specific actions will be required for this purpose. Yet such a change does not imply abandoning the objective of growth, which had generally oriented the development strategies of the fifties and sixties. In fact, economic growth will be necessary for the long-term viability of policies aiming to improve the lot of the underprivileged. But the reconciliation of the two objectives of economic growth and social justice will be possible only if priority is given to increasing the productivity of the poorest. In this respect the development of agriculture, on which the vast majority of these destitute depend, will play a fundamental role.

If I have particularly insisted in this book on the necessity of increasing the productive capacity of the poorest, it is because this aspect has frequently been overlooked in the formulation and implementation of certain development strategies. In several countries, the excessive importance given to the welfare of the destitute — to the detriment of policies aiming to increase their productive capacity — has led to the arrest of economic development. While giving priority to measures intended to increase the productivity of the poor, we must not forget, however, that, within the "nonproductive" government programs, a reorientation toward these categories of people is also necessary. In the areas of education, health, or water supply, for instance, government policies — and especially public expenditures — will have to be reoriented toward the social categories which have the greatest need for them.

Taken one by one, the measures I have outlined above may appear of a limited nature, and one may wonder whether they would actually be sufficient to rectify the serious shortcomings of the past thirty years and counteract the many problems of the coming decades. I would like to suggest, however, that, far from being limited in scope, these policies are, in fact, of a rather far-reaching nature. Carried out in isolation, of course, each of them is unlikely to be very effective — one may even question whether it would have any impact at all. If, however, these policies are implemented as parts of a coherent strategy, the overall program is likely to appear much more formidable; it will also be incomparably more effective. Could we indeed call limited a strategy that would combine an integrated, effective family planning program, a vigorous policy for developing domestic energy resources (including large-scale reforestation programs), a real (as opposed to the fashionably rhetorical) priority to rural development, the organization of small farmers' cooperatives, the implementation of large-scale, productive rural works, a labor-intensive industrialization scheme favoring small-scale enterprises, and a flexible, efficient export development program? If, in addition, one believes that, in countries where land distribution is skewed, agrarian reform is an absolute prerequisite, and if one also doubts the possibility of such a reform being successfully carried out by peaceful means, one must recognize that the whole strategy represents much more than piecemeal and limited reformism.

One could of course still argue that, in spite of its far-reaching nature, such a strategy might not be sufficient to avert the future problems looming large over the end of the century. Because of the seriousness of these impending crises, I cannot be completely certain that even this strategy will be able to check them. I am convinced, however, that if we do not implement it, we will soon be overwhelmed by these very problems. And I also think that the alternative "blueprints for survival" variously proffered, whether of a capitalist or a Marxist persuasion, do not provide us with the answers to the failures of the past and the issues of the future.

This book on the development of the Third World is mainly concerned with the economic strategies of these countries. It is clear that the prime responsibility for their development will lie with the Third World nations themselves and that their economic performance will depend mostly on their own efforts. Yet the international community has an important responsibility, and the industrial countries' policies will in part determine the results obtained by the developing countries. In this respect also the last decade has marked a turning point, to the extent that it has enabled us to understand more clearly the interdependence which now unites all the nations. It is clear today that the countries of the "North" can no longer formulate their economic policies without reference to the countries of the "South," any more than the latter can define their development strategies without taking into account the situations and actions of the industrial nations.

Just as it is essential now to reconsider growth in the developing countries, it is also necessary to redefine the economic relations between rich and poor nations in an interdependent world. Today the developed countries can no longer afford to ignore the Third World nations; the development of the latter has ceased to be exclusively their own preoccupation and now directly concerns the whole international community. During the last decade we have understood more clearly the importance of the Third World and discovered the dimensions of our mutual dependence. We must now transform this passive interdependence into an active solidarity.

NOTES

INTRODUCTION

1. See the report of the Independent Commission on International Development Issues, *North-South: A Program for Survival* (Cambridge: MIT Press, 1980), p. 24. Hereafter the report will be cited as *Brandt Report*.

CHAPTER 1

1. Paul Bairoch, *The Economic Development of the Third World since 1900* (London: Methuen, 1975).

2. Simon Kuznets, *Economic Growth of Nations* (New York: W. W. Norton, 1965).

3. Bairoch, *Economic Development of the Third World*. Kuznets, *Economic Growth of Nations,* estimates that, over the long term, annual growth rates of today's developed countries since the beginning of their industrialization have been around 3% for GDP and 2% for per capita GDP.

4. Paul N. Rosenstein-Rodan, "International Aid for Undeveloped Countries," *Review of Economics and Statistics,* May 1961. Also see Hollis Chenery and Alan Strout, "Foreign Assistance and Economic Development," *American Economic Review,* September 1966, for another series of projections which, on the whole, have also been surpassed by the actual results.

5. Resolution 1710 (XVI) of the U.N. General Assembly, December 1961.

6. Resolution 2626 (XXV) of the U.N. General Assembly, October 1970.

7. Calculated from figures given in David Morawetz, *Twenty-five Years of Economic Development, 1950 to 1975* (Baltimore: Johns Hopkins University Press, 1977).

8. By using some simple algebra again, it can easily be shown that the absolute gap will continue to increase until the ratio of the two per capita GDPs is equal to the inverse of the ratio of their respective growth rates.

9. Morawetz, *Twenty-five Years of Economic Development,* found that the correlation coefficient between the rankings in 1950 and 1975 of 77 countries was 0.91.

10. Leaving aside the particular cases of Kuwait and Libya, in 1950 the absolute gap (measured in 1974 values) between Somalia ($37 per head) and Israel ($1,090) amounted to some $1,050; in 1975 the gap (again expressed in 1974 values) between Rwanda ($81 per head) and Israel ($3,287) was three times as much. See Morawetz, *Twenty-five Years of Economic Development.*

11. For an analysis of this process, see Alain Barrère, *Le Développement divergent: Essai sur la richesse et la pauvreté des nations* (Paris: Economica, 1978).

12. The "poorest countries" referred to here are those whose per capita GDP was below $200 in 1970.

13. The rapid growth of these countries' real GDP per capita in the first half of the last decade was essentially due to the increase in relative oil prices. In the future, such growth rates of their per capita GDP are as unlikely as a new quadrupling of oil prices within a one-year time span.

14. "Development Trends since 1960 and Their Implications for a New International Development Strategy," *United Nations Journal of Development Planning* (New York) no. 13 (1979).

15. See General Agreement on Tariffs and Trade, *International Trade, 1980/81* (Geneva, 1981). Also World Bank, "World Trade and Output of Manufactures," Staff Working Paper, Washington, D.C., January 1979, and *World Development Report* (Washington, D.C., 1981).

16. In 1979, the contribution of agriculture to the developing countries' GDP amounted to some $375 billion, while the share of manufacturing represented about $370 billion. The whole industrial sector (which includes manufacturing) contributed approximately $835 billion.

17. In 1979, the relative gap between the GNP per capita of Singapore and that of Bangladesh was about 43 to 1; the gap vis-à-vis the latter would come to 81 to 1 for Saudi Arabia and 190 to 1 for Kuwait. As a reminder, the relative gap between developed and developing countries was, at the time, approximately 13 to 1.

CHAPTER 2

1. See, for instance, Food and Agriculture Organization (FAO), *Agriculture: Towards 2000* (Rome, 1979); Shlomo Reutlinger and Marcelo Selowsky, *Malnutrition and Poverty,* World Bank Staff Occasional Paper (Baltimore: Johns Hopkins University Press, 1976); Joseph Klatzmann, *Nourrir dix milliards d'hommes?* (Paris: Presses Universitaires de France, 1975).

2. There seems to be a broad consensus that the number of malnourished persons increased over the sixties; however, it is less clear whether their proportion in the Third World's population also augmented during the same period.

3. See "Development Trends since 1960 and Their Implications for a New International Development Strategy," *United Nations Journal of Development Planning,* no. 13, 1979; and *Agriculture: Towards 2000.*

4. David Morawetz, *Twenty-five Years of Economic Development, 1950 to 1975* (Baltimore: Johns Hopkins University Press, 1977), recalls that, in Ghana (at the time, the Gold Coast), the question was mentioned in all important reports on education from 1842 up to the 1957 independence.

5. See in particular ibid. and "Development Trends since 1960."

6. Morawetz, *Twenty-five Years of Economic Development.* The sixteen indicators used were: per capita calorie supply (as a percentage of requirement), per capita protein supply, per capita protein supply from animal or pulse, infant mortality rate, death rate at 1 to 4 years, life expectancy at birth, population per nursing person, population per doctor, population per hospital bed, average number of persons per room, percentage of dwellings without piped water, percentage of dwellings with access to electricity, adult literacy rate, primary school enrollment ratio, secondary school enrollment ratio, and vocational school enrollments as a percentage of secondary school enrollments.

7. See Overseas Development Council, *The United States and World Development: Agenda 1977* (New York: Praeger, 1977); see also the volumes *Agenda 1979* and *Agenda 1980.*

8. See Morawetz, *Twenty-five Years of Economic Development;* also World Bank, "Two Studies of Development in Sub-Saharan Africa," Staff Working Paper, October 1978.

9. In 1976, the poorest 40% of the population were receiving 16.9% of the national income. (In the United States, the corresponding percentage was 15.2% in 1972.) See Hollis Chenery et al., *Redistribution with Growth* (London: Oxford University Press, 1974).

10. While the poorest 20% of the population was not receiving more than 5% or 6% of China's total income around 1929-1933, its share now presumably exceeds 10%. See "The Chinese Experience," in Keith Griffin and Azizur Khan, coordinators, *Poverty and Landlessness in Rural Asia* (Geneva: International Labor Office, 1977).

11. Morawetz, *Twenty-five Years of Economic Development;* World Bank, "Two Studies of Development in Sub-Saharan Africa"; Griffin and Khan, *Poverty and Landlessness in Rural Asia.*

12. Montek Ahluwalia, "Rural Poverty in India," in World Bank, "India: Occasional Papers," Staff Working Paper, May 1978.

13. Griffin and Khan, *Poverty and Landlessness in Rural Asia.*

14. In most cases, this poverty line is defined as the income required to ensure a given nutritional minimum.

15. For Pakistan, Stephen Guisinger and Norman L. Hicks ("Long-Term Trends in Income Distribution in Pakistan," *World Development* 6 [1978]) conclude that there was a trend towards an improving distribution of income during the 1960s (although distribution might have worsened during the 1970s). For Sri Lanka, Lal Jayawardena (in Chenery et al., *Redistribution with Growth*) concludes that income distribution improved over the two previous decades. For India, finally, a more exhaustive study by Ahluwalia ("Rural Poverty in India") concludes that, while the number of "absolute poor" in the countryside increased, the proportion of these poor within the rural population did not consistently change in any recognizable direction over time.

16. Asian Development Bank, *Rural Asia: Challenge and Opportunity* (New York: Praeger, 1977), p. 63.

17. In this respect, it is sobering to compare the somewhat pessimistic tone of the Asian Development Bank survey cited in n. 16 (above) with that of the study on the same subject the bank carried out ten years before — at a time when the first stirrings of the Green Revolution were thought to be portents of a bountiful future. (Asian Development Bank, *Asian Agricultural Survey* [Tokyo: University of Tokyo Press, 1969; Seattle: University of Washington Press, 1969]).

18. World Bank, *Accelerated Development in Sub-Saharan Africa: An Agenda for Action* (Washington, D.C., 1981), and "Two Studies of Development in Sub-Saharan Africa." See also International Labor Office, "Rural Poverty in the Third World" (Geneva, 1979); this document provides some — admittedly spotty — information indicating that poverty has increased in the rural sectors of many African and Latin American countries.

19. U.N., Economic Commission for Latin America, *El Desarollo economico y social y las relaciones economicas externas de America Latina* (E/CEPAL/1061), February 1979. "Poverty" is here defined as the incapacity to buy an unspecified basket of goods and services assuring the satisfaction of basic needs. "Absolute poverty" corresponds to an income that does not permit the acquisition of the food required for even a minimum nutritional standard.

CHAPTER 3

1. See, for instance, Herman Kahn and Anthony J. Wiener, *The Year 2000* (New York: Macmillan, 1967); also Paul N. Rosenstein-Rodan, "The Have's and Have-not's around the Year 2000," in Jagdish Bhagwati et al., *Economics and World Order: From the 1970s to the 1990's* (New York: Macmillan, 1972).

2. The amount of this financial assistance went from $17.6 billion in 1970 to $25.4 billion in 1981 (all values in constant 1981 dollars). See Organization for Economic Cooperation and Development (OECD), "Resources for Developing Countries in 1981 and Recent Trends," mimeograph (Paris, 1982).

3. OECD, *Development Cooperation: 1981 Review* (Paris, 1981). In OECD jargon, "nonconcessional flows" include the flows of private capital and the flows of public funds transferred under terms close to market conditions.

4. The commission chaired by the former West German chancellor Willy Brandt stressed the importance of this problem (see *Brandt Report,* p. 240). Its concern is apparently shared by many commercial banks as well as by the International Monetary Fund and the World Bank.

5. Arthur Lewis, *The Theory of Economic Growth* (Homewood, Ill.: Richard D. Irwin, 1953), p. 9. One has to underline, however, that the interest in economic growth, no matter how deep, never became exclusive. See Deepak Lal, "Distribution and Development: A Review Article," *World Development* 4, no. 9 (September 1976), for a critique of certain overly simplistic presentations of the situation prevailing in the fifties and sixties. David Morawetz also argues that, in the late forties and early fifties, economists had a less narrow conception of "development" than in the following years: see his *Twenty-five Years of Economic Development, 1950 to 1975* (Baltimore: Johns Hopkins University Press, 1977).

6. By and large this has been the attitude of the Indian government until fairly recently. The Pakistani government, however, took the problem more seriously, doubtless in part because of the sharp decline in the amount of food aid this country received in 1966–1967 under PL 480 assistance.

7. Gunnar Myrdal, *Asian Drama* (New York: Pantheon Books, 1968). See also, by the same author, *The Challenge of World Poverty* (New York: Vintage Books, 1970).

8. V. M. Dandekar and Nilakantha Rath, *Poverty in India,* Indian School of Political Economy (Bombay: Economic and Political Weekly, 1971).

9. Irma Adelman and Cynthia Morris, *Economic Growth and Social Equity in Developing Countries* (Stanford: Stanford University Press, 1973), p. 189.

10. Tripartite World Conference on Employment, Income Distribution, Social Progress, and the International Division of Labor, *Program of Action* (Geneva, June 1976), para. 1.

11. *Brandt Report,* p. 271.

CHAPTER 4

1. Michael Noelke, *Europe–Third World: The Interdependence File* (Brussels: Commission of the European Communities, 1979). The minerals considered here are aluminum, lead, copper, zinc, tin, manganese, nickel, tungsten, and iron.

2. Thus, the average reduction on nonpreferential tariffs for manufactures is one-fourth for developing countries' exports as against one-third for the overall average of all industrial products. See General Agreement on Tariffs and Trade, *The Multilateral Trade Negociations of the Tokyo Round* (Geneva, 1979).

3. See World Bank, *World Development Report* (Washington, D.C., 1981).

4. In 1979 and 1980, official development assistance of OPEC countries amounted on average to 1.41% of their GNP; the corresponding percentage was 0.36% for the industrialized countries of the Organization for Economic Cooperation and Development (OECD) and 0.12% for the industrialized socialist countries. During the same period, OPEC aid represented about one-fifth of the total financial assistance received by developing countries. See OECD, *Development Cooperation: 1981 Review* (Paris, 1981).

5. As a reminder, financial assistance of socialist countries amounted, over the last few years, to less than $2 billion per annum.

6.   While the idea of a collective self-reliance has been frequently discussed in developing countries over the last years, very little has been accomplished so far. This, of course, is not to say that nothing can be done or that nothing will be done. I think, however, that in the future, actions in this direction will be aimed more at increasing the economic relations among developing countries (especially in the fields of trade and finance) than at any "delinking" between these countries and the developed ones. Such an overall evolution would, naturally, not exclude the possibility of certain countries or regions electing, during the same time, to follow an autarkic development strategy.

7.   See *The Limits to Growth: A Report for the Club of Rome's Project on the Predicament of Mankind* (New York: New American Library, 1972).

8.   *Towards Full Employment and Price Stability: A Report to the OECD by a Group of Experts* (Paris, June 1977), p. 14.

9.   See, for instance, Dennis Gabor and Umberto Colombo, *Beyond the Age of Waste: A Report to the Club of Rome* (Elmsford, N.Y.: Pergamon Press, 1978).

10.   W. W. Rostow, *Getting from Here to There* (New York: McGraw-Hill, 1978). The ideas of Kondratieff, who was writing in the 1920s, evidently did not tally with the Marxist dogmas, since these affirm that capitalist economies are subject to increasingly violent crises, until their final collapse and the subsequent advent of socialism. This might be why, according to Solzhenitsyn (*Gulag Archipelago*), Kondratieff finished his days in a prison camp.

11.   Herman Kahn, *World Economic Development: 1979 and Beyond* (New York: Morrow Quill Paperbacks, 1979).

12.   In French in the English text. Kahn chose this expression to contrast this period with those preceding it in the economic history of industrialized countries: La Belle Epoque (1886–1913), La Mauvaise Epoque (1914–1947), La Deuxieme Belle Epoque (1948–1973).

13.   OECD, *Interfutures — Facing the Future: Mastering the Probable and Managing the Unpredictable* (Paris, 1979). Hereafter this study will be cited as *Interfutures*.

14.   *The Global 2000 Report to the President: Entering the Twenty-First Century* (Washington, D.C.: Government Printing Office, 1980), hereafter cited as *Global 2000 Report;* World Bank, *World Development Report* (Washington, D.C.) 1980 and 1981 issues.

CHAPTER 5

1.   Leon Tabah, "Changement dans la trajectoire démographique mondiale" (mimeograph), U.N. Department of International Economic and Social Affairs, Population Division, 1979. The fourteen countries here considered are Barbados, Chile, Costa Rica, Cuba, Fiji, Hong Kong, Jamaica, Mauritius, Panama, Malaysia, Dominican Republic, Singapore, Trinidad and Tobago, and Tunisia.

2.   The eight large countries here considered are China, India, Indonesia, Mexico, Brazil, Pakistan, Bangladesh, and Nigeria.

3.   The net reproduction rate is defined as the number of daughters a woman would have, under prevailing fertility and mortality patterns, who would survive to the mean age of childbearing.

4.   Tomas Frejka, *The Future of Population Growth: Alternative Paths to Equilibrium,* Population Council, (New York: John Wiley, 1973).

5.   *Brandt Report,* p. 113.

6.   See, for instance, *Interfutures;* Ruth W. Arad et al., *Sharing Global Resources* (New York: McGraw Hill, 1979); and R. G. Ridker and E. W. Cecelski, *Resources, Environment, and Population: The Nature of Future Limits* (Washington, D.C.: Population Reference Bureau, 1979).

7.   These figures do not include the People's Republic of China. See United Nations, *The World Population Situation in 1979* (New York, 1980).

8. Phyllis T. Piotrow, "Population Policies for the 1980's," in Georges Tapinos and Phyllis T. Piotrow, *Six Billion People* (New York: McGraw Hill, 1978). Also World Bank, "Family Planning Programs: An Evaluation of Experience," Staff Working Paper, July 1979.

9. See, for instance, William Rich, *Smaller Families through Social and Economic Progress* (Washington, D.C., Overseas Development Council, 1973). Rich shows that in several developing countries birthrates markedly declined even though family planning programs were relatively recent or even, in certain cases, nonexistent. A characteristic common to all these countries, however, was that the *whole* of their population apparently benefited from economic and social advances, much more so than in most other developing countries, for instance. See also Rashid Faruquee, "Sources of Fertility Decline: Factor Analysis of Inter-Country Data," World Bank Staff Working Paper, February 1979. Faruquee's conclusion is that, while family planning programs *are* important in fertility decline, economic and social development is by far the most influential factor.

10. See, for instance, United Nations, *World Population Trends and Policies: 1979 Monitoring Report* (New York, 1980), vol. 1, chap. 8. For an analysis of the influence of education, see Susan H. Cochrane, *Fertility and Education: What Do We Really Know?,* World Bank Staff Occasional Paper (Baltimore: Johns Hopkins University Press, 1979).

11. Rich, *Smaller Families through Social and Economic Progress.* This study also provides other analyses contrasting the demographic evolution of countries such as Taiwan, Barbados, Singapore, Uruguay, Cuba, Costa Rica, and China on one hand, and Venezuela, Brazil, and other Latin American countries on the other.

CHAPTER 6

1. See, among others, Dennis Gabor and Umberto Colombo, *Beyond the Age of Waste* (Elmsford, N.Y.: Pergamon Press, 1978); *Interfutures; Global 2000 Report;* Workshop on Alternative Energy Strategies, *Energy: Global Prospects, 1985–2000* (New York: McGraw Hill, 1977); Herman Kahn, *The Next 200 Years* (New York: William Morrow, 1976); and World Energy Conference, Conservation Commission, *Report on World Energy Demand, 1985–2020* (London, 1977).

2. These resource estimates, given by *Interfutures,* naturally depend on underlying price assumptions. For the sake of simplicity, these are not repeated here since I only want to compare the orders of magnitudes of present and future demands with those of existing resources. The estimates of commercial energy's world consumption in 2000 come from World Bank, *World Development Report* (Washington, D.C., 1980).

3. According to the International Energy Agency, the ratio of the growth rate of energy consumption to the GNP growth rate decreased from 1.01 in 1973 to 0.86 in 1979 in industrialized (OECD) countries. Oil consumption per $1 million (constant 1975 value) of GNP went from 471 to 402 tons during the same period. Partly as a result of energy conservation, the industrial countries imported in 1980 only 18% more oil than they did in 1970, despite a 37% rise in their real GNP.

4. According to the World Energy Conference, *Report on World Energy Demand,* and *Interfutures,* world oil production should level off between 1990 and 2000 and then decrease by half between 2000 and 2020. The Workshop on Alternative Energy Strategies, *Energy,* estimates that this plateau should in fact be reached sooner, possibly as soon as 1985.

5. The energy potential of the socialist countries taken as a whole (China included) appears quite high. Besides its potential in oil production, the U.S.S.R. has the largest natural gas reserves in the world; it is already the second world producer and the third exporter of gas. China's oil reserves are thought to be at least twice as large as Russia's, and this Far Eastern country is also the third coal producer in the world.

6. The corresponding proportion is about 50% for the industrialized market economies and about 30% for the nonmarket developed economies.

7. In 1980, the net fuel import bill of oil-importing developing countries reached $74 billion. See World Bank, *World Development Report* (Washington, D.C., 1981); also World Bank, "Energy Options and Policy Issues in Developing Countries," Staff Working Paper, August 1979, and World Bank, "Global Energy Prospects," Staff Working Paper, August 1981.

8. See World Bank, *A Program to Accelerate Petroleum Production in the Developing Countries* (Washington, D.C., 1979).

9. In the United States, for instance, the cost of drilling wells rose two and a half times between 1970 and 1976, and the cost of other operations has risen in proportion.

10. Investment in coal mining has traditionally been financed by public or private sources within the developing countries themselves. Since 1973, a few multinational corporations have undertaken to explore and develop coal resources in developing countries (with the aim of exporting the eventual production, however).

11. An example of the first possibility would be the aluminum plants built near the Volta River in Ghana; an example of the second, the sharing of electricity between Uganda and Kenya, or between Brazil and Paraguay.

12. On average, the capital cost of a hydropower installation is one and a half times higher, per kilowatt-hour of installed capacity, than that of a thermal plant.

13. Per kilowatt-hour of installed capacity, the capital cost of a nuclear plant is 1.5 to 2.5 times higher than that of a thermal plant.

14. The U.S. Geological Survey has estimated that known reserves of oil shale yielding more than 10 gallons of oil per ton amount to the equivalent of about 100 billion barrels of oil in Africa, as many in Asia, and 800 billion barrels in Latin America.

15. To the development of energy resources should of course be added energy conservation programs. Such programs have a very significant potential in developing countries, particularly in the transport and industry sectors (which, together, represent some 80% to 90% of these countries' consumption of commercial energy). In this respect, it would be desirable that these countries increase energy prices on their domestic markets, so as to encourage conservation efforts. (So far, for instance, the prices of petroleum products in these countries have been, on average, below the prices prevailing in developed countries.)

16. The proportions here given for Africa exclude South Africa. See World Bank, "Prospects for Traditional and Nonconventional Energy Sources in Developing Countries," Staff Working Paper, July 1979, and World Bank, *Renewable Energy Resources in the Developing Countries* (Washington, D.C., November 1980).

17. The following quotation from Plato's *Criteas* shows that the philosopher had a good understanding of the problem: "There are mountains in Attica which can now keep nothing more than bees, but which were clothed not so very long ago with fine trees, producing timber suitable for roofing the largest buildings; the roofs hewn from this timber are still in existence. There were also many lofty cultivated trees, while the country produced bountiful pastures for cattle. The annual supply of rainfall was not then lost, as it is at present, through being allowed to flow over a denuded surface to the sea. It was received by the country in all its abundance, stored in impervious potter's earth, and so was able to discharge the drainage of the hills into the hollows in the form of springs or rivers with an abundant volume and a wide distribution. The shrines that survive to the present day on the sites of extinct water supplies are evidence for the correctness of my present hypothesis."

18. *Global 2000 Report*, 1:26. The total area of the Third World forest amounts to some 1,200 million hectares. See World Bank, *Forestry,* Sector Policy Paper (Washington, D.C., 1978); also *Global 2000 Report*.

19. In addition to their human costs, these floods also entail substantial economic and financial costs. In India, for instance, devastations due to floods represent every year a cost

of some $140 to $170 million. See *World Conservation Strategy,* (Geneva, 1980), jointly published by the United Nations Environment Program, the International Union for Conservation of Nature, and the World Wildlife Fund.

20.   From a range of $300 to $5,000 per watt of peak production in the early seventies, this cost has fallen to some $15 today. The U.S. Department of Energy forecasts that it should come down to 50 cents per watt (of peak production) by 1985.

21.   *Brandt Report,* pp. 83–84.

CHAPTER 7

1.   The figures cited for grain imports of developing countries vary according to the definition chosen for these countries and to the method used for measuring these imports (gross or net of all exports from exporting developing countries); thus, frequent confusions arise. I give here the figures of the Food and Agriculture Organization, a specialized agency of the United Nations; these figures concern the whole Third World (China included) and are net of exports from exporting developing countries. Both sets of figures (net or gross) are interesting in their own right. Gross figures are more appropriate if we are concerned with the problem of food import financing, while net figures will be relevant if we are looking into the question of the availability, in developed countries, of the grain required for these imports. Net grain imports of developing countries consist mostly of wheat, since the rice exports and imports are approximately equal.

2.   On a three-year average, grain consumption per head amounted to 144 kilograms in 1960–1962, 151 in 1970–1972, and 142 in 1975–1977. See World Bank, "Behavior of Food Grain Production and Consumption in India, 1960–1977," mimeograph (Washington, D.C., 1979), for a statistical study of this apparent contrast between the growth of production and the stagnation of consumption.

3.   For an interesting and comprehensive presentation of the Green Revolution, see Sterling Wortman and Ralph W. Cummings, Jr., *To Feed This World* (Baltimore: Johns Hopkins University Press, 1978). For lack of a better term, I use the word *technology* here to cover the set of agricultural practices entailing the utilization of high-yield varieties with the required accompanying inputs (water and fertilizers in particular).

4.   In 1944, Mexico imported 163,000 tons of corn and 432,000 tons of wheat. It exported 497,000 tons of corn in 1965 and some 276,000 tons of wheat per year from 1962 to 1965. See Wortman and Cummings, *To Feed This World.*

5.   Over the last decade, the question, Who benefits from the Green Revolution? has been hotly debated — as has been the related issue of the employment impact of farm mechanization in the areas where high-yield varieties were being used. Without entering into this debate here, I shall nonetheless indicate that, in my view, there is no single answer to these questions that would be valid in all countries and all areas. Thus, farm mechanization has often been labor-saving and, to this extent, may have aggravated an existing situation of underemployment; in certain cases, however, the use of tractors made possible the cultivation of an additional crop, hence increasing the crop intensity and the labor requirements per unit of land.

6.   Asian Development Bank, *Rural Asia: Challenge and Opportunity* (New York: Praeger, 1977), p. 2. Similarly, it is interesting to contrast Lester Brown's *Seeds of Change* (New York: Praeger, 1970), published around the same time, with the subsequent books of this economist.

7.   Among the best known of these estimates are those of Wageningen University (P. Buringh, H.O.J. Van Heemst, and G. J. Staring, *Computation of the Absolute Maximum Food Production of the World,* [Wageningen, Netherlands: Agricultural University, 1975]) and of the U.S. President's Science Advisory Panel on the World Food Supply (*The World Food Problem* [Washington, D.C.: Government Printing Office, 1967]). A comprehensive presentation of these estimates (as well as an optimistic analysis of the world food future) is

given in Marylin Chou et al., *World Food Prospects and Agricultural Potential* (New York: Praeger, 1977). Like all resource estimates, those concerning arable areas depend on assumptions made on development costs — assumptions which at times are not explicitly stated. Joseph Klatzman, *Nourrir dix milliards d'hommes?* (Paris: Presses Universitaires de France, 1975), thinks that these costs would often be prohibitive and concludes that the global cultivated area could be increased only by approximately one-fourth.

8.   The development costs here mentioned are those of the University of Wageningen study cited in the preceding note. A 1% annual increase in the developing countries' cultivated area throughout the next twenty years would imply a yearly increment of about 8.2 million hectares, with an average development cost of some $1,600 per hectare. In 1975, total agricultural investment in all developing countries amounted to some $12 to $16 billion.

9.   This does not imply, of course, that developed countries are free from this kind of problem. Thus, it is estimated that, in the United States, some 40 million hectares of arable land have deteriorated since 1935 to such an extent that they are now unfit for cultivation.

10.   See *World Conservation Strategy* (Geneva, 1980).

11.   Root crops supply some 30% of the calorie intake of the sub-Saharan population. For an analysis of the specific problems of African agriculture, see World Bank, *Accelerated Development in Sub-Saharan Africa: An Agenda for Action* (Washington, D.C., 1981).

12.   On this subject, see, for instance, Lester Brown, *The Twenty-Ninth Day* (New York: W. W. Norton, 1978).

13.   On the illusions of "organic" agriculture and, in particular, on the feasibility of doing without fertilizer and insecticide, see Klatzmann, *Nourrir dix milliards d'hommes?* and also René Dumont, *La Croissance de la famine* (Paris: Seuil, 1975). Certainly, excessive use of fertilizers and pesticides must be checked; however, it would be naive to think we could do completely without these chemical inputs.

14.   There are exceptions, of course. Thus, in certain cases, it may be difficult to do without tractors if a particular task must be completed within a limited time period (for instance, when the land has to be rapidly prepared for a second crop). Another exception concerns the pumping of water from deep tubewells, which requires an electric or a fuel pump.

15.   Fertilizers and farm machinery represent some 90% of the consumption of commercial energy in agriculture. On this subject, see the special chapter, "Energy and Agriculture" in Food Agriculture Organization (FAO) *The World Situation of Food and Agriculture* (Rome, 1976).

16.   See Organization for Economic Cooperation and Development (OECD), "Nutrition and Agriculture," mimeograph (Paris, 1976) a background study for the Interfutures project.

17.   For more information on the competition between food and fuel crops, see Lester Brown, "Food or Fuel: New Competition for the World's Cropland," Worldwatch Paper no. 35, Washington, D.C., March 1980, from which the previous paragraphs are largely inspired. Also, World Bank, *Alcohol Production from Biomass in the Developing Countries,* September 1980.

18.   Thus the Wageningen University study (Buringh, Van Heemst, and Staring, *Absolute Maximum Food Production*) estimates the maximum grain production of the world at about thirty times its present level. Klatzmann, *Nourrir dix milliards d'hommes?,* thinks that, in the long run, world food production could be multiplied by five. As a matter of fact, it has been estimated that the potential of our planet would be sufficient to satisfy the food requirements of 40 billion people (Roger Revelle, "The Resources Available to Agriculture," *Scientific American* 235, no. 3 [September 1976]) or even 150 billion (Colin Clark, *Population Growth and Land Use* [New York: St. Martin's Press, 1967]).

19. See, for instance, FAO, *Agriculture: Towards 2000* (Rome, 1979); World Bank, "Developing Country Foodgrains Projection for 1985," Staff Working Paper, November 1976; U.S. Department of Agriculture, *Alternative Futures for World Food in 1985* (Washington, D.C.: Government Printing Office, 1978); International Food Policy Research Institute (IFPRI), *Food Needs of Developing Countries: Projections of Production and Consumption to 1990* (Washington, D.C., 1977); *Global 2000 Report*. For 1990, for instance, IFPRI estimates that the developing countries' net deficit in the production of major staples should be between 83 million and 107 million metric tons — the same order of magnitude as the FAO's projection (90 million tons).

20. In this respect, the leveling of yields of the main crops in the United States during the last decade is certainly alarming.

21. As a reminder (see n. 1, above), one should consider the gross (and not the net) deficit when analyzing the problem of food import financing. According to the FAO the gross deficits projected for 1990 and 2000 would exceed the net deficits by more than 20 million tons.

22. U.S. National Academy of Sciences, *World Food and Nutrition Study: The Potential Contributions of Research* (Washington, D.C., 1977).

23. See Klatzmann, *Nourrir dix milliards d'hommes?* also FAO, *Agriculture: Towards 2000;* and OECD, "Nutrition and Agriculture."

24. With regard to single-cell proteins, the problems of taste and potential health hazards still have to be resolved (in the case of eventual production for human consumption, in particular). In addition, their production costs have risen sharply in the wake of last decade's oil price increases. Herman Kahn, in his *The Next 200 Years* (New York: William Morrow, 1976) and in Chou et al., *World Food Prospects and Agricultural Potential,* sets much store by the potential of these nonconventional foods, but leaves completely aside the problem of insolvent demand.

25. FAO, *Agriculture: Towards 2000.*

26. World Food Conference, Resolution I, "Objectives and Strategies of Food Production," Rome, 1974.

27. *Global 2000 Report,* 1:2.

28. Presidential Commission on World Hunger, *Preliminary Report,* Washington, D.C., December 1979, p. III.3.

29. *Brandt Report,* p. 73.

CHAPTER 8

1. Hollis Chenery et al., *Redistribution with Growth* (London: Oxford University Press, 1974), p. xiii.

2. In attempting to estimate the number of absolute poor in the world, the World Bank and the Organization for Economic Cooperation and Development have used the notion of purchasing power parity (PPP) defined by Irving B. Kravis, a concept that takes account of the variations among countries due to exchange rates and structural differences. Per capita incomes expressed in nominal U.S. dollars have thus been transformed into "real" incomes expressed in PPP. The selected poverty threshold was $200 in 1970 PPP, which corresponds to a per capita income of $50 to $75 (in 1970 nominal dollars), depending on the countries.

3. *Brandt Report,* p. 57.

4. See Michael Lipton, *Why Poor People Stay Poor* (London: Temple Smith, 1977).

5. This estimate of the share of the rural population in total population comes from World Bank, *Rural Development,* Sector Policy Paper (Washington, D.C., 1975).

6. For instance, the proportion of primary schools offering the complete number of grades is lower in the countryside than in the cities. See World Bank, *Education,* Sector

Policy Paper (Washington, D.C., 1980), for further information on the differences between town and country in this field.

7. The situation is, on the whole, different in sub-Saharan Africa. In most countries of this region, the very concept of land distribution among several individual owners often cannot be directly used, since there still exist relatively large land resources and traditional systems of collective land tenure. Ownership systems are now evolving, however; already in some African countries (Botswana, Gabon, or Cameroon, for instance), land distribution is apparently less equalitarian today than in certain Asian countries like Sri Lanka or South Korea. See International Labor Office, "Rural Poverty in the Third World" (Geneva, 1979).

8. For a presentation of these theories, see Christian Morrisson, *La Répartition des revenus dans le Tiers-Monde* (Paris: Cujas, 1968).

9. Simon Kuznets, "Economic Growth and Income Inequality," *American Economic Review* 45, no. 1 (March 1955). Kuznets himself stated that his article was "perhaps 5% empirical information and 95% speculation."

10. Simon Kuznets, "Quantitative Aspects of Economic Growth of Nations: Distribution of Income by Size," *Economic Development and Cultural Change* 11, no. 2, pt. 2 (January 1963).

11. See, for instance, Hollis Chenery and Moises Syrquin, *Patterns of Development, 1950-1970* (London: Oxford University Press, 1975); Montek Ahluwalia, "Income Inequality: Some Dimensions of the Problem," in Chenery et al., *Redistribution with Growth;* idem, "Inequality, Poverty, and Development," *Journal of Development Economics* 3, no. 3 (December 1976); Irma Adelman and Cynthia Morris, *Economic Growth and Social Equity in Developing Countries* (Stanford: Stanford University Press, 1973); Edmar L. Bacha, "The Kuznets Curve and Beyond: Growth and Changes in Inequalities," mimeograph prepared for the Bellagio seminar on income distribution (Bellagio, Italy, April 1977).

12. Thus Adelman and Morris, *Economic Growth and Social Equity*, arrived at the conclusion (mentioned in Chapter 3, above) that the first stages of development were accompanied by a decline in the absolute income of the poorest. Their study was sharply criticized, however, for the methodology followed as well as for the quality of the data used. Subsequent studies (for instance, Ahluwalia, "Inequality, Poverty, and Development") showed, on the basis of more reliable data and of a less objectionable methodology, that the *absolute* income level of the poorest would in fact rise at all stages of economic development if changes in income distribution were to take place over time according to a U-curve law corresponding to that estimated from cross-country data.

13. See, for instance, Ahluwalia, "Inequality, Poverty, and Development."

14. It is interesting to note, however, that in Brazil, income distribution deteriorated in the sixties (during the import-substitution phase) but that there may have been some improvement during the export-oriented phase of the seventies. See World Bank, "The Distribution of Income in Brazil," Staff Working Paper, September 1979.

15. See, for instance, Ahluwalia, "Inequality, Poverty, and Development."

16. An implicit assumption of such a statement is that birthrates are higher among the poorest population categories — which is usually the case. If these rates were similar in all social strata, the negative effect of population growth on farm size would presumably be felt equally by rich and poor farmers alike.

17. See, for instance, Chenery and Syrquin, *Patterns of Development, 1950-1970;* Ahluwalia, "Inequality, Poverty, and Development"; Adelman and Morris, *Economic Growth and Social Equity.*

18. See Keith Griffin and Azizur Khan, coordinators, *Poverty and Landlessness in Rural Asia* (Geneva: International Labor Office, 1977), for more specific data on the deterioration that occurred in these two countries.

19.   Ahluwalia, "Rural Poverty in India." In this study, Ahluwalia regressed, for four-teen Indian states, the proportion of the rural population living in poverty, on two explana-tory variables: agricultural production per rural inhabitant and time. He thus showed that there was a significant negative relationship in seven states between poverty level and per head agricultural production, while the relationship was not significant for the other states. For half the states, there was a positive correlation between time and poverty level, indi-cating that in these states, at constant agricultural production per head, a trend towards impoverishment would prevail.

20.   Neoclassical economists might add to this list the utilization of a progressive system of direct or indirect taxation. Whatever the theoretical potential of such a system (and its importance, in practice, in developed countries), there now exists an abundant literature showing that its effectiveness as an income redistribution tool has been quite limited in the developing world.

21.   See T. N. Srinivasan, "Development Policies and Levels of Living of the Poor: Some Issues," mimeograph, World Bank, May 1977; Irma Adelman and Sherman Robin-son, *Income Distribution in Developing Countries* (London: Oxford University Press, 1978); David Morawetz, *Twenty-five Years of Economic Development, 1950 to 1975* (Baltimore: Johns Hopkins University Press, 1977); Griffin and Kahn, *Poverty and Landlessness in Rural Asia;* Wahidul Haque et al., "Towards a Theory of Rural Develop-ment," United Nations, Asian Development Institute, 1975; International Labor Office, "Rural Poverty in the Third World"; U.N. Economic Commission for Latin America, *El Desarollo economico y social y las relaciones economicas externas de America Latina* (E/CEPAL/1061), February 1979.

22.   P. Bardhan in the annex "India," in Chenery et al., *Redistribution with Growth,* p. 261. And yet this book can hardly be considered a revolutionary pamphlet!

23.   World Bank, *World Development Report* (Washington, D.C., 1978), p. 33.

24.   Thus, the World Bank calculations assume that the share of the *increment* in national income going to the poorest 60% of the population would increase from 18%-25% (the present average percentage) to 45%. This last proportion has been achieved, over the recent years, only by a few developing countries such as Sri Lanka and South Korea; even Taiwan realized a slightly smaller percentage (42% from 1964 to 1972). See World Bank, "Growth and Poverty in Developing Countries," Staff Working Paper, December 1978, and *World Development Report* (Washington, D.C., 1979).

25.   *Global 2000 Report,* 1:1.

CHAPTER 9

1.   World Bank, "Global Estimates for Meeting Basic Needs: Background Paper," mimeograph, August 1977.

2.   Among the advocates of this strategy, some are quite willing to recognize the short-comings, or even the naivete, of most of the literature on this subject. See, for instance, Mahbub Ul Haq, "Basic Needs: A Progress Report," mimeograph, World Bank, August 1977; T. N. Srinivasan, "Development Policies and Levels of Living of the Poor: Some Issues," mimeograph, World Bank, May 1977; Paul Streeten and Shahid Javed Burki, "Basic Needs: Some Issues," *World Development* 6, no. 3 (1978). In any case, there is some contradiction (not always perceived by the proponents of this approach) in a strategy that gives much importance to freedom or participation—which are given the status of full-fledged "basic needs"—while apparently implying a significant level of government intervention.

3.   For marginalists, the correct term here would, of course, be "utility" instead of "satisfaction."

4.   Theodore W. Schultz was one of the first to recognize the importance of education as a "human investment"; see, for instance, his *Economic Value of Education* (New York:

Columbia University Press, 1963). Gunnar Myrdal subsequently attacked this concept of human investment as too narrow for Third World countries and defended the view that, in these countries, many other so-called consumption expenditures (in nutrition and health in particular) improved productivity and, to this extent, could be considered as investment: see *Asian Drama* (New York: Pantheon Books, 1968), and *The Challenge of World Poverty* (New York: Vintage Books, 1970). On the importance of nutrition and health for workers' productivity, see also World Bank, "Iron Deficiency Anemia and the Productivity of Adult Males in Indonesia," Staff Working Paper, April 1974; and idem, "Nutrition and Health of Indonesian Construction Workers," Staff Working Paper, April 1973.

5. From 1952 to 1974, value added in the agricultural sector presumably grew at an average annual rate of 3.4%, while population increased by 2.1% per year. In these conditions, agricultural value added per head must have increased by one-third between these two dates. Most of the information used here comes from World Bank, "Industrialization, Technology, and Employment in the People's Republic of China," Staff Working Paper, August 1978; and Thomas Rawski, *Economic Growth and Employment in China* (London: Oxford University Press, 1979).

6. In the seventies, the poorest 20% of the population were obtaining, from the food ration program, some 20% of their calorie consumption, corresponding to 15% of their income.

7. During the ten years following the Arusha declaration, GNP grew at an annual rate of about 4.5%. In 1979, GNP per head was approximately $260.

8. From 1970 to 1977, agricultural production grew by 3.2% per year and population by 3.0%.

9. As a percentage of GDP, gross fixed capital formation, which in 1965 amounted to 12.9%, represented 24.2% in 1971 but subsequently decreased to some 20%. Public savings, which in 1967-1969 amounted to +1.6% of GNP, came down to -1.8% in 1974-1975.

10. *Brandt Report*, p. 128.

CHAPTER 10

1. See Paul Bairoch, *Révolution industrielle et sous-développement* (Paris: S.E.D.E.S., 1963); also by the same author, *Le Tiers-Monde dans l'impasse* (Paris: Gallimard, 1971), and "Agriculture and the Industrial Revolution," in *The Fontana Economic History of Europe* (London: Collins, 1969).

2. Thus, growth in agricultural productivity started in England well before the beginning of the enclosure movement (particularly important between 1760 and 1780), which, of course, in turn accelerated this productivity increase.

3. See, for instance, Paul Mantoux, *La Révolution industrielle au XVIIIᵉ siècle,* (Paris: Editions Genin, 1959), for further information on the social origins of the eighteenth-century industrialists.

4. Paul Bairoch, *The Economic Development of the Third World since 1900* (London: Methuen, 1975). For Africa, Latin America, and Asia, these indices apparently decreased between 1922-1926 and 1960-1964.

5. Bairoch (ibid.) estimates at some 40% the increase in productivity during the "agricultural revolution" stage. This would correspond to a productivity index of about 5 at the beginning of this phase.

6. On the experiences of South Korea and Taiwan, see, for instance, Hollis Chenery et al., *Redistribution with Growth* (London: Oxford University Press, 1974); also World Bank, "Growth and Equity in Semi-Industrialized Countries," Staff Working Paper, August 1979. On Taiwan see John C. H. Fei, Gustav Ranis, and Shirley W. Y. Kuo, *Growth with Equity: The Taiwan Case* (London: Oxford University Press, 1980).

7. Exports of manufactures increased (in current dollars) at an average annual rate of 42% between 1967 and 1974, passing from $163 million to $1,900 million.

8. See Martin Karcher, "Unemployment and Underemployment in the People's Republic of China," *China Report*, no. 11, September–December 1975; John Gurley, "Rural Development in China, 1949–1972," *World Development* 3, nos. 7–8 (July–August 1975); Thomas Rawski, *Economic Growth and Employment in China* (London: Oxford University Press, 1979).

9. Thus several studies on Latin American countries show that average family size in rural areas and small towns is almost twice as large as in big cities.

10. On this subject see World Bank, "Labor Force, Employment, and Labor Markets in the Course of Economic Development," Staff Working Paper, June 1979.

11. Thus, industrial value added and employment increased in the Third World at annual rates of 8.4% and 3.8%, respectively, between 1960 and 1970. In the developed countries, the corresponding rates between 1895 and 1920 were, respectively, 3.6% and 1.5% approximately.

12. World Bank, *World Development Report* (Washington, D.C., 1979). For further information on the impact of industrialization on employment, see David Morawetz, "Employment Implications of Industrialization in Developing Countries: A Survey," *Economic Journal* 84, no. 335 (September 1974).

13. In percentages, the breakdown of the Indian labor force was as follows in 1921 and 1971:

	1921	1971
Agriculture	73.1	73.8
Mining and manufactures	9.0	9.8
Others	17.9	16.4
	100.0	100.0

14. Government of India, *Draft Five-Year Plan, 1978–1983* (New Delhi, 1978), pp. 83–84.

15. Between 1960 and 1970, industrial value added in low-income countries increased by 6% a year; industrial employment increased about half as fast. At this rate, the industrial sector, which today provides employment to some 11% of these countries' labor force, is presumably absorbing every year an additional 0.33% of this labor force and would be absorbing 0.50% instead if the growth rates of industrial value added and employment suddenly increased by half. As compared to this, the annual growth of these countries' labor forces should approximate 2.1% per annum in the coming years.

16. See the special chapter on employment prospects in Latin America over the next two decades in the 1977 report of the Inter-American Development Bank, *Progreso Economico y Social en America Latina* (Washington, D.C., 1977); by the same institution see also, *Tendencias Demograficas y de Urbanizacion en America Central y Panama* (Washington, D.C., 1978). The 1979 report of the U.N. Economic Commission for Latin America, *El Desarollo economico y social y las relaciones economicas externas de America Latina* (E/CEPAL/1061), February 1979, also provides useful information on this subject.

17. John Maynard Keynes, *The General Theory of Employment, Interest, and Money* (New York: Harcourt, Brace and World, 1964), p. 383.

18. Quesnay, of course, cannot be accused of displaying anti-agriculture biases, since, for him, farmers were the only "productive class." Through his economic table, he was able to show how an increase in the expenditures or the production of one "class" augmented the production of the others. His table was in any case neutral, since it did not give any priority or preference to industry's linkage effects on agriculture over the opposite linkage.

19. Adam Smith, *Inquiry into the Nature and Causes of the Wealth of Nations* (Lon-

don: Dent, 1970), 1:337 and 362. Regarding agriculture, Smith displays an ambivalence typical of classical economists. On the one hand, he thinks that a country's interests coincide with those of its landowners. On the other, he prefers industry to agriculture, mostly because the former can better utilize the advantages of a large market, owing to its economies of scale. See *The Wealth of Nations*, 3, chaps. 1 and 4.

20. Albert O. Hirschman, *The Strategy of Economic Development* (New Haven: Yale University Press, 1958), pp. 109-10.

21. "A habit of indolence naturally prevails. The greater part of the land lies uncultivated. What is cultivated, yields not its utmost for want of skill and assiduity in the farmers" (David Hume, *Writings on Economics* [Madison, 1955], p. 47). In addition, Hume accuses the landowners of neither saving nor investing and of squandering their incomes. According to Marx and Engels, peasants, if they fight against the bourgeoisie, do so only in order to save their existence as a part of the middle class. "They are therefore not revolutionary, but conservative. Nay more, they are reactionary, for they try to roll back the wheel of history" (Karl Marx and Friedrich Engels, *Manifesto of the Communist Party* [Baltimore: Penguin Books, 1967], p. 91). Similarly, Engels accuses peasants of being "the strongest pillar not only of the parliamentary corruption in Paris and Rome but also of Russian despotism" (Friedrich Engels, *The Peasant Question in France and Germany*, in Karl Marx and Friedrich Engels, *Selected Works*, 2 vols. [Moscow: Foreign Languages Publishing House, 1951], 2:381).

22. Examples given in Theodore W. Schultz, *Economic Crises in World Agriculture* (Ann Arbor: University of Michigan Press, 1965).

23. C. Peter Timmer and Walter P. Falcon, "The Political Economy of Rice Production and Trade in Asia," in Lloyd G. Reynolds, ed., *Agriculture in Development Theory* (New Haven: Yale University Press, 1975).

24. This section is substantially inspired by the analyses of Michael Lipton in *Why Poor People Stay Poor* (London: Temple Smith, 1977).

25. This, of course, is not to say that rural exodus is an unmixed blessing. In any case, a comparison of labor marginal productivity in the agricultural and the urban sectors should take into account the considerable "disutilities" caused by the uncontrolled growth of cities.

26. The gross marginal capital/output ratio is the ratio of one year's gross investment to the increment in gross value added of this year over the previous one. A ratio smaller in agriculture than in the other sectors thus indicates that the same amount of gross investment will create a higher value added in this sector than in the others; in this sense it can therefore be said that the productivity of capital is higher in agriculture. Michael Lipton (*Why Poor People Stay Poor*) carried out similar computations for seven countries, using capital instead of investment, and arrived at the same conclusion.

27. See Paul A. Samuelson, *Economics* (New York: McGraw Hill, 1964).

28. This is still another economic policy for which the fathers of classical economic theory could, in all fairness, be held partly responsible. During the famous debate about the Corn Laws and their abolition, Ricardo's authority contributed — with the use of often questionable arguments — to the legitimation of policies protecting the sole industrial sector at the expense of agriculture.

29. Yet another idea which goes back to the classical economists!

30. International "experts" too often tend to ignore or minimize these problems in the name of an economic logic insufficiently sensitive to human and political realities. One could of course argue that governments tend, on the contrary, to give too much weight to these "realities" and overlook the long-term economic costs of the strategies they follow.

31. Thus farm workers are often paid in kind (at least partly) with meals or food; to this extent, they will be less directly affected by an increase in food prices.

32.   It is thus frequently the case that the main beneficiaries of these programs belong to the so-called middle class (which, in reality, as Myrdal explained, is only a part of the upper class). The reduction or elimination of the food rations going to these social categories would, without additional cost, free a substantial volume of food for the requirements of the genuinely needy.

33.   Assuming that for *public* investment the same relation holds (between the gross marginal capital/output ratio in the agricultural sector and the corresponding ratios in the other sectors) as exists between the same ratios for *all* investment (i.e. public and private; see n. 26, above), a "marginalist" management of public finances would lead to an increase in the share of government-financed investment in the agricultural sector (where the ratio is smaller) at the expense of the other economic sectors.

34.   For a study on the economic profitability of agricultural research, see Theodore W. Schultz, *Economic Growth and Agriculture* (New York: McGraw Hill, 1968); also Robert E. Stevenson and Yoav Kisley, *Agricultural Research and Productivity* (New Haven: Yale University Press, 1975).

35.   The "Training and Visit" system promoted by the Israeli expert Daniel Benor enabled several Asian countries to achieve unprecedented yield increases. The economic rates of return of these operations have often been above 50% or even 100%. See Daniel Benor and James Q. Harrison, *Agricultural Extension,* World Bank (Washington, D.C., May 1977).

CHAPTER 11

1.   In the Philippines, agricultural production grew at an annual rate of 3.8% between 1957 and 1971; during the same period the average real income per family of the poorest fifth of the rural population decreased by more than 10% (see Keith Griffin and Azizur Khan, coordinators, *Poverty and Landlessness in Rural Asia* (Geneva: International Labor Office, 1977). In El Salvador, agricultural production increased by 3.4% per year between 1961 and 1975; during the same time, the real income of households cultivating less than one hectare (42% of the rural population) fell by 20% (see International Labor Office, "Rural Poverty in the Third World," [Geneva, 1979]).

2.   Asian Development Bank, *Rural Asia: Challenge and Opportunity* (New York: Praeger, 1977), pp. 231-32.

3.   For this prejudice (since it *is* a prejudice), classical and Marxist economists can — again — be held partly responsible. Thus Adam Smith thought that, on the whole, big landowners were more prone to innovate in their work methods than were small farmers. Ricardo shared this opinion; he also thought that large farms could provide more employment per hectare. Marx and Engels, and Lenin after them, accused small farmers of not accumulating capital, of not innovating, and of not lending themselves to cooperative types of production. In general, these statements were not backed by statistical data. When they were (in the case of Lenin, for instance) their interpretation was at times questionable (see Michael Lipton, *Why Poor People Stay Poor* [London: Temple Smith, 1977]).

4.   "All else being equal" is, of course, a condition which will not be satisfied, since a real land reform is bound to change completely the economic and social system prevailing in the rural areas. But these changes, if they can be for the worse (because of the social and political turmoil the reform may trigger), can also, if they are properly organized, controlled, and supervised, represent an actual improvement (by establishing, in particular, the supporting institutions which will permit an effective rural development).

5.   See Asian Development Bank, *Rural Asia;* also Griffin and Khan, *Poverty and Landlessness in Rural Asia.* As a reminder for the noneconomist reader, the average saving rate (of a person, say) is the ratio of his total saving to his total income. His marginal saving rate would be the ratio of the increment in saving (corresponding to some increment in

income) to this incremental income itself. If the marginal saving rates are approximately equal for various farmers and if wᵉ further assume that the land reform will not cause any change in yields, a transfer of land from rich to poor farmers will correspond to a similar transfer of income, and the resulting increase in the poor farmers' saving will equal the decrease in the saving of the rich.

6. By way of a numerical example, let us assume that a big farmer has a marginal saving rate of 0.30 and gets a net income of 1,000 pesos per hectare, while a small farmer has a marginal saving rate of 0.25 but, because of his more intensive work, obtains a net income of 1,400 pesos per hectare. The transfer of one hectare from the big to the small farmer would decrease the former's saving by 300 pesos (0.30 × 1,000 pesos) but would increase the saving of the latter by 350 pesos (0.25 × 1,400 pesos), wherefrom a *net* increase in total saving of 50 pesos.

7. During the period of the land reform implementation, the ratio of net investment to national income apparently increased remarkably quickly, going from 1% or 2% in 1949 to about 20% in 1953. See John Gurley, "Rural Development in China, 1949–1972," *World Development* 3, nos. 7–8 (July–August 1975).

8. See, for instance, World Bank, *Land Reform,* Sector Policy Paper (Washington, D.C., 1975); also World Bank, "Land Reform in Latin America: Bolivia, Chile, Mexico, Peru, and Venezuela," Staff Working Paper, April 1978.

9. I was able to observe personally that, in India and Bangladesh, for instance, it is not unusual for an extension worker to be boarding at the house of some rich farmer. In return, this worker will help his host as an agricultural adviser or, in some cases, as a preceptor for his children.

10. For a study of the Chinese experience with agrarian reform and farmers' organization, see Gurley, "Rural Development in China, 1949–1972," and Neville Maxwell, "Learning from Tachai," also in *World Development* 3, nos. 7–8 (July–August 1975).

11. See International Labor Office, "Rural Poverty in the Third World"; Asian Development Bank, *Rural Asia;* and Griffin and Khan, *Poverty and Landlessness in Rural Asia,* for statistical data on the increase in the number of agricultural workers and landless laborers in these countries.

12. Data given in World Bank, *Land Reform.* By way of comparison, the corresponding average is 1.63 hectares in Europe and 21.5 in the United States.

13. World Bank, "Public Works Programs in Developing Countries: A Comparative Analysis," Staff Working Paper, February 1976, p. 72.

14. The above-mentioned World Bank study (ibid.) concludes, on the basis of data from several Asian countries, that as an average (and taking into account the benefits of both the investment and the operation phases), the ratio of the owners' benefits to those of the workers was 3.2 for irrigation works, 3.0 for land reclamation, and 4.3 for drainage.

15. See Erik P. Eckholm, *Losing Ground: Environmental Stress and World Food Prospects* (New York: W. W. Norton, 1976).

16. Even in Tunisia, where a very substantial and sustained program was carried out, the percentage reached only 2.4% on average between 1959 and 1969.

17. See World Bank, "Industrialization, Technology, and Employment in the People's Republic of China," Staff Working Paper, August 1978, and idem, "Public Works Programs in Developing Countries." For China, it can be estimated, on the basis of an average working period of 1.5 to 2 months per worker (of these public works campaigns), that the employment created amounted to some ten days per member of the Chinese labor force. The corresponding figure would be one day in India and Bangladesh and three days in South Korea and Morocco.

18. Rural works may have created each year on average some 5 billion man-days of work, amounting to about 20 million full-time jobs. As a comparison, employment in the

Chinese rural industries presumably adds up to some 10 to 17 million jobs (see the next section of this chapter).

19. Thus R. S. Eckhaus, "The Factor-Proportions Problem in Underdeveloped Countries," *American Economic Review* 45 (September 1955): 544, wrote twenty-five years ago: "I should now like to suggest that the use of the 'modern' techniques is not necessarily irrational emulation but the result of real limitations in the technological choices available, and that this, in turn, is a major source of labor employment problems in underdeveloped areas."

20. See, for instance, United Nations Industrial Development Organization (UNIDO), *World Industry since 1960: Progress and Prospects* (New York, 1979); World Bank, *Employment and Development of Small Enterprises,* Sector Policy Paper (Washington, D.C., 1978); International Labor Office, *Technology and Employment in Industry* (Geneva, 1975); and David Morawetz, "Employment Implications of Industrialization in Developing Countries: A Survey," *Economic Journal* 84, no. 335 (September 1974).

21. World Bank, *Employment and Development of Small Enterprises,* p. 15.

22. See UNIDO, *Technologies from Developing Countries,* Development and Transfer of Technology Series no. 7 (ID/208) (New York, 1978).

23. Thus UNIDO, *World Industry since 1960,* indicates that studies of at least twenty-five developing countries show this elasticity to vary between 0.5 and 1.2.

24. As quoted in Van Der Veen, "A Study of Small Industries in Gujarat State, India," Cornell Agricultural Economics Occasional Paper no. 65, May 1973, p. 1.

25. Administrative Reforms Commission, *Report on Small Scale Sector,* Government of India, 1970, p. 8.

26. Asian Development Bank, *Rural Asia,* p. 290.

27. For information on the policies of the two latter countries, see World Bank, "Small-Scale Enterprises in Korea and Taiwan," Staff Working Paper, April 1980.

28. UNIDO, *World Industry since 1960,* p. 285. See also Jon Sigurdson, "Rural Industrialization in China," *World Development* 3, nos. 7–8 (July–August 1975).

29. This increase in demand will be all the more significant since its elasticity with respect to agricultural production is apparently quite high. See *Rural Enterprise and Non-Farm Employment,* World Bank Paper, January 1978.

30. For instance, Gunnar Myrdal (in *Asian Drama* [New York: Pantheon Books, 1968], pp. 1366–84) and John Mellor (in *The New Economics of Growth* [Ithaca, N.Y.: Cornell University Press, 1976], pp. 104–6) advocate such a "reformist" strategy.

CHAPTER 12

1. Samir Amin, *Accumulation on a World Scale* (New York: Monthly Review Press, 1974). The quotation given here is my translation from the French original, *L'Accumulation a l'échelle mondiale* (Paris: Anthropos, 1970), p. 58.

2. See Gunnar Myrdal, *Economic Theory and Underdeveloped Regions* (London: Duckworth, 1957); Raùl Prebisch, "Commercial Policy in the Underdeveloped Regions," *American Economic Review Papers and Proceedings,* May 1959.

3. Ragnar Nurkse, "Patterns of Trade and Development," in *Equilibrium and Growth in the World Economy* (Cambridge, Mass.: Harvard University Press, 1961), pp. 289 and 310.

4. See, for instance, World Bank, "World Trade and Output of Manufactures," Staff Working Paper, January 1979, and Francoise Brochart-Martinie, *Les Exportations de produits manufacturés des pays en developpement: Facteurs et tendances* (Clermont-Ferrand, France: CERDI, 1979).

5. The seventeen countries or areas considered in Table 12.2 produce some 65% of the

developing countries' manufactured exports. Within the Third World's exports of capital-intensive manufactures, the share going to other developing countries (including OPEC) is larger and has grown faster than the share going to developed countries.

6. These countries are Spain (22.3% of developing countries' exports of capital goods in 1979), Singapore (17.5%), Korea (15%), Hong Kong (11.8%), and Brazil (11.3%). See World Bank, "The Changing Composition of Developing Countries' Exports," Staff Working Paper, January 1979, for a detailed presentation of developing countries' exports.

7. World Bank, *World Development Report* (Washington, D.C., 1981), p. 30.

8. On average between 1967 and 1972, exports to other developing countries represented some 19% of total exports of developing countries; in 1980 this percentage had gone up to 27%.

9. Thus only one-sixth of the total trade in manufactured goods among developing countries is taking place among Latin American countries or among countries in sub-Saharan Africa — the only two regions where regional integration programs ever achieved any real significance.

10. If the indirect linkage effects (corresponding to the labor needed for the production of the inputs supplied to exporting industries by other firms) are taken into account, the *net* employment effect could reach 900,000 additional jobs for the developed countries of the Organization for Economic Cooperation and Development (OECD). See OECD, *The Impact of the Newly Industrializing Countries on Production and Trade in Manufactures* (Paris, 1979). For France, see Yves Berthelot and Gérard Tardy, *Le Défi économique du Tiers-Monde,* La Documentation Française (Paris, 1978).

11. See Albert Fishlow, "A New International Economic Order: What Kind?" in Albert Fishlow et al., *Rich and Poor Nations in the World Economy* (New York: McGraw Hill, 1978). Other statistical evidence is given in Bela Balassa, "Export Incentives and Export Performance in Developing Countries: A Comparative Analysis," *Weltwirtschaftliches Archiv* 114 (1978). Bela Balassa measured the Spearman rank correlation coefficient between export growth and GNP increase for a sample of seventeen countries; this coefficient was 0.82 for the 1960–1966 period and 0.93 for 1966–1973.

12. Although less often mentioned among the benefits of export development, improved utilization of existing capital is an important consequence of export-oriented policies. It is evidenced by the fact that the incremental capital-output ratios (ICOR) are significantly lower for exporting countries. Thus for 1960–1973, these ratios were 1.76 for Singapore, 2.10 for South Korea, and 2.44 for Taiwan, while they reached 5.49 for Chile and 5.72 for India. Such differences in ICOR are especially important for developing countries, since capital is particularly scarce there. See Bela Balassa, "Export Incentives and Export Performances in Developing Countries."

13. As a reminder, the total labor force of developing countries represented some 850 million people in 1980. See World Bank, "World Trade and Output of Manufactures"; and William Tyler, "Manufactured Exports and Employment Creation in Developing Countries: Some Empirical Evidence," *Economic Development and Cultural Change* 24, no. 2 (January 1976).

14. See William Tyler, "Manufactured Exports and Employment Creation"; percentages vary from 1% for Brazil in 1969 to 17% for Taiwan in the same year. For Brazil, see also, by the same author, *Manufactured Export Expansion and Industrialization in Brazil,* Kieler Studien 134 (Kiel, Germany, 1976).

15. For Taiwan, see Tyler, "Manufactured Exports and Employment Creation"; for South Korea see Larry Westphal, "The Republic of Korea's Experience with Export-Led Industrial Development," *World Development* 6, no. 3 (1978). It may be safer not to try to compare across countries results obtained with methodologies which are not strictly iden-

tical. Also, these proportions change rapidly in countries with fast-growing exports: thus in 1960 South Korea's exports were accounting for only one out of every thirty jobs.

16. The ratio between the work content of one unit of value added for export and the corresponding content of one unit of value added for the domestic market is about 1.07 for Brazil, 1.93 for Colombia, 2.09 for Indonesia, and 2.21 for Thailand. See Anne O. Krueger, "Alternative Trade Strategies and Employment in Developing Countries," *American Economic Review* 68, no. 2 (May 1978).

17. Tyler, "Manufactured Exports and Employment Creation," p. 370.

18. During this period, the percentage of imports financed by exports was about 82% for the poorest countries and 86% for the others.

19. The World Bank forecasts that, over the next decade, the fuel import bill of the oil-importing developing countries will represent about one-fourth of their export earnings (26.3% in 1980) in spite of a significant increase in the volume of these exports. See *World Development Report, 1981.*

20. See Carlos Diaz-Alejandro, "Delinking North and South," in Fishlow et al., *Rich and Poor Nations in the World Economy.*

21. Adam Smith, *Inquiry into the Nature and Causes of the Wealth of Nations* (London: Dent, 1970), 2:121–22 (bk. 4, chap. 7).

22. Samir Amin, "Développement autocentré, autonomie collective et ordre économique international nouveau: quelques réflexions," in *L'Occident en désarroi: Ruptures d'un système économique,* ed. Xavier Greffe and Jean-Louis Reiffers (Paris: Dunod, 1978).

23. This statement, I must add, should not be construed as a criticism. To make a (presumably inappropriate) parallel, the emotional aspects of racial problems do not lend themselves easily to a rational discussion. Yet no one would pretend that these aspects are not important and can be overlooked.

24. For an unbiased presentation of the implications of various development strategies for a country's economic and political independence, see Michael Roemer, "Dependence and Development Strategies," *World Development* 9, no. 5 (1981).

25. Historically, the expansion of the multinationals has followed — or led — the strategies of the developing countries: exploitation of natural resources, then creation of import-substituting industries, and finally development of export industries. In 1967, half of the Third World's foreign investment was in Latin America.

26. Angus Hone, "Multinational Corporations and Multinational Buying Groups," *World Development* 2, no. 2 (February 1974). Also see United Nations, Economic and Social Commission for Asia and the Pacific, *Regional Development Strategy for the 1980's,* Bangkok, March 1980; and, for South Korea, Westphal, "The Republic of Korea's Experience with Export-Led Industrial Development."

27. Westphal, "The Republic of Korea's Experience with Export-Led Industrial Development," p. 362.

28. See Richard Burnett and Ronald Muller, *Global Reach: The Power of the Multinational Corporations* (Beaverton, Ore.: Touchstone Press, 1974), a book which can hardly be considered favorable to the multinationals.

29. See, for instance, World Bank, "A 'Stages' Approach to Comparative Advantages," Staff Working Paper, May 1977. Also Hollis Chenery, "Transitional Growth and World Industrialization," in *The International Allocation of Economic Activity,* ed. Bertil Ohlin et al. (London: Macmillan, 1977).

30. In South Korea, for instance, it seems that the capital intensity of manufactured exports markedly increased after 1968, when exports of such products as cement, steel, or fertilizers rapidly expanded. See Larry Westphal and Kwang Suk Kim, "Industrial Policy and Development in Korea," World Bank Staff Working Paper, August 1977. On Singapore's experience, see Cheah Hock Beng, "Export-Oriented Industrialization and

Dependent Development: The Experience of Singapore," *Institute of Development Studies Bulletin* 12, no. 1 (December 1980).

31. For two conflicting views about the role of the multinational corporations in this field see Amin, "Développement autocentré, autonomie collective et ordre économique international nouveau: quelques réflexions," and UNIDO, *World Industry since 1960: Progress and Prospects* (New York, 1979).

32. Donald B. Keesing, "Trade Policy for Developing Countries," World Bank Staff Working Paper, August 1979, p. 165.

33. See General Agreement on Tariffs and Trade (GATT), "Adjustment Trade and Growth in Developed and Developing Countries," *GATT Studies in International Trade,* no. 6. Imports from developing countries still represent only a small share of the developed countries' total imports, even for labor-intensive goods. Thus for fourteen developed countries, imports from developing countries made up, on average, only 13.5% of their total imports of labor-intensive products in 1970. See Ranadev Banerji, "The Export Performance of the Less Developed Countries," *Weltwirtschaftliches Archiv,* no. 3 (1974).

34. For a sector study of the effect of the developed countries' protectionism on Third World's exports see Juergen Donges and James Riedel, "The Expansion of Manufactured Exports in Developing Countries: An Empirical Assessment of Supply and Demand Issues," *Weltwirtschaftliches Archiv,* no. 1 (1977). The authors arrive at the conclusion that "apart from textiles, clothing and footwear, constraints on the demand side do not at present appear to be quite so severe as developing countries seem to believe."

35. World Bank, *World Development Report* (Washington, D.C., 1981), p. 115.

36. For more information about the impact of export-oriented policies on exports and GNP growth after the 1974–1975 crises see Bela Balassa, André Barsony, and Anne Richards, *Policy Responses to External Shocks in Developing Countries* (Paris: OECD, 1981). Also Bela Balassa, "The Newly-Industrializing Developing Countries after the Oil Crisis," World Bank Staff Working-Paper, October 1980 and idem, "Structural Adjustment Policies in Developing Economies," World Bank Staff Working Paper, July 1981.

37. World Bank, *World Development Report* (Washington, D.C., 1979), p. 22.

38. See Westphal, "The Republic of Korea's Experience with Export-Led Industrial Development," and Westphal and Kim, "Industrial Policy and Development in Korea." It was in fact only after 1970 that Japanese investment markedly increased in South Korea. The only exception to the absence of preferential treatment for Korean firms consisted, during the Vietnam War, in admitting Korean exporters as bidders in the U.S. Army tender procedures outside of U.S. territory.

39. Westphal and Kim, "Industrial Policy and Development in Korea," p. 5–13.

40. It is presumably not too difficult to see (on a theoretical plane at least) how a high level of protection of the domestic market will discourage entrepreneurs from making the efforts required to attack foreign markets, which are always more hazardous than the domestic one. But, since a priori arguments often look a bit suspicious, it may be reassuring to see that empirical studies support this theoretical reasoning. Thus Thomas Morrison ("Manufactured Exports and Protection in Developing Countries: A Cross-Country Analysis," *Economic Development and Cultural Change* 25, no. 1 [October 1976]) shows, with a statistical regression across countries, that there is an inverse relation between export performance and level of protection.

41. Certain of these studies tried to trace the evolution of exports back to responses to changes in the incentive policies. Thus Donges and Riedel, "The Expansion of Manufactured Exports in Developing Countries," found that in eight out of twelve exporting countries, a statistically significant change in the export trend followed the establishment of an incentive system for manufactured exports. Other studies, on the contrary, compared the evolution of several countries (or several sectors within the same country) with different

incentive systems. For instance, Westphal and Kim, "Industrial Policy and Development in Korea," measured the economic incentives offered in Korea to different industrial exports and concluded that, on the whole, exports increased faster for the goods receiving a higher level of incentive.

42.   See, on this subject, Bela Balassa and Michael Sharpston, "Export Subsidies by Developing Countries: Issues of Policy," *Commercial Policy Issues,* November 1977.

INDEX

Africa: agricultural production in, 13, 142; economic growth of, 9-10, 19; education in, 24; energy resources of, 79-82; external financing of oil-price shocks in, 37; food production and consumption in, 23, 87-88, 92-93, 101, 105-6; income distribution and growth in, 29, 32-33, 111; industrial production in, 15, 205; labor force growth in, 149-50; land reserves in, 96-97; North, 23, 93; population growth in, 61, 64-65

Agricultural credit, 158-59, 170

Agricultural production: and economic theory, 44-45, 151-58; growth of, 12-13, 19-20; and income distribution, 119-21; and population growth, 68, 148-51. *See also* Agricultural productivity; Agriculture; Food

Agricultural productivity: and development strategies, 128, 134, 148, 158-63, 201; and land reform, 165-69; role in the industrialization process of, 44-45, 140-54. *See also* Agricultural production; Agriculture; Food

Agriculture: and basic needs, 134-38; and cooperatives, 171-72; employment in, 68, 112-13, 149-51, 160, 166-67; and energy supply, 102-4; extension services in, 161, 169; and income, 30-31, 95, 119-20, 153, 156, 182; investment in, 97, 157-58, 160-62, 167, 170; and poverty, 119-20, 134, 148; price struc-

ture in, 154-55, 159-60; research in, 92-93, 101, 161, 169; and small farmers, 114-16, 169-73, 182. *See also* Agricultural production; Agricultural productivity; Food; Land distribution; Landless workers; Land reform

Alcohol, 84, 103-4

Algeria: development strategy of, 146-47; Physical Quality of Life Index in, 26

Andean Market, 198

Andhra-Pradesh (Indian state of), income distribution in, 30

Argentina: agricultural employment in, 167; grain exports of, 89; income distribution in, 29; and multinational firms, 198; nuclear power installation in, 80

Arusha declaration, 136

Asia: agricultural productivity in, 92-96, 101, 142, 153-54, 160; economic development in, 10, 45; education in, 24; energy resources of, 79-80, 84; evolution of rural poverty in, 30-31; income distribution and growth in, 29, 111, 120-21, 200; industrial production in, 15-16, 142-44; labor force growth in, 150, 172; land distribution in, 114-15, 120-22; land reform in, 165, 168, 183; land reserves in, 96-97; malnutrition in, 23, 108; multinational firms in, 197; population growth in, 60-61, 64; rural works in, 173-76

235